JEWS ON THE MOVE

SUNY Series in American Jewish Society in the 1990s
Barry A. Kosmin and Sidney Goldstein, Editors

This series is based on the Council of Jewish Federations 1990
National Jewish Population Survey.

JEWS ON THE MOVE

Implications for Jewish Identity

Sidney Goldstein and Alice Goldstein

STATE UNIVERSITY
OF NEW YORK
PRESS

Published by
State University of New York Press, Albany

Production by Susan Geraghty
Marketing by Fran Keneston

Printed in the United States of America

For information, address State University of New York Press,
State University Plaza, Albany, N.Y., 12246

Library of Congress Cataloging-in-Publication Data

Goldstein, Sidney, 1927–
    Jews on the move : implications for Jewish identity / Sidney
Goldstein and Alice Goldstein.
        p.   cm.—(SUNY series in American Jewish society in the
1990s)
    Includes bibliographical references and index.
    ISBN 0–7914–2747–1. — ISBN 0–7914–2748–X (pbk.)
    1. Jews—United States—Migrations. 2. Migration, Internal—
United States. 3. Jews—United States—Identity.   I. Goldstein,
Alice. II. Title. III. Series.
E184.J5G636 1995
304.8'089'924073—dc20   95-5830
                                                                          CIP

10 9 8 7 6 5 4 3 2 1

To our grandchildren,
Allison, Penina, Michaela, Nathaniel,
Avi, Asher, and Talya

whose commitments to Judaism and migration experiences
will help to shape American Jewry in the 21st century

CONTENTS

TABLES

ILLUSTRATIONS

FIGURES

MAPS

FOREWORD

Jews on the Move: Implications for Jewish Identity is the first monograph to be published in the series "American Jewish Society in the 1990s," based on the Council of Jewish Federation's (CJF) landmark 1990 National Jewish Population Survey. The survey yielded a vast array of statistical data on the demographic, social, and religious characteristics of the Jewish American population. It is being used to provide, in a number of monographs, an in-depth assessment of the major changes and trends in Jewish American life as it approaches the end of the century. To a degree, this monograph series parallels past undertakings by teams of social scientists who analyzed the demographic and social data emanating from United States decennial censuses. A monograph series focussing on the Jewish population is, however, unique. Although a national survey similar in nature had been conducted in 1970, that project yielded comparatively few reports and those were in limited areas of concern.

Recognizing the importance of a comprehensive assessment of the total Jewish American population as the basis for an effective planning agenda, the concept of a national Jewish population survey in 1990 was first considered in 1986 by CJF's National Technical Advisory Committee on Jewish Population Studies (NTAC). The idea was further promoted the following year at the World Conference on Jewish Demography held in Jerusalem, at which plans were developed for a worldwide series of national Jewish population studies undertaken in or around the decennial year. An American survey was seen as a key component of this series. In 1988, CJF officially agreed to conduct a national Jewish population survey in 1990, parallel to the federal decennial census. ICR Survey Research Group of Media, Pennsylvania, was commissioned to conduct the three-stage survey.

In contrast to the 1970 national study, NTAC decided to insure public access to the 1990 National Jewish Population Survey (NJPS) data as early as possible and to actively encourage

xxi

wide use and analysis. The success of that effort is evident in the large number of analyses that have been completed or are in process. To date, more than 150 items extensively based on NJPS, such as journal and magazine articles, dissertations, and papers for professional meetings, have been written. These encompass such varied topics as aging, apostasy, the baby boom generation, children, comparisons with international Jewry, comparisons with the larger American population, denominations, fertility, gender equality, geography, intermarriage, Israel connections, Jewish education, Jewish identity, life cycle, mobility, occupation, philanthropy, Sephardim, social stratification, and women's roles. A number of these topics are expected to appear as monographs in the series.

From the outset, NTAC envisioned that a number of scholars would independently produce monographs utilizing NJPS data for in-depth assessment of topics having special relevance for the understanding of Jewish life in America. While planning for the various stages of NJPS, NTAC therefore concurrently acted to identify potential monograph writers. Public notices were placed in a variety of academic journals and invitations were conveyed through a network of professionals, both within and outside of Judaic disciplines. Although funds were raised for the data collection, survey execution, and data processing, no financial support was available for subsidizing data analyses, except for a summary report, *Highlights of the CJF 1990 National Jewish Population Survey*. Thus, potential monograph writers knew from the beginning that they would be participating on a voluntary basis, dependent on whatever resources they could themselves muster. The dedication of the authors to the completion of their respective monographs is gratefully acknowledged. While drawing on basically the same set of data, authors were free to establish their own analytic categories and to apply their own perspectives in interpreting the data. They were also encouraged to draw not only on NJPS, but also on comparative data from other sources, such as local community surveys.

In selecting authors, efforts were made to insure coverage of key issues and a diversity of topics and to avoid serious overlap in coverage of the same topic. A screening and approval process, in collaboration with the editors at SUNY Press, was administered by the series editors, Dr. Barry Kosmin, Director of Research at the Council of Jewish Federations and Director of the Mandell L. Berman Institute—North American Jewish Data Bank (NAJDB) at City University of New York Graduate Center; and Dr. Sidney Goldstein, Chair of NTAC and G. H.Crooker University Professor Emeritus and Professor Emeritus of Sociology at Brown University.

Jeff Scheckner, Administrator of NAJDB and Research Consultant at CJF, with the help of the series editors, coordinated the activities of the monograph writers by arranging meetings at which authors discussed technical aspects of the data and their preliminary findings, fielding daily inquiries about the data set, and circulating periodic informational updates. Much of this activity was necessitated by the fact that NJPS is both a large data set with a complex weighting system (see Appendix A) and that definitional issues complicate any analysis of contemporary Jewish populations. The work of the monograph authors was further enhanced through the coordination of a "buddy" system by which other scholars associated with NJPS provided academic peer review to authors at various stages of manuscript preparation.

The intense interest generated by the initial release of NJPS findings has already significantly affected deliberations within the Jewish American community among communal service workers, religious and educational professionals, and lay leaders. At the same time, the results of early reports have elicited considerable attention among those in the larger American community whose interests focus on the changing religio-ethnic composition of the population and the role of religion in America. This series is intended to provide a comprehensive, in-depth evaluation of American Jewry today, some one hundred years since the massive waves of Jewish immigrants from Eastern Europe began to change the size and character of Jewry in the United States. During the intervening decades, continual change has been the hallmark of the community. The profile of the Jewish population in the 1990s that NJPS delineates both provides a historical perspective and points to the challenges of the future.

Barry Kosmin
Graduate Center, City
University of New York and
Council of Jewish Federations
New York, NY

Sidney Goldstein
Population Studies and
    Training Center
Brown University
Providence, RI

January 1995

PREFACE

As social scientists with special interests in demography, our research over the past two decades has focussed heavily on two quite diverse populations, the people of China and the Jews of the United States. China, with its 1.1 billion people, has the largest population in the world and is very determined to control growth to insure a better quality of life for its people. By contrast, American Jewry today numbers just under 6 million persons and is much concerned with questions of continuity and identity in the face of low fertility, high rates of intermarriage, and assimilatory tendencies. In both situations, migration has become an important dynamic leading to large scale redistribution of the population.

For us, as scholars, this has presented new challenges and new opportunities: how to assess the extent, direction, characteristics, causes, and effects of population movement in the context of the larger concerns that confront China in the one instance and American Jewry in the other. A major reason why such assessments are so problematic has been a lack of appropriate information on the mobility behavior of either populations. By coincidence, within a few years of each other, both China and the Jewish American community recognized the importance of generating adequate statistics to allow evaluation of the patterns of migration and their impact. And so, this monograph, *Jews on the Move*, parallels research reports that we have prepared on migration and urbanization in China. In both cases, our hope has been that the resulting insights will provide a firmer basis for improving the quality of life of the people who constitute the focus of the analyses.

As committed Jews, we believe that fuller attention to the role of migration in the redistribution of Jewish Americans is a key to understanding the dynamics underlying changes in the structure of the Jewish American community and in levels of individual identity. The research reported in this volume has therefore allowed us to pursue our general scholarly interests in an area which overlaps significantly with personal concerns we have regarding the future vitality of the Jewish American community. We are grateful for this opportunity because we believe that planning on the basis of the facts rather than on myths and wishful thinking is the best way to cope with the challenges the community faces.

The data for this analysis come from the 1990 National Jewish Population Survey (NJPS), sponsored by the Council of Jewish Federations (CJF). In the absence of official census data on religion, this "self-study" of the Jewish population was undertaken to meet the needs of the Jewish American community for a firm, factual basis for assessing its position in the closing decade of the twentieth century and for effective planning for the transition to the twenty-first century. The strong support given to NJPS by CJF's lay and professional leadership testifies to their concern and foresight in their efforts to maintain a vital Jewish community. We are most grateful to the members of the CJF's National Technical Advisory Committee on Population Studies (NTAC), which the senior author chaired, for their dedication and arduous work in developing the design of the survey and in insuring successful completion of the field work. The wide use to which the collected data have already been put—in shaping the agenda of discussion within the organized community, in scholarly research, and in planning at the national and local levels—document the value of their efforts as well as those of the ICR Survey Research Group of Media, Pennsylvania, and the Mandell Berman Institute of the North American Jewish Data Bank (NAJDB) at the Graduate School and University Center of the City University of New York, which, respectively, had responsibility for implementing the research design and insuring proper processing and distribution of the survey data. Dr. Barry Kosmin, Research Director of CJF and Director of the Berman Institute at NAJDB, Jeffrey Scheckner of the CJF Research Department, and Ariella Keysar, Research Fellow at NAJDB, deserve special mention for the key roles they played at all stages of the research in insuring the highest quality data set and easy access to it.

The richness of NJPS-1990 is perhaps best indicated by the large array of publications and presentations at professional meetings that followed in the years immediately after release of the data set. Concurrently, plans were made for a monograph series designed to exploit in depth a wide range of topics of interest both to the scholarly community and to planners in the Jewish community. This monograph is the first in a series to be published by SUNY Press on American Jewish society in the 1990s. We are grateful to SUNY Press (Albany) for agreeing to sponsor this series and to Rosalie Robertson and her sucessor, Christine Worden, for their help in organizing the series.

Because this is only one of many monographs that will draw on the NJPS-1990 data, a challenge we faced in undertaking this research was to avoid too much overlap with those monographs that will focus on topics closely related to migration. The various monographs are intended to complement rather than duplicate each other. The plan for a monograph focussing on the geography of American Jews, for example, explains why minimum attention has been given in this report to the relation between migration and community size. An ongoing project by Uzi Rebhun at the Hebrew University, comparing the migration patterns revealed by the 1970–71 and 1990 National Jewish Population Studies accounts for the minimal attention given in our assessment to the 1970 statistics. We hope that these complementary reports will soon be available and that interested readers will use them in combination with this monograph.

Our endeavor benefitted greatly from the efforts of a number of persons. At the Population Studies and Training Center of Brown University, Dr. Xiushi Yang helped immeasurably in preparing computer tabulations and statistical analyses of the data, as did Lori Hunter in preparing the graphic material. Irene Gravel was very generous with her time in expertly organizing computer files for the analysis. Following a review system developed by NTAC, Drs. Barry Kosmin (CJF and NAJDB), Sergio Della Pergola (Hebrew University), and Ira Sheskin (University of Miami) served as initial reviewers of the manuscript. We are most appreciative to them for their comprehensive, incisive criticisms; they proved most helpful in preparing the manuscript for external review. We are grateful, too, for the reactions received from three anonymous reviewers selected by SUNY Press; their comments were very valuable in completing revisions of the manuscript for publication. Thanks, too, to Dr. Joseph Waksberg for the special contribution he has made to this and the other monographs in the series by preparing the methodological appendix outlining the study design. To Christine Worden, editor of the series, we are indebted for the care with which she handled the monograph and for seeing it through to publication.

During the years in which the National Jewish Population Study was being planned and the subsequent period when the survey was conducted and our analysis of the migration data undertaken, we became the grandparents of seven lovely children born to our Beth, David, and Brenda and their spouses, Raphael, Sarah, and David. Like many of the individuals represented in our analysis, our children and grandchildren have experienced migration; they currently live in three different states far from our own Rhode Island. Despite their dispersion, we are delighted and grateful that our family ties remain strong, as do our children's and grandchildren's commitments to Judaism. In the hope that this monograph will in its small way contribute to a better understanding of the dynamics of change in the Jewish American community and to insuring its continued strength in the decades ahead, we dedicate this volume to our grandchildren. They represent the future; we trust that, as they move through life, they will themselves be dedicated to maintaining a strong Jewish identity and helping others do the same.

CHAPTER 1

Introduction

Internal migration has become a major dynamic responsible for the growth or decline of many Jewish communities and for the redistribution of the Jewish population across the American landscape in a pattern quite different from that characterizing American Jewry earlier in the century. Indeed, internal migration together with generational change are closely interrelated with many of the other demographic, social, and economic changes that affect the ties of individuals to the larger Jewish community; and in many instances, migration helps to explain these changes.

For many years, the Jewish American press and, indeed, leaders of the Jewish American community have believed that the major *demographic* challenges facing American Jewry were the effects of high intermarriage rates and very low fertility. While these concerns persist, high levels of geographic mobility and major shifts in residential distribution are now recognized as also having significant relevance for the vitality of the Jewish community, both locally and nationally. America's Jews are highly mobile. They are increasingly dispersed across the major regions of the United States, across a growing number of metropolitan areas, and away from center cities to suburbs and exurban areas as well as to smaller cities and towns. Their redistribution presents new challenges to the national Jewish community and to individual Jews (cf. DellaPergola, 1991; Cohen, 1988).

That such mobility has raised concerns is clearly evident in newspaper headlines such as "Population Shifts Create New Problems for Jewish Federations"; "South Dakota's Lone Rabbi Travels Far and Wide to Sell Judaism to All"; "Jewish Outposts in Dixie"; "A Growing Trend: Jewish Population Moving from Northeast to Sun Belt"; "Being Jewish Where There Is No Jewish Community." High levels of population mobility and greater geographic dispersion are thus compounding the challenges to the demographic and socioeconomic vitality of the Jewish community raised by high intermarriage rates and low fertility.

1

The problems caused by mobility extend not just to the community, but affect individual Jews as well (cf. Moore, 1994). The sense of isolation or disconnectedness that movement may engender is captured very well in an essay by Jay Neugeboren (1994:95). "[W]e often prized the distance . . . we created between our world and the world of our parents. . . . I had, obviously, made use of my American freedoms—my freedom of choice and freedom from discrimination—to gain education and amenities denied my parents. . . . And yet, it seemed, my very freedoms had led me to a time and place in which I felt, to my surprise, small connection."

The freedoms identified by Neugeboren are an integral part of the factors resulting in high levels of mobility. The high educational level of Jewish Americans and the kinds of careers they can now pursue, coupled with broad freedom of choice about where to live, have increasingly resulted in movement away from parental family and place of origin; this often also means movement out of centers of Jewish concentration (S. Goldstein, 1990). The primacy of considerations other than ties to place and kin when career decisions are made is caught in an exchange reported by journalist Mark Patinkin (1980):

> Occasionally, students will call me to talk about [my profession]. . . .
> "You looking anywhere specific?" I'll ask.
> "If there's a job, I'll go," they'll say.
> When I graduated, I pretty much felt the same way. . . .
> The call we hear is for the best job, not the closest ties. It doesn't mean we're growing colder, just more mobile.

Such geographic mobility may weaken ties to a particular Jewish community by reducing the opportunites for local integration while increasing opportunities for greater interaction with non-Jews. Moreover, the migration effects of both changing education and occupational patterns may be compounded by changes in marital and fertility behavior. If Jews marry at later ages, if more Jews choose not to marry at all, if marital disruption increases, and if fertility remains low, conditions conducive to locational stability may continue to weaken so that even higher levels of longer-distance movement may result.

While geographic mobility has been a striking feature of Jewish history from the very inception of the Jewish people in biblical times, population movement is certainly not unique to Jews. It accounts for the settlement and current population configuration of the North American continent. The migration of Jewish Americans must therefore be seen within the generally high mobility rates that characterize American society: about one in five Americans change their residence annually.

Such mobility for Americans as a whole has been attributed (Gober, 1993) to a number of factors: a longstanding tradition of immigration that fosters, once initial ties are severed, a "culture of migration" in which attitudes, values, and institutions are conducive to further movement; a high premium placed on personal freedom, which includes the freedom to move; and having housing markets and public policies that facilitate mobility. Such cultural features stimulating mobility are reinforced by wide opportunities for higher education, the character of employment and labor turnover and transfers in industrial and commercial enterprises, and such life cycle features as late marriage, living independent of parental households, low fertility, high divorce rates, and retirement.

Other factors affecting mobility in the 1990s have been identified by Peter Drucker (1994:72–73) as related to the rise of the "knowledge society." Old communities, like the family and village, have ceased to perform the social tasks delegated to them in the past, and have been replaced by organizations. But organizations do not generate the loyalties of their members in the way that the old communities did. "By definition, a knowledge society is a society of mobility. . . . People no longer have roots." To the extent that Jews participate heavily in the knowledge society, they may also be disproportionally affected by its rootlessness.

For the individual and the community, frequent and widespread mobility can have both positive and negative effects. These are effectively summarized by Gober (1993:4), who points out that one school of thought sees the freedom associated with migration as leading to greater innovation as a result of the synergism of people from a variety of backgrounds sharing ideas and expertise. Others argue that high mobility can be disruptive by leading to social isolation, a breakdown in family life, the loss of a sense of community, and the development of, to use Vance Packard's (1972) term, a "nation of strangers." Most geographic mobility combines both features, depending on particular circumstances.

THEORETICAL PERSPECTIVES

Wade Clark Roof (1976), in his critical assessment of traditional religion in contemporary society, argued that in the absence of a religiously based moral order, structural-functional interpretations of commitment in terms of role and status positions appear to be less than satisfactory in explaining traditional religion in modern, industrial society. Instead, he proposed that social sectors in modern life, in which traditional symbols and rituals are meaningful, provide an alternative approach for explaining the social basis of religion in a secular order. In doing so, he turned to the local community as a sphere in modern society that still persists "as a complex system of friendship and kinship networks, formal and informal associations, as well as symbolic attachments, very much rooted in family life and ongoing socialization processes" (197). Roof stressed the importance of locality attachments and participation by citing Luckmann (1967) to the effect that the locality is a micro-universe around which experiences may be structured and interpreted in the modern world: "The local community in modern mass society offers an individual opportunities for nurturing and maintaining the 'private' life, set aside and somewhat distinct from the public sectors of society" (Roof, 1976:206).

Complicating the formulation of the role of community as the context for religious expression are the changes that have occurred in attitudes and behavior among the generation born during the "baby boom" years. Roof (1993) has shown how their experiences have led to a transformation of the role of religion that in the 1990s includes a reemergence of spirituality, religious pluralism, and beliefs and practices that draw on a variety of sources. These changes have created a new desire for networks and community within which to realize religious expressions. This emerging set of religious affiliations and practices has great relevance to any assessment of the impact of migration; relocation from one community to another may break the connections that tie the individual to the local religious community.

The relation among migration and levels of community involvement and extent of Jewish identity may be affected by three processes that generally affect differences between migrants and nonmigrants at origin or destination, regardless of the particular attitudinal or behavioral traits being assessed (cf. S. Goldstein and

A. Goldstein, 1983): *selectivity, adaptation,* and *disruption.* The selectivity perspective views the differentials as having existed before migration occurred. The adaptation response is seen as manifesting itself after migration in response to the conditions of the host population and to facilities in the place of destination. The third perspective (disruption) argues that the migration process itself largely accounts for whatever differentials exist, and these differentials are therefore likely to dissipate with increased duration in place of destination.

In the case of Jewish migration, the *selectivity* model assumes that, compared to nonmovers at origin, migrants are less affiliated in their community of origin and generally less identified with Judaism; they may therefore be less reluctant or even more motivated to move elsewhere. This perspective suggests that, even after all other key variables (such as education and occupation) affecting mobility are controlled, such persons would be more mobile because of their weaker ties to the Jewish community. Moreover, the character of the selection process may change with time, as the strength and nature of individual ties to the community change with the meaning of identity in individual lives. Over time, and especially as migration becomes more common, the migrants may become more typical of the population as a whole so that the differentials associated with the selection process may become less distinct.

The *adaptation* model assumes that Jewish migrants differ minimally from the Jewish population at origin and bring with them to their new destination those attitudes and behavioral traits characteristic of Jews at origin. However, once exposed to the new opportunities and facilities at destination, and after sufficient interaction with the population living there, the migrants are likely to adopt the attitudes and behavior of the "host" population. The major variable here, of course, is who constitutes the host population. If the motives for migrating include the desire to discard one's original identity, then the move may include a concerted effort to "disappear" into the larger community and to avoid contact with the Jewish community. If, on the other hand, there is a desire to maintain or even strengthen Jewish identity and participation, then a concerted effort may be made to search out other Jews, to join Jewish groups, and to live in Jewish neighborhoods. The success of such efforts will depend both on the strength of the motivation and on the degree to which the host community extends a facilitating hand. The combination of circumstances will determine whether, in fact, the incoming individuals and families differ from or come to resemble the nonmigrant Jewish population in their Jewish characteristics.

We would not expect a uniform pattern among all in-migrants since substantial variation is likely in the motives for moving and in the priorities given to maintaining Jewish identity. For example, in Washington, D.C., Ressler (1993) found that expression of Jewish identity was initially greater among migrants to the capital, but diminished with time spent in Washington. Evidently, the identificational norms of the host community, which involved low levels of affiliation, were conveyed to and adopted by the new residents. The eventual lower levels of involvement of the in-migrants may, on the other hand, be in response to creation of informal networks with other Jews; once created, the formal structure would no longer be as important.

Moreover, duration of residence in itself constitutes a major variable as do the size of the Jewish community, the nature of its facilities, and the extent of difference between sending and receiving communities. As Cohen (1983) points out, a new area of residence may have a "contextual impact," including the effect of such factors as the socioeconomic composition of the area's population, the maturity of the area's institutions, the density of Jewish population, and the proximity to major Jewish communities and central institutions. Some, like Goldscheider (1986), have argued that weakened ties to the formal Jewish community are replaced by other sources of ethnic and identificational cohesion; movement into areas of lower Jewish density may reflect constraints of economic factors and housing markets, but not necessarily a desire to assimilate. Nonetheless, the nature of the adaptation made and the extent to which assimilation does occur will undoubtedly be influenced by contextual factors.

A variation of the adaptation model is the *socialization* model. It also assumes that adaptation to the patterns characterizing the host community will occur, but only after considerable length of residence at destination, often involving one or more generations. Duration of residence in any given location may be limited, however, with extensive repeated movement; the opportunity for integration and adaptation may therefore be seriously restricted.

These two perspectives point to conditions at places of origin or destination as the key variables affecting migrant attitudes and behavior in comparison to those of nonmigrants. The *disruption* model, by contrast, holds that the migration process itself may be responsible for observed differentials. The differentials would therefore be sharpest immediately following the move and lessen with longer duration of residence, since the disruptive effects of migration are likely to dissipate over time.

Several factors may help to explain the disruptive character of the migration process for Jews. To the extent that community ties within the Jewish population are expressed through membership in temples/synagogues, enrollment of children in educational programs, participation in local organizations, and contributions to local philanthropic activities, a high degree of population movement, especially when it is repeated with some frequency, may disrupt existing patterns of participation or weaken the loyalties they generate.

Reflecting breaks in social ties, in neighborhood cohesion, in school and occupational connections, and in affiliations, the move itself may be sufficiently stressful from a sociopsychological perspective as to interfere with integration into the new setting. Lack of familiarity with resources of the Jewish community and lack of a sense of loyalty to the new location and community may also retard the adaptation process. Sociological research has suggested, for example, that recent migrants to a community are much less active in its formal organizational structure than are long-term residents (Zimmer, 1955; Goldscheider, 1986). In a study of Greater Orlando, Florida, for example, Sheskin (1993) found that membership in a synagogue increased from 21 percent of those who had lived in the area less than five years to at least 38 percent for those with longer residence.

Although participation eventually increases, the adjustment may take from three to five years, and sometimes migrants never reach the same level of participation as persons who grew up in the community. Moreover, if a significant proportion of in-migrants anticipate that they are likely to remain in the community only a few years, the financial and sociopsychological costs involved in becoming members of organized groups and in developing new linkages may discourage efforts to participate and affiliate, thereby exacerbating the disruptive effects of the move. Such costs as initiation fees and required contributions to building funds may serve as barriers to affiliation for newcomers who expect to remain in the community only a few years.

Observances within the home may be less affected by the move than those involving interaction with the larger community, but even the former may depend on the ease with which access is gained in the new setting to Jewish facilities and to the personal contacts and organizations that often facilitate such access. With the passage of time, the migrant may either resume earlier patterns of behavior or adapt to the new contextual conditions and opportunities. Depending on the degree and nature of initial disruption, the development of linkages with both the Jewish community and the larger community may be difficult and prolonged, and the disruptive effects could have a permanent impact.

The problem may be especially acute in smaller communities, where newcomers are often seen as potentially invigorating the local Jewish community. Yet, as Barry Marks (1975) observed, if the newcomers anticipate moving out again in a few years, they contribute little to their current community: "Many of our newcomers . . . still identified primarily with their former communities and spend one or more weekends a month out of town. . . . I've seen a good deal of mobility in the past year—families barely established in [the community] on the move once again" (212).

The selection, adaptation, and disruption processes are not mutually exclusive. Thus, the patterns of affiliation, observance, and other Jewish activities of migrants at the time of a given survey can, in fact, reflect the cumulative effects of all three processes. To isolate any one requires a very rich set of longitudinal data as well as detailed information on the contextual features of the various areas from which and to which the migrants have moved; this is well beyond the possibilities of the data from the 1990 National Jewish Population Survey that form the basis of this assessment. While the possible roles of the respective processes in explaining differentials between migrants and nonmigrants and among migrants belonging to subcategories of the Jewish population will be suggested and explored as far as the data allow, definitive answers are not likely.

Migration may also have a positive impact on the individual and the community. It could help enhance the Jewish identity of individuals by bringing them to communities with more extensive facilities and fuller opportunities for interaction with other Jews. Those Jews wishing to have easy access to other Jews and to Jewish facilities—like synagogues/temples, schools, and kosher butchers—may opt to shift residence from areas of weak Jewish life to areas that are more Jewish. This may be especially true of Orthodox and, to a lesser degree, of Conservative Jews. Some of the movement from smaller towns to larger cities and from states and regions more heavily secular to those containing higher proportions of observant Jews may reflect such concerns.

At the same time, by bringing additional population to smaller communities or to declining ones, migration can also provide the kind of "demographic transfusion" and minimum population density needed to help maintain or to develop basic institutions and facilities essential for a vital Jewish community. This would be especially true if the in-migrating Jews have a strong Jewish identity and can assume leadership roles and provide models for the less committed. Migration may also have a positive effect by bridging the traditional age and affiliation cleavages that characterize some communities, thereby providing the social cement needed to hold the community together and to enhance Jewish continuity across the generations (Lebowitz, 1975). Whether mobility varies among the denominational subsegments of the Jewish community and between these groups and those identifying as secular Jews also has significance for ties to the larger community and for individual identity.

Jaret (1978), using data from Chicago, found that geographic mobility has different impications for Reform/nonaffiliated and for Orthodox/Conservative Jews. For the former, mobility was linked to reduced ethnic identification and participation. Among the latter, mobility apparently did not necessarily mean ethnic detachment, and even promoted ethnic participation. If these differentials can be generalized, any substantial change in the degree to which Jews identify with, and are committed to, their ethnic community could well be associated with both higher levels of residential mobility and lower levels of social participation. Cause and effect remain to be determined.

In interviews conducted in Iowa, New Jersey, and Oregon in 1972 on the relation between geographic mobility, social integration, and church attendance, Welch and Baltzell (1984) found that geographic mobility inhibits attendance indirectly through disrupting an individual's network of social ties and bonds of community attachment. The authors suggest that a reference group perspective may be useful in interpreting the observed patterns. Migrants may experience resocialization pressures as they encounter community norms that might deemphasize formal church attendance. Adoption of these norms, rather than disruption per se, may therefore be responsible for the change in behavior. Exposure to a variety of norms in the new social setting may encourage a relativistic perspective that allows individuals to evaluate new norms more critically and to choose new styles of behavior (cf. de Vaus, 1982). As the authors stress, full evaluation of the process requires data that allow attention to localism, multiple measures of past and present attendance, community religious norms, and propensity for norm violation.

Concurrently, mobility may contribute to the development of a national Jewish society, characterized by greater population dispersion and by greater population exchange among various localities (Goldstein, 1991). Both processes require more effective networking among locations in order to insure continuing opportunities and stimuli for mobile individuals and families to maintain their Jewish identity and their links to the Jewish community, regardless of where they live or how often they move from place to place. Greater dispersion, especially to smaller communities and to more isolated ones, also requires development of methods to insure that such communities are better able through their own facilities or through links to other, larger communities to service the social, psychological, economic, health, and religious needs of both their migrant and nonmigrant populations (Goldstein, 1990).

EVIDENCE FROM PAST STUDIES

Community Studies in the 1960s

Despite migration's importance for understanding the dynamics of population change both nationally and in individual communities, little attention was given to Jewish population movement in most studies undertaken before the 1970s (Goldstein, 1971:34–52). Some insights were provided by studies of individual Jewish communities, but to the extent that each community is unique in some respects, the possibility of generalizing to the total Jewish American population was limited. National data first became available from the results of the 1970/71 National Jewish Population Study (NJPS-1970/71). These findings reinforced those from earlier community studies which suggested that, judged either by the proportion of population born outside the community of residence or by the length of time individuals had resided in the area of enumeration, high levels of mobility characterized American Jewry.

The 1963 Detroit study (Mayer, 1966a), which ascertained the place of birth of the resident population, found that only one-third of the total Jewish population of Detroit was born in the city; 28 percent were foreign-born; and 36 percent had moved to Detroit from other places in the United States, with over half of these coming from other cities and towns in Michigan. A similar finding emerged from the 1964 Camden, New Jersey, study (Westoff, 1964): only one-third were born in the Camden area, and almost 60 percent had moved there from elsewhere in the United States. The small balance of foreign-born reflected the area's more recent growth as a place of Jewish residence, partly as a suburb of Philadelphia.

The 1963 Greater Providence study (Goldstein, 1964), which encompassed almost all of Rhode Island's Jewish population, found that 60 percent of all Jews living in the area were born in the state. Of the 40 percent who were born elswhere, 16 percent were foreign-born and 24 percent originated in other states. Virtually identical patterns emerged for Springfield, Massachusetts (Goldstein, 1968).

Mobility can also be measured by length of residence in the area. The 1964–65 Milwaukee study (Mayer, 1966b), for example, found that 60 percent of the city's Jews had been living in their current residence for less than ten years and 40 percent for less than five years. These data suggest a high degree of residential mobility, although they did not specify whether it took the form of intraurban mobility or migration across larger distances. The 1965 Boston study (Axelrod, Fowler, and Gurin, 1967) also suggested a high degree of mobility. Half the population had lived at their present address for less than ten years, and almost one-third for five years or less. The age statistics confirmed that, like the general American population, the highest mobility characterized those in their twenties; 70 percent of Boston's Jews age 20–29 had lived at their surveyed address less than five years compared, for example, to 10 percent of those age 60–69. Further reflecting the high mobility of Boston's Jews, 34 percent intended to move in the near future. Part of the high mobility in the Boston area reflects the high concentration there of college/university students.

The 1969 Columbus, Ohio, study (Mayer, 1970) was among the first to document that levels of mobility varied between the older, more concentrated areas of settlement and the newer, less densely Jewish areas. The former were inhabited more by persons who were born in the community, and who were also characterized by lower educational levels, were more likely businessmen than professionals, and were inclined toward more traditional religious beliefs and practices. The results suggested that the importance of religion as a basis for selecting areas of residence was diminishing in favor of socioeconomic criteria. This in turn suggested a greater dispersion of the Jewish population in the future, as the traditional forces that had led to settlement in areas of high Jewish density weakened and as the motivations for mobility that characterized the American population as a whole also came to characterize the Jewish population.

A few studies also suggested that the rising educational level of Jews and changes in their occupational profiles could contribute to an increasing rate of population movement. For example, statistics from Toledo, Ohio (Rosen, 1970), indicated that national operations had brought to Toledo a surprisingly large number of Jewish men in managerial positions, and that the local university had had a substantial increase in the number of Jewish faculty. At the same time, 45 percent to 60 percent of young Jews raised in Toledo had moved to distant cities after college graduation to begin employment.

Based on the experience of the general American population, the pattern identified by the Toledo study seemed likely to become more typical of the Jewish population, resulting in increasing migration levels and increasingly higher rates of repeated movement by the same persons. General migration studies of the American population had already documented higher than average mobility of professionals and other highly educated persons because of the unequal regional demands for their talents and their greater responsiveness to opportunities around the country. Moreover, as the Toledo report on the national corporations suggested, many national firms had adopted company policies of relocating staff, especially executives and professionals, as the needs of the firm's various branches changed and as a way of upgrading ranks. As the proportion of Jews holding such positions increased, the rate of Jewish population mobility was likely to increase, too.

This possibility had been recognized by Glazer and Moynihan (1963:150) as early as 1963: "The son wants the business to be bigger and better and perhaps he would rather be a cog in a great corporation than the manager in a small one. He may not enjoy the tight Jewish community with its limited horizons and its special satisfactions—he is not that much of a Jew any more." Status may thus be the drawing force of third-generation Americans, just as financial success was the major consideration of second-generation Americans. The decline in discriminatory practices and the greater availability of executive and professional positions formerly closed to Jews were also expected to stimulate the greater geographic dispersal of those Jews willing to develop occupational careers outside the communities where they were raised.

That this was already happening in the 1960s was strongly suggested not only by the Toledo data but also by evidence from the 1963 study of Greater Providence (Goldstein, 1964). Among the surveyed families, only one-third of the sons age 40 and over were living outside Rhode Island, compared to half of the sons age 20–39 and almost two-thirds of those under age 20. Although fewer daughters lived away from their parental community, the basic age differentials paralleled those characterizing the sons.

These data clearly suggested a weakening in the kinship ties of Jewish Americans, as measured by a greater tendency of children to live at some distance from parental family. They supported Gerhard Lenski's (1963) thesis that one of the best indicators of the changing importance attached to family and kin groups by modern Americans is their willingness to leave their native community and move elsewhere. Since most migration is motivated by economic and occupational considerations, he suggested, migration serves as an indicator of the strength of economic motives compared to kinship ties. In modern society the continual removal of economic rewards out of the hands of kin and extended family groups lessens the dominance of Jewish families over the socioeconomic placement of its young. The changing kinship relations, coupled with more fluid labor markets, contributed to higher mobility rates. To the extent these trends could be expected to persist, they pointed to increased mobility in future decades. The 1987 Rhode Island study (Goldscheider and Goldstein, 1988), for example, found that almost 60 percent of all respondents' sons and daughters age 25–64 lived outside the state, well above the 1963 level and with minimal differences by gender.

While the data from these individual community studies provided valuable insights into the extent and character of Jewish population movement, they also documented clearly that mobility levels varied considerably among communities, depending on size, location, the age of the Jewish settlement, the age structure of the Jewish population, and the availability of Jewish facilities and resources. They also suggested that the pull of living in areas inhabited by other Jews and serviced by Jewish institutions remained strong even while the attraction of being part of more integrated areas and of taking advantage of the full range of residential, social, educational, and occcupational opportunities was gaining momentum. The latter forces might have become more important in influencing whether Jews moved and in their choice of destination. To the extent that new areas of residence had lower Jewish population and institutional density, increased mobility might have impinged seriously on the cohesiveness of the Jewish community and on the likelihood that migrating Jews would retain a strong Jewish identity. Indeed, it might be in part responsible for increasing rates of intermarriage and assimilation.

Yet, the community studies in themselves, while highly suggestive of the extent and impact of migration, could not adequately or fully document the process or its effects nationally. In addition to varying on a wide range of characteristics, individual communities differed significantly in the survey sampling methods used to identify the Jewish population, in the questions and definitions employed, and in the way the data were tabulated. This lack of standardization created serious difficulties in attributing differences in migration patterns among communities to the actual characteristics of the communities or to differences in research designs and analytic methods. Undoubtedly, both factors were operating in most cases.

Individual community studies were also of limited value because they usually encompassed only one side of the mobility picture. Relying on samples of the population resident in the community at the time of the survey, only in-migrants to the community were assured coverage. Persons who had moved away were not generally encompassed by the studies, except in surveys that asked about household members, especially children, who had out-migrated. However, even here the picture was incomplete; when entire households had moved away they were completely missed. For all these reasons, local studies made generalizations to the national scene difficult if not dangerous.

The 1970/71 National Jewish Population Survey

A national survey that covers both areas of out-migration and in-migration and that relies on the best possible sampling procedures, with appropriate definitions and questions, is able to overcome the limitations of community studies. The decision by the Council of Jewish Federations and Welfare Funds to undertake a National Jewish Population Survey in 1970/71 provided an opportunity to realize these goals more effectively than had heretofore been possible (Massarik, 1992).

The study was designed to sample the entire Jewish population of the United States, including marginal and unaffiliated Jews as well as those closely identified with the organized Jewish community, in every geographic region of the country, and generally from every Jewish community with an initially estimated population of 30,000 or more (Massarik and Chenkin, 1973). Interviews were also conducted in appropriate proportions in medium-sized and small Jewish communities, and special efforts were made to contact Jewish households in a sample of counties which had until then been assumed to contain few Jewish households.

Two types of samples were used: (1) an "area probability sample," collected by contacting and screening many thousands of households on a door-to-door basis to identify those including a Jewish member; and (2) a "list sample" based on households known to have at least one Jewish member through inclusion of the household on lists either furnished by Jewish communities or developed specifically for the study. The two sample groups were combined through proper weighting to provide the needed balance between marginal Jews and those directly associated with their Jewish community. A total of 7,179 households were included in the national sample, encompassing a weighted sample size of 33,165 individuals.

The wide range of questions included in the omnibus survey included several on mobility. They provided the basis for obtaining information on lifetime migration (based on comparison of place of residence in 1970/71 and place of birth), mobility between 1965 and the time of the survey, and the last move. Information was also obtained on mobility expectations in the five years following the survey. Background data on the socioeconomic characteristics of the surveyed population allowed assessment of differentials between migrants and nonmigrants (Goldstein, 1981).

Unfortunately, the data from NJPS-1970/71 were not as fully analyzed as the richness of its contents justified.[1] The limited evaluation did, however, document relatively high mobility rates: one quarter of the native-born Jewish population was living in a state other than that in which they were born, a level of interstate lifetime movement quite similar to that of the native-white population of the United States. Eight percent of the adult population had moved interstate within the 5–6 years immediately preceding the survey, and as many as one-third of the entire adult population were living in a town or city other than that in which they had resided in 1965. The observed patterns of redistribution indicated a migration loss of Jews for the Northeast, minimum net change in the Midwest, and migration gains for the South and the West, as well as substantial decreases in the concentrations in central cities and a more generally dispersed Jewish population (Goldstein, 1982).

The tendency for migration rates to be higher for those with more education and for education to be positively correlated with movement involving greater distance (see chapter 4) confirmed earlier suggestions that higher levels of enrollment in colleges and universities would be an important factor in Jewish mobility levels and patterns. Such a conclusion was reinforced by the observed occupational differentials, which pointed to a positive association between white-collar employment and levels and distance of migration.

The continuation of a high degree of movement in future years was also suggested by the answers to questions on anticipated moves. Of the total population, 16 percent indicated plans to move within at least five years, but as many as six out of every ten adults age 25–29 expected to do so. Such high rates are obviously related to the family formation and career stages of persons in this cohort. The rates declined with increasing age.

The evaluation of the NJPS-1970/71 data supported the thesis that Jewish population mobility had to be considered a key variable in any assessment of the future vitality the Jewish American community.

Community Studies after NJPS-1970/71

Between NJPS-1970/71 and NJPS-1990, no other full-scale study of the national Jewish population was undertaken that allowed detailed attention to migration. As a result, insights about changes in this twenty-year interval again must be derived from community studies. They continued to document high levels of mobility. Since several communities that had given attention to migration in their first survey undertook second and, in the case of Boston, third surveys between 1970 and 1990, some assessment could be made of the persistence of earlier patterns.

Only selected evidence from these studies need be cited here. The 1972 Dallas survey (Maynard, 1974) found that only 35 percent of the population were born in Dallas, and a high percentage of these were children. Over half the Jewish population had moved to Dallas from other parts of the United States, and an additional 14 percent were foreign born. Consistent with the patterns of regional redistribution noted earlier, almost one-quarter of the U.S.-born migrants to Dallas originated in the Northeast, and just over one quarter in the Midwest. Similarly, the 1976 Greater Kansas City survey (*Jewish Population Study*, 1979) found that "not only are the majority of household heads not born in Kansas City, but there is little tendency for this proportion to increase among the younger people."

Evidence from northern New Jersey suggested that weakening kinship ties were associated with high levels of mobility (Verbit, 1971). Only about one-quarter of the sons and daughters among those children living outside their parental home remained in the same general area, and an additional quarter were living in other areas of the state. What is most important is that as many as 25 percent were residing in parts of the United States outside New York, Pennsylvania, and New Jersey, pointing to the substantial dispersion of family members.

That the levels of migration were increasing for the Jewish population was strongly suggested by the 1987 Rhode Island survey (Goldscheider and Goldstein, 1988), a study similar to that conducted twenty-four years earlier for Greater Providence. The 1987 study found that only one-third of those surveyed had lived in Rhode Island all their lives, compared to about half of those surveyed in 1963. The highest migration rate characterized younger adults; seven out of every ten persons age 18–45 were in-migrants to Rhode Island. This compared to only 36 percent of this age range in 1963. Of the American-born Jews living in Rhode Island in 1987, 45 percent were born in other states, compared to only one-quarter in 1963. Moreover, more of the migrants living in the state in 1987, especially the younger population, came from more distant parts of the United States than in 1963: 28 percent from outside New England, compared to only 14 percent in 1963.

As in 1963, the redistribution patterns also affected movement of Jews away from Rhode Island. Six of every ten children living away from parental home were living outside the state. In contrast to 1963, by 1987 almost equal proportions of children in all age groups were living outside the state. That such separation was no longer exceptional for younger groups corroborates other evidence of increasing Jewish mobility levels over the past several decades. Similarly, considerable out-migration seems to have characterized middle-aged and older persons. Even after taking account of mortality, the number of older persons enumerated in 1987 was considerably below the number projected on the basis of the population surveyed in 1963. The substantially higher percentage of Rhode Island Jews who were in-migrants in the state by 1987 compared to 1963, the out-migration of others, and the greater dispersal of the population within the state, all represent an accentuation of patterns observed a quarter century earlier.

The 1987 Rhode Island data also showed that recent migrants had lower levels of Jewish organizational affiliation than did those who had always lived in the state. The relation between recency of migration and synagogue/temple membership was especially clear: for persons under age 65, migration was associated with lower levels of affiliation, especially in the period immediately following settlement in the new community.

Rhode Island is clearly not typical of the country as a whole, but in the past changes in the general population of the state have often preceded those in the nation as a whole. The changing patterns of Jewish mobility behavior may thus also anticipate changes that will come to characterize American Jewry as a whole, or at least reflect the ongoing processes in the older sections of the nation, including the Northeast and the Midwest.

Boston is unique in having undertaken surveys decennially since 1965. Moreover, the data from the 1965 and 1975 Boston studies have also been the subject of intensive analyses by Steven

Cohen (1983) and Calvin Goldscheider (1986). Unfortunately, the treatment of migration in the three surveys was not uniform, making comparisons across time difficult.

The 1965 survey used length of residence in present home as its measure of mobility. It found that 31 percent of the Greater Boston population had lived in their present home for less than five years and half had done so for less than ten years. Although these data point to a high level of mobility, they do not distinguish between local and longer-distance movers. Indicative of future mobility, 34 percent of the total population reported definite or tentative plans to move within the next two years, but most of the intended movement was expected to occur within the Greater Boston area, especially to newer suburbs.

The results of the 1975 survey, as reanalyzed by Goldscheider (1986), pointed to considerably higher mobility among Jews than non-Jews in the area. Only one-fifth of the Jews but almost four out of every ten non-Jews had lived in their community for twenty years or more; moreover, higher mobility characterized every age group of the Jewish population. As many as four in ten Jews, but only one-quarter of the non-Jews, resided in their 1975 community less than three years. This rose to over three-fourths of the Jews age 18–29, compared to half of the non-Jews.

That Jews were highly mobile was corroborated by the data on their origins. Four in ten of the Jewish population were born in the United States but outside the Boston metropolitan area, compared to only 29 percent of non-Jews. This picture of substantial movement from outside the Greater Boston area persisted when the assessment was based on comparison of place of residence in 1975 compared to ten years earlier. Almost one-third of the Jews, but only 22 percent of the non-Jews, lived outside the metropolitan area.

The Boston data also pointed to substantial differences between migrants and nonmigrants in various indicators of Jewishness. For example, whereas 66 percent of those who had lived in Boston city ten years earlier reported that most of their friends were Jewish, only 33 percent of those migrating from outside the metropolitan area did so. Whereas 55 percent of the former valued living in a Jewish neighborhood, only one-third of the migrants did. Fifteen percent of the 10-year Boston residents were nondenominational, in contrast to 40 percent of the migrants from outside the metropolitan area. Synagogue attendance, however, showed minimal difference.

On the basis of his in-depth analysis, however, Goldscheider (1986:57) concluded that "while there appears to be a relationship between migration and disaffection from the Jewish community, that relationship is mainly because movers are younger and more educated. The net effects of migration per se are weak, except among those with the shortest durations of residence." Since, for many migrants to a community, residence does not extend to more than a few years, the opportunities to integrate more fully may be limited. The much lower levels of Jewishness characterizing such recent migrants may, in fact, be indicative of a longer term situation for those who experience frequent movement.

In this respect, Stephen Cohen's (1983:111) conclusions, also using the Boston data, but with different types of analyses, seem relevant:

[H]igh residential mobility . . . is a crucial factor influencing communal affiliation. Movers are indeed less often affiliated than nonmovers. In part this is so because movers are initially different from—primarily younger than—the residentially stable. Indeed, this process of self-selection is the principal reason why recent movers contribute less often to philanthropic causes. However, joining a synagogue is a much more localistic activity than participating in Jewish charitable drives. As a result, synagogue membership is adversely affected by residential mobility as well as by the antecedents of mobility (especially age and life cycle).

In particular, the residentially mobile disrupt their ties to family, friends, and formal institutions; and they take five or more years to reestablish those ties in their new residential locales. Moreover, they are likely to move to those areas where residential mobility is high and where, as a consequence, established informal networks and mature communal institutions are relatively rare.

The 1985 statistics on mobility for the Boston community pointed to continued high levels of mobility—quite similar, in fact, to those of 1975 (Israel, 1987). As in 1975, the highest rates of mobility characterized the younger segment of the population, partly reflecting the heavy concentration of students enrolled in educational institutions in the area. Moreover, four out of every ten adults thought it very or fairly likely that they would move out of the Greater Boston area within the next ten years. Of these, almost one in five named Florida as a likely destination and 16 percent the West or Southwest. Only 19 percent designated places in New England as a likely choice; 28 percent pointed to New York, New Jersey, and other Atlantic Seaboard areas.

The 1985 survey also found that migration had an impact on the integration of individuals into the organized life of the community. Of those who were living in the same locality in the Boston area in both 1975 and 1985, 63 percent were not affiliated with any Jewish organization, and 18 percent belonged to two or more. By contrast, of those who had moved to Greater Boston during this ten-year period, 86 percent were not affiliated, and only 4 percent belonged to two or more organizations. These differentials were especially pronounced among the middle-aged. The 1985 Boston data thus suggested that population turnover had become an important feature of the Jewish community, with all that this implies for levels of integration and continuity.

The findings about the extent of mobility and its impact on Jewish affiliation and identity based in individual communities may not be typical of the larger American scene. Nonetheless, the consistency of patterns identified by diverse community surveys was highly suggestive of more universal features of the process. Full evaluation of the relation between migration and Jewish affiliation and continuity required national data.

An approach to a national analysis was undertaken by Gary Tobin (1993). His comparative assessment was based on community studies completed in the mid- and late–1980s, encompassing all regions of the United States; it is not, however, fully representative of the country as a whole because of the selective character of the communities covered (e.g., New York and Los Angeles were not included nor was there adequate representation of Jewish communities with populations under 20,000). The study lent strong support to the evidence already cited from individual communities: A substantial proportion of Jews moved in recent years, and the general patterns of redistribution paralleled those of the general American population even while retaining some unique features.

Tobin (1993) found that the two dominant areas of growth were southern Florida and California, but that the nature of movement to Florida was changing. While climate and health considerations accounted for the moves of a majority of the migrants (Sheskin, 1982), more of the recent movers were attracted by work-related factors and the desire to be near a large Jewish community. The chain reaction process of migration obviously was operating in Florida, with growing communities attracting still more migrants (Sheskin, 1987).

For other communities in the United States, such as Pittsburgh; Boston; Washington, D.C.; Columbus; and Atlantic City, work-related/economic considerations were found to be the primary explanation for in-movement. Jews were seeking to take advantage of the special opportunities afforded by local economies to utilize their aquired skills and/or to realize their aspirations for a better livelihood. Yet Tobin pointed out that not all boom communities have attracted Jews. He speculated that part of the reason may be the absence of a critical mass to serve as a magnet. Such communities would not provide access to a full range of Jewish community services; their lack apparently acted as a deterrent to residence for those interested in strong Jewish identification.

The community surveys pointed to a substantial flow of migrants from other cities and from other regions of the country to the communities under study (Tobin, 1993). For most communities, a large majority of the population was not born in the city of current residence. As many as 85 percent of Washington's Jews, for example, were not born in the area, and 30 percent of the in-migrants had lived there less than five years. In Denver, as many residents had been born in New York as had been born in Denver—22 percent in each. Over half of Denver's population originated in the East and the Midwest. Similarly, in San Francisco about one-quarter of the respondents were born in New York, and just slightly more in California. If the children of these respondents had been included, the percentage born in the San Francisco area would have been higher.

In addition to documenting the extensive redistribution of Jewish population across the country, Tobin's comparative evaluation is valuable in emphasizing that the regional variations in redistribution are linked to age and the contextual features of the individual places of destination. The attraction of Florida and Arizona to the older population are cases in point. The educational opportunites concentrated in the Boston area and associated opportunities for employment in the advanced high-technology industries located there help to explain the flow of younger migrants to this area of New England, although the latter attraction waned with the poorer economic conditions in the late 1980s and early 1990s. The New Jersey suburbs of New York, and undoubtedly the Connecticut ones, too, are characterized by a large influx of families at the younger stages of the life cycle seeking better environments in which to rear children. Even sexual preferences may influence the direction of movement, as evidenced by the high proportion of gays and lesbians contributing to the growth of the San Francisco Jewish community.

Evaluating his findings, Tobin (1993:16–18) pointed to their implications for the migrants and the community. He emphasized that the segmentation by age resulting from the selective character of movement to particular localities may have consequences in terms of delivery of needed services; for example, communities may be unable to support services for large concentrations of the aged. Indeed, some sunbelt communities have already put pressure on communities of origin and on the national community to share in the costs of providing such services. It is argued that since these retirees had spent most of their lives in other locations and donated to the insitutions in those communities, it is unfair that the new community of residence be expected to underwrite the full costs of the postretirement needs of the newcomers.

Furthermore, if Jews move to places with less developed institutional and organizational infrastructures, these newer areas of Jewish settlement will have difficulty providing strong links to the community. This would especially be the case since the patterns of settlement in areas of in-migration tend to be much more dispersed than they are in the older sections and cities of the country from which the migrants are coming.

A related concern revolves about the greater difficulty that the places of destination may have in fundraising, in part because the newcomers are not easily identified and integrated, in part because they have not yet developed loyalties to their new locality, and in part because the financial resources of the migrants, especially for some of the aged, may not be as great as they were before they moved. They may also have adopted a different lifestyle that attaches less value to integration into the Jewish community and support for its institutions. In Florida, for example, they may have moved into condominiums that are heavily, if not exclusively Jewish, thereby reducing the need to turn to Jewish institutions for social support.

Tobin has suggested that the continued redistribution of Jews in the United States may weaken Jewish community life. He concluded that special efforts must be made to strengthen Jewish organizations and institutions and possibly to shift resources from the older regions of Jewish settlement in the Northeast and Midwest to the more recently settled areas to help develop the organizational and institutional infrastructure needed to support Jewish networks and to facilitate the integration of incoming Jews.

Although assessments of Jewish life in America in the 1970s and 1980s, based on the findings of individual community studies, yielded valuable insights, continuing concerns persisted about the acccuracy and comprehensiveness of these studies and the conclusions drawn from them. Over time, the quality of the studies has improved considerably: they have better sampling procedures; have more extensively used standardized definitions, questions, and tabulations; and have achieved greater analytic sophistication (Goldstein, 1987a). Yet, since not all communities adhered to the same standards or followed the same procedures, comparisons and aggregation of results across regions or the nation remain difficult. Moreover, although more communities are covered by such surveys, some large communities had still not been surveyed in the 1980s. Even more serious, representation of smaller communities was inadequate. Furthermore, the individual surveys were undertaken in diverse years so that cumulating the results or treating the studies as if they all referred to the same point in time ran the risk of overlooking significant changes that might have occurred in social and economic conditions in the larger society or within the Jewish community which may have affected the attitudes and behavior with respect to migration and other topics being studied.

THE 1990 NATIONAL JEWISH POPULATION SURVEY

These concerns, and especially the growing interest of the Council of Jewish Federations (CJF) in the emergence of a national Jewish community (Sidney Hollander Memorial Colloquium, 1987) led to the decision in 1988 to undertake a national Jewish population survey in 1990, to coincide with the national decennial census. The survey was to take full advantage of the work during the preceding several years of the CJF's National Technical Advisory

Committee on Population Studies (NTAC). It had been engaged in developing a standardized core questionnaire for use in community studies as well as better sampling methods to insure maximum coverage of affiliated and unaffiliated Jews and to allow assessment of gains and losses attributable to intermarriage and assimilation. The work of the Committee was greatly enhanced by the efforts of the Mandell L. Berman North American Jewish Data Bank (NAJDB), jointly created by the Council of Jewish Federations and the Graduate School of the City University of New York.

In close coordination with Federation plannners, NTAC designed the questionnaire to be used in the national survey, drawing heavily on core questionnaires developed earlier. Given the omnibus character of the survey and the limited time available for the telephone interviews, no particular topic, including migration, could be covered in great depth. (For a broad summary of the NJPS-1990 methodology and findings, see Kosmin et al., 1991.)

The sample design was intended to ensure the widest possible coverage of the Jewish population, encompassing all types of Jews, ranging from those strongly identifying themselves as Jewish, at one extreme, to those on the margins of the community or even outside it, at the other; it sought to include born Jews who no longer considered themselves Jewish and the non-Jewish spouses/partners and children of Jewish household members, as well as other non-Jewish members of the household.

The Survey Methodology

With this broad coverage in mind, the CJF commissioned ICR Survey Group of Media, Pennsylvania, to undertake a national sample survey of approximately 2,500 households drawn from a qualified universe of households containing at least one person identified as currently Jewish or of Jewish background.[2] A three-stage data collection process was employed to achieve this goal. Since the universe of Jewish households was not known, Stage I involved contacting a random sample of 125,813 American households using computer-assisted telephone interviewing. The sampled households represented all religious groups in continental United States as well as secular households; the Jewish households were identified among them (Kosmin and Lachman, 1993).

In addition to traditional census-type questions on sociodemographic, economic, and household characteristics, the screening survey included four questions, asked in the following order, to determine Jewish qualification of each household for later in-depth interview:

1. What is your religion? If not Jewish, then. . . .
2. Do you or anyone else in the household consider them-selves Jewish? If no, then. . . .
3. Were you or anyone else in the household raised Jewish? If no, then. . . .
4. Do you or anyone else in the household have a Jewish parent?

A positive answer to any of these questions qualified the house-hold for initial classification as "Jewish" and therefore as eligible for follow-up contacts in Stage II. Of the 125,813 randomly selected households screened in Stage I, 5,146 households con-tained at least one person who qualified as currently Jewish or who was of Jewish background as determined by the screening questions.

During Stage II, the inventory stage, attempts were made to recontact households in order to requalify potential respondents and to minimze loss to follow-up between the initial screening, which for some households had begun as much as a year before the final round of interviews. A total of 2,240 households from the early months of screening were covered in Stage II. (The remain-der were covered as part of Stage III.) During this procedure, a number of potential respondents dropped out of the sample pool due to changes in household composition or disqualification upon further review of their "Jewish" credentials.

Consistent with the original goal of a total sample of 2,500 households for the in-depth study, the final interviewing stage of the survey, conducted in May–July 1990 to coincide with the United States census, yielded a total of 2,441 completed interviews with qualified respondents. Persons qualified to be respondents in the survey if they indicated they were Jewish by religion, consid-ered themselves Jewish, or were born/raised Jewish. Households were included in the sample only if they contained at least one qualified respondent. During Stage III, the 2,441 qualified respon-dents were interviewed using the extensive questionnaire prepared by NTAC for in-depth assessment of their sociodemographic and economic characteristics and of a wide array of attitudinal and behavioral variables related to Jewish identity. The survey instrument collected information about every member of the household. Thus the study was able to ascertain basic data about the 6,514 persons in the surveyed households, both Jews and non-Jews. More detailed information, and especially attitude questions, referred only to the adult respondent who was chosen randomly from among the currently Jewish or Jewish background members of the household age 18 and over.

Appropriate weighting procedures were applied to the data so that the sample reflected the total United States population in each category, based on U.S. Bureau of the Census statistics. The weighting procedure automatically adjusted for noncooperating households as well as those who were not at home when the interviewer telephoned and for households that did not have telephones or had multiple lines. (See appendix A for a fuller discussion of the sampling and weighting procedures as well as discussion of nonsampling errors and sampling variability.) The weighted sample encompasses 8.1 million individuals. Some of these were persons who were of Jewish background but not Jewish at the time of the survey; others were never-Jewish members in the substantial number of mixed-marriage households and in other units in which Jews and non-Jews lived together.

NJPS-1990 has the great advantage of providing information on all these persons. It thereby allows scholars and planners the option of including or excluding particular subcategories from any given analysis, depending on its purpose. An opportunity is thereby provided to compare and evaluate the characteristics and attitudinal and behavioral traits of those in the core Jewish population, those on the margins, and those who switched religion, as well as those non-Jews who are living with current and former Jews.

For such purposes, the Jewish *core population* will be subdivided into three groups: (a) those born Jewish and reported as Jewish by religion; (b) the secular-ethnic Jews—those born Jewish but not reporting themselves as Jewish by religion and not reporting any other religion; (c) Jews by choice—those formally converted to Judaism and those simply choosing to regard themselves as Jewish. (Since the criteria for conversion vary among denominations, this analysis does not try to distinguish between the two subgroups of Jews by choice.) The currently *peripheral population* (sometimes termed non-Jews) also consists of three subgroups: (a) adults who were born or raised Jewish but who had switched to another religion at the time of the survey; (b) persons who reported Jewish parentage, but who were raised from birth in another religion (some of these and of those who switched religion consider themselves Jewish by ethnicity or background); (c) persons who were not and had never been identified as Jewish by religion or ethnic origin. Of the total households covered, 84 percent included at least one person identified as a core Jew; the remaining 16 percent were households that consisted of only those identifed as peripheral population and included at least one person identified as a Jew by background or descent.

The interviews collected a vast array of information from the 2,441 respondents. Their answers reflect a subjectivity factor on two levels. First, respondents applied their own interpretation to the questions, and second, they replied in terms that were personally meaningful. Readers must be aware that respondents fit themselves into constructs and categories in terms of their own understanding, experience, and environment, rather than the official ideology of religious movements. This is particularly true of questions dealing with attitudes and practices, which are inevitably more ambiguous than demographic characteristics such as age, education, and place of birth. In this context, we must accept the fact that in the United States religion and ethnicity are voluntary expressions of identity. Consequently, many people exhibit and report inconsistencies in their behavior and attitudes with respect to normative expectations. This analysis accepts their answers as reported.

Migration Data in the Survey

A full assessment of the extent of population movement and its impact on Jewish affiliation and identity ideally requires a full residential history, attention to the reasons for movement, and the levels and patterns of affiliation and identity both before and after the move. Information should also be available on the contextual situations before and after migration (i.e., the "Jewish" characteristics of the places of origin and destination). Such comprehensive information is precluded by the competition for space and time in an omnibus questionnaire such as NJPS-1990, designed to collect a wide array of information on the national community in a 30–

35 minute telephone interview. In-depth assessment of migration and its impact must await a survey designed specifically for that purpose.

However, the inclusion of an important core set of questions on residence and migration in NJPS-1990 (see appendix B), together with the wide array of information collected on other demographic variables as well as on behavioral and attitudinal indicators of Jewish identity, means that NJPS-1990 offers the best opportunity yet available to assess the national levels of Jewish population movement and the effects such movement has on redistribution of the population across the regions of the country and between metropolitan and nonmetropolitan areas. Such data allow assessment of the volume and direction of the different migration flows. Combined use of the data on mobility, socioeconomic characteristics, and selected behavioral and attitudinal indicators of Jewish identity allows evaluation of the extent to which migrants differ from nonmigrants and the ways in which movement may affect identity and do so differently for the varied subsegments of the Jewish population. This monograph exploits the NJPS-1990 material for such purposes.

Some of the questions on migration used in the survey referred to all household members; others were restricted to the respondents.[3] Those asked of all members include: country of birth, and state of birth for those born in the United States; year of migration to the United States of the foreign born; for those age 18 and over, country of birth of mother and father; and number of grandparents born in the United States. (The latter two sets were designed largely to allow measurement of the generation status of the household members.) The respondents were asked a broader array of questions: year of movement to the current address; year of movement to current city or town of residence; whether the respondent had, previous to the last move, lived in the same city/town, a different place in the same state, a different state, or a different country; if the previous residence was a different state or country, the specific name was obtained; if the move was within the state, the previous zip code was obtained. Paralleling a question in the United States census, respondents were also asked where they were living five years before the survey (May 1985), and detailed information was obtained similar to that noted for last place of residence. For all respondents, the zip code of current residence was obtained, thereby allowing classification of the residence by type/size of location.

To assess the likely future redistribution of the population and the relation between past and future mobility, respondents were also asked whether they thought it very, somewhat, or not at all likely that they would move within the next three years and, if so, what the likely destination (within state, other state, other country) would be. Finally, to take account of bilocal residence, repondents were also asked whether they spent more than two months of the year away from their present residence; if so, whether it was in one or in more places, in which state or country most of that time was spent, and whether a home was owned in that location.

ANALYSIS PLANS

The data derived from these questions provide a wealth of information for the assessment of migration patterns and their impact, current and potential, on both the migrants themselves and on their communities. Such an assessment will be undertaken using four basic migration perspectives: (1) lifetime migration, defined as changes in residence between place of birth and place of residence in 1990; (2) recent migration, defined as changes between 1985 and 1990; (3) combined use of lifetime and five-year migration data to define duration of residence and multiple moves; (4) future movement as indicated by responses to the question on the likelihood of a move in the next three years. The major thrust of the assessment will be on moves that involved a change in community and state of residence, since the major interest is in the effect of migration on the redistribution of the population and the impact of movement on Jewish affiliation and identity. Minimum attention will therefore be given to residential movement within the same location, and local movers will generally be treated as nonmigrants, with which the migrant population will be compared. The basic thesis is that the longer the distance moved, the more recent the move, the more frequently that moves are made, and the more likely a future move is anticipated, the lesser will be the integration into the new community and the greater the impact on Jewish identity.

We will turn first to the volume and direction of redistribution measured in terms of lifetime and recent mobility. In doing so, we will give particular attention to the impact of such movement on the regional distribution of the Jewish population, on the extent of repeat migration, and on the likely level of future mobility. Once the levels and direction of migration are established, the analysis will proceed to assess whether the migrant population differs in its sociodemographic and economic characteristics from the nonmigrants and, if so, what implications these differences have for their communities of origin and destination and for future migration patterns. Included are such variables as age, gender, education, occupation, and marital status.

Next, the assessment of differentials is extended to variables indicative of Jewish identity. These include denominational affiliation, Jewish education, intermarriage, visits to Israel, and Jewish ritual practices. Integration into the community of destination is evaluated through comparison of migrants and nonmigrants with respect to such indicators as organization membership, volunteer work, synagogue/temple affiliation, and philanthropic giving. Whenever appropriate, these evaluations of differentials and integration take account of both past and likely future mobility. Multivariate analyses are used to control for the effects of key background variables, such as age, gender, education, occupation, and marital status. The monograph ends with attention to the overall implications of the findings for the future vitality of the American Jewish community and for community efforts to strengthen Jewish identity and continuity.

CHAPTER 2

Numbers, Distribution, and Mobility

The fluid nature of the Jewish American population is at the heart of the 1990 National Jewish Population Survey (NJPS) findings. The number of Jews, their composition, and their geographic distribution across the nation depend on who is counted as in or out of the Jewish population. From a policy perspective, this raises questions about how the community can retain those at the core; how it can draw in those at the margin; whether it should attempt to bring back those who have left; and if it should attempt to influence those who must choose whether or not to be Jewish. Depending on how these questions are resolved over the next several decades, the Jewish population can potentially grow substantially or decline sharply.

CHANGING NUMBERS, 1970/71 TO 1990

At no time in American history has there been a complete enumeration of the nation's Jewish population. Any statistics on the number of Jews in the United States are therefore estimates. Given the complexity of identifying who is Jewish, the estimates vary considerably, depending on the inclusiveness or exclusiveness of the criteria used and their success in identifying the various subsets of the population. The results of NJPS-1990 indicate that, depending on the criteria used, the number of Jews in the United States varies from a low of 5.5 million to a high of 6.8 million, or even up to 8.2 million if we choose to include the gentile members of "Jewish households." In fact, some analysts of the 1990 data may conclude that there are far fewer than 5.5 million Jews if they apply *halachic* criteria. Such inherent differences in data collected for a particular year, and even more so when criteria vary among surveys conducted in different years and communities, make any evaluation of changes over time difficult if not impossible.

The 1970/71 National Jewish Population Survey (NJPS-1970/71) counted persons as Jewish if they had been born Jewish, had a parent who had been born Jewish, or regarded themselves as being Jewish. It estimated the national Jewish population to be 5.4 million, or 2.9 percent of the total American population. Lazerwitz's (1978) later adjustment of this estimate took account of housing units whose religion could not be ascertained and of biases resulting from area sample cut-offs in field sampling. The resulting estimates showed the total Jewish population to range between 5.6 and 6.0 million. (Lazerwitz's medium estimate was 5.8 million.) Since no adjustments were ever made for the socioeconomic subcategories of the 1970/71 population, it seems advisable to continue to use the 5.4 million original estimate in any comparisons undertaken here between the results of that survey and those of the 1990 survey. Readers should keep in mind the adjustments that Lazerwitz generated and advocates.

The comparative statistics on population and households for the 1970/71 and the 1990 surveys clearly indicate that the extent of change in the twenty-year interval varies sharply depending on the criteria used to classify individuals as Jewish (table 2.1). Under the broadest definition, the population in Jewish households increased by 40.2 percent, from 5.85 to 8.20 milllion. This is a faster rate of growth than even the total American population, which increased by 22.4 percent during the same interval. However, much of this growth in the "Jewish" population reflects the very large increase in the number of gentiles living with Jews.

If the comparison is restricted to individuals who are either currently Jewish or of Jewish descent, the increase is much smaller, from 5.48 to 6.84 million, or 24.8 percent. Here, too, the indicated growth may be misleading since almost one in five of the 6.84 million are not currently Jewish. The impressive growth within this category is largely attributable to the growing number of persons who are Jewish by descent but currently adhere to a different religion or to no religion at all.

Restricting the comparison to those currently Jewish—that is, the core population—only a slight increase has occurred in the Jewish population since 1970, from 5.42 million to 5.51 million, or 1.8 percent. This is a far slower rate of growth than that of the American population as a whole. On the other hand, these statistics indicate that the sharp declines in the Jewish population that some scholars anticipated after the 1970/71 survey have not been

Table 2.1
The Jewish Population in the United States, 1970 and 1990

	1970	1990	Percent Change
Total Population in Jewish Households	5,850,000*	8,200,000**	+40.2
Total Jews: Currently Jewish and Jewish Background	5,480,000	6,840,000***	+24.8
Total Core Jews: Currently Jewish Religion/ Identification	5,420,000	5,515,000	+1.8
Number of Households with One or More Jews	1,950,000	3,186,000	+63.4
U.S. Resident Population	203,211,000	248,710,000	+22.4
U.S. Households	63,449,000	91,947,000(est)	+44.9
Jews as a Percent of U.S. Population			
Total Population in Jewish Households	2.9	3.3	
Total Jews	2.7	2.7	
Total Core Jews	2.7	2.2	
Average Household Size			
Total Households with Jews	3.0	2.6	-13.3
Entirely Core Jewish Households	NA	2.2	
Mixed Households	NA	3.2	
Households with No Core Jews	NA	2.7	
Total U.S. Households	3.1	2.7	-12.9

* Includes 50,000 institutionalized population.
** Includes 100,000 institutionalized and unenumerated population.
*** Includes 700,000 children under age 18 of Jewish descent who are currently not being raised as Jews.

realized. Little more than stability has been achieved, and that is probably due to immigration from overseas. However, if Lazerwitz's adjusted medium estimate of 5.78 million Jews in 1970/71 is more accurate than the lower 1970/71 estimate used here, then compared to our 1990 data, the population did decline in the twenty-year interval by about 4.6 percent.

Reflecting the high rates of intermarriage and the consequent large increase in the number of households containing a Jew (two Jews marrying each other form one household, whereas two Jews who intermarry form two households), the number of households in 1990 (3.19 million) far exceeded the number identified in the 1970/71 survey (1.95 million). Again, we must stress that half a million of the households included in the 1990 survey contained no core Jew.

Just as the absolute number of Jews varies, their percentage of the total U.S. population will also vary depending on criteria used to identity the "Jewish population." If the broadest definition is used, including gentiles, then the proportion has risen from 2.9 percent in 1970 to 3.3 percent in 1990; for some purposes (e.g., political), this may be the relevant statistic. However, if we restrict the comparison to persons of Jewish descent and preference, the proportion remains unchanged at 2.7 percent. If the comparison is limited to those identified as core Jews, it decreases from 2.7 percent in 1970 to only 2.2 percent twenty years later. (The drop would be even sharper if Lazerwitz's adjusted 1970 statistics were used.) Unless the currently non-Jewish members of "Jewish households" are included in the count, Jews will clearly constitute a smaller percentage of the total population.

Nonetheless, according to estimates emanating from the National Survey of Religious Identification (Kosmin and Lachman, 1993), based on data obtained from the screening phase of NJPS-1990 on the religious composition of the total American population, Jews remain easily the third largest major religious group in the United States. Restricted to the adult population and to those professing a religion, that survey found 86.5 percent of the population to be Christian (26.5 percent identified as Catholic and 55.7 percent as Protestant; the balance reported "Christian") and 1.8 percent Jewish. The remainder of the adult population was distributed among a number of other groups (e.g., Muslims, Buddhists, Hindus) as well as among agnostics and those reporting no religion. No single other religion exceeded 0.5 percent of the total adult population. Thus, although a small minority in comparison to the overwhelming Christian majority in America, Jews clearly constitute the predominant minority religious group in the nation.

While total numbers are important, for our analysis of migration the distribution of the population is more relevant. The value of NJPS-1990 for assessing the redistribution of the population is greatly enhanced by the opportunity to compare Jews belonging to different identity subcategories of the core population and, in turn, to compare these with the peripheral population segment of the national sample.

DISTRIBUTION PATTERNS

Regional Distribution

In 1900, during the midst of the mass immigration of Jews from Eastern Europe, estimates indicate that 57 percent of American Jewry lived in the Northeast, in contrast to the 28 percent of the total American population (table 2.2). Moreover, virtually all the Jews in the Northeast were in New York, Pennsylvania, and New Jersey. New York alone accounted for 40 percent of the national total, reflecting New York City's role as the key port of entry from Europe and the magnetic effect of the social/economic networks provided to the incoming migrants by the dense Jewish settlements that already existed in New York City.

The North Central region (Midwest) accounted for the next largest number of Jews—about one-fourth. By contrast, one-third of the total American population lived in this region in 1900. Compared to the general population, Jews were also underrepresented in the South, where 14 percent were located, largely in Maryland. Florida at that time had only 3,000 Jews. The proportion of Jews in the West in 1900 was identical to that of the general population, just over 5 percent. The heavy westward movement had obviously not yet begun.

The continued mass immigration from Eastern Europe during the first decades of the twentieth century was interrupted by World War I and largely terminated in the 1920s as a result of quota laws controlling immigration, especially from Eastern and Southern Europe. Nonetheless, between 1900 and 1930 the Jew-

Table 2.2
Distribution of Total United States and Jewish Population, by Regions, 1900, 1930, 1971, and 1990

Region	1900 Jewish[a]	1900 United States[b]	1930[c] Jewish	1930[c] United States	1971[d] Jewish	1971[d] United States	1990[e] Jewish	1990[e] United States
Northeast	56.6	27.7	68.3	27.9	63.2	24.1	50.6	20.4
New England	7.4	7.5	8.4	6.6	6.7	5.8	7.1	5.3
Middle Atlantic	49.2	20.3	59.9	21.3	56.5	18.3	43.6	15.1
North Central (Midwest)	23.7	34.6	19.6	31.4	12.1	27.8	11.2	24.0
East North Central	18.3	21.0	15.7	20.5	9.8	19.8	9.2	16.9
West North Central	5.4	13.6	3.9	10.9	2.3	8.0	2.0	7.1
South	14.2	32.2	7.6	30.7	11.5	30.9	19.3	34.4
South Atlantic	8.0	13.7	4.3	12.8	9.3	15.1	16.4	17.5
East South Central	3.3	9.9	1.4	8.0	0.7	6.3	0.7	6.1
West South Central	2.9	8.6	1.9	9.9	1.5	9.5	2.2	10.8

West	5.5	5.4	4.6	10.0	13.2	17.1	18.8	21.2
Mountain	2.3	2.2	1.0	3.0	0.9	4.1	2.6	5.5
Pacific	3.2	3.2	3.6	7.0	12.3	13.0	16.3	15.7
Total United States								
Percent	100.0	100.0	100.0	100.0	100.0	100.0	100.0	100.0
Number (in 1,000s)	1,058	75,994	4,228	123,203	6,059	203,212	5,981	248,710

a American Jewish Year Book. 1900. "Jewish Statistics," *American Jewish Year Book*, Vol. 1, pp. 623–624.
b U.S. Bureau of the Census. 1961. *1960 Census of Population*, Vol. 1, *Characteristics of the Population*. Washington, D.C.: Government Printing Office, pp. 1–16.
c Linfield, H.S. 1931. "Statistics of Jews," *American Jewish Year Book*, Vol. 33, p. 276.
d Chenkin, Alvin. 1972. "Jewish Population in the United States, 1971," *American Jewish Year Book*, Vol. 7, pp. 384–392. Data were not published for 1970. United States distribution refers to 1970.
e Kosmin, Barry, and Jeff Scheckner. 1991. "Jewish Population in the United States, 1990," *American Jewish Year Book*, Vol. 91, pp. 204–224.

Map 2.1
Regions of the United States

ish population of the United States experienced a fourfold increase. Jews became heavily concentrated in the large cities of the Northeast. By 1930, the Northeast region contained 68 percent of the American Jewish population, primarily in New York. The other regions of the country all contained smaller proportions of the Jewish population than they had at the turn of the century, with the sharpest drop in the South, down to only 8 percent of the total. The Far West continued to encompass the smallest percentage of Jews, remaining at 5 percent, although the proportion of the total American population living in the Western states doubled between 1900 and 1930. Jews clearly lagged behind the general population in the westward movement.

These patterns of distribution across the United States partly reflect the degree to which various regions were perceived as being hospitable to Jews. New York and the Northeast had long been areas of Jewish settlement with a comparatively liberal attitude towards immigrants and widespread support services. By contrast, the South was economically depressed during the decades of mass immigration and had an active anti-Semitic movement in the KKK. It thus had little to offer either newly arrived Jewish immigrants or Jews who were looking for better economic opportunities away from the East Coast.

With the great reduction in immigration after the 1920s, internal movement became increasingly important in redistributing the Jewish population among regions of the country. Jews in large measure followed the pattern of redistribution characterizing the population as a whole. Succeeding decades witnessed a continuous decline in the percentage living in the Northeast and particularly sharp rises in the proportions living in the West and to a lesser extent in the South.

For 1971, based on counts provided by local communities, the *American Jewish Year Book (AJYB)* reported 63 percent of the population lived in the Northeast and one-fourth in the sunbelt states of the South and the West, about twice the 1930 level; the Midwest had declined to only 12 percent of the total (Chenkin, 1972). NJPS-1970/71 found a slightly higher percentage (64 percent) in the Northeast, and considerably more in the Midwest (about 17 percent), and fewer in the sunbelt (19 percent). The difference has never been satisfactorily resolved (Massarik, 1974). Although the South and the West, according to both the *AJYB* and NJPS-1970/71, still contained proportionally fewer Jews in 1970 than did the general population, the differences in distribution had considerably narrowed since the 1930s. The data for 1970 clearly indicated that the high mobility levels of American Jews and their increasing dispersion across the United States presented new challenges to the national and local communities and to individual Jews (Goldstein, 1982). Indeed, migration had by the 1970s become the major dynamic responsible for the growth or decline of many individual Jewish communities in the United States and for the changing distribution of the Jewish population among regions of the country and among metropolitan areas.

The trend in redistribution documented for 1970/71 has continued (table 2.3). By 1990, according to NJPS estimates, considerably fewer core Jews were living in the Northeast—only 43.6 percent. The South and the West together accounted for 45.1 percent, almost equally divided between them. The Midwest contained the smallest percentage of Jews—only 11.3 percent of the total.[1] This overall distribution pattern shows a major realignment of the Jewish population and supports the assumption that Jews have, perhaps in accentuated form, participated in the movement out of the Northeast and Midwest to the South and West that have generally characterized the American population in the 1970s and 1980s (Long, 1988:137–188).

While Jews remain heavily concentrated in the Northeast, the changing regional distribution suggests that Jews feel increasingly accepted in America and are paralleling mainstream America in shifting to the Sunbelt (cf. Newman and Halvorson, 1979; Ritterband, 1986). This similarity in patterns of redistribution seems likely to continue as Jews enter occupations requiring mobility because of the limited opportunities available in particular areas of the country, as physical proximity to family becomes less important for third and higher generation Jews than had been the case for the first and second generations, and as living in areas of high Jewish density assumes lower priority for many Jews. In an ecological sense, therefore, the population seems likely to become a more "American population," with all this implies in terms of assimilation.

Some insights into these speculations are provided by the information available from NJPS-1990 on the regional distribution by type of Jewish identity. Differences in regional distribution cannot, however, be ascribed entirely or even mainly to the effects of selective migration. They may well stem from differences in the

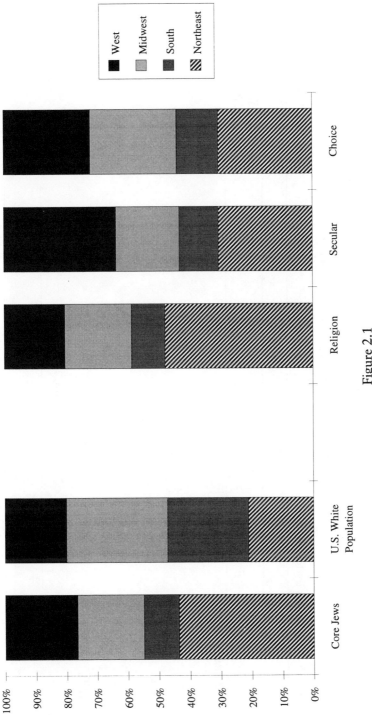

Figure 2.1
Region of Residence of Core Jewish Population and U.S. White Population, 1990

Table 2.3
Region of Residence of Population by Jewish Identity

Percent Distribution by Region

Core Jewish Population

Region	By Religion	Secular	By Choice	Total	Total U.S. White Population
Northeast	47.8	30.4	30.4	43.6	21.1
Midwest	10.8	12.7	13.5	11.3	26.1
South	21.7	20.4	27.9	21.6	32.8
West	19.7	36.6	28.2	23.5	20.0
Total Percent	100.0	100.0	100.0	100.0	100.0
Total Number (in millions)	4.10	1.12	0.18	5.40	199.7

Peripheral Population

Region	Switched Religion	Jewish Background*	Gentiles	Total
Northeast	25.2	28.4	36.6	32.3
Midwest	22.6	14.7	13.8	14.9

South	31.0	29.8	23.8	26.9
West	21.2	27.1	25.8	26.0
Total Percent	100.0	100.0	100.0	100.0
Total Number (in millions)	0.21	1.12	1.35	2.68

Percent Distribution by Jewish Identity

	Core Jewish Population			Peripheral Population				
	By Religion	Secular	By Choice	Switched Religion	Jewish Background*	Gentiles	Total Percent	Total Number (in millions)
Northeast	60.8	10.6	1.7	1.7	9.8	15.4	100.0	3.22
Midwest	43.9	14.1	2.5	4.8	16.3	18.5	100.0	1.01
South	47.1	12.7	2.7	3.5	17.6	17.0	100.0	1.89
West	41.1	20.8	2.6	2.3	15.5	17.7	100.0	1.96
Total	50.7	13.9	2.3	2.7	13.8	16.7	100.0	8.08

*Includes 700,000 children under age 18 of Jewish descent being raised in another religion.
Note: In this and succeeding tables, the total percentages may not add exactly to 100.0 due to computer rounding of individual percentages.

historical development of various Jewish communities, to variations in socioeconomic and denominational composition, to the size of local Jewish communities, and to localized norms regarding intermarriage and conversion.

NJPS-1990 shows that, in a comparison of core Jews and peripheral population, more of the core Jews (44 percent) are concentrated in the Northeast, which includes the New York, New Jersey, and Pennsylvania areas of original heavy immigrant settlement; only 32 percent of the peripheral population reside in the Northeast. By contrast, relatively more of the peripheral population live in each of the other three regions. This finding suggests that regions outside the Northeast either attract a disproportional number of the marginal Jews or that conditions in these regions are more conducive to marginality and the intermarriages that result in gentile spouses and children living in the same household as one or more core Jews.

The sharp differences among the subgroups of core Jews support such a conclusion. Whereas almost half of the Jews by religion are concentrated in the Northeast, less than one-third of the secular Jews and those who are Jews by choice are located there. Clearly, the Northeast, while no longer the majority area of Jewish residence in the United States, is by far the dominant location of persons identifying themselves as Jewish by religion. Both secular Jews and Jews by choice are relatively more likely to live in each of the other regions. The differences are particularly sharp for the West. Such variable distribution may have serious implications for the future strength of the Jewish identity of those living in the different regions.

Variations in regional distribution also characterize the non-Jewish members of the sampled households. Quite a low proportion (just over one-quarter) of those who switched out of Judaism and those of Jewish descent who grew up in and now practice another religion live in the Northeast; this percentage is considerably below that of Jews by religion and even below that of secular Jews and Jews by choice. Many more of the non-Jews live in the Midwest and the South than do any of the core identity groups. However, while somewhat more live in the West than is true of Jews by religion, the percentage of both secular Jews and Jews by choice in the West exceeds the percent of the switchers from Judaism and of those of Jewish descent but now non-Jews.

Gentile household members, unlike the other non-Jewish members, are relatively more concentrated in the Northeast and less so in the Midwest and South. In fact, their distribution pattern quite closely parallels that of the Jews by choice. Whether this stems from high rates of marriage to secular Jews remains to be determined in an in-depth assessment of intermarriage patterns.

The net result of the differential regional concentrations of the various identity subgroups is that the Jewish identificational composition of the different regions also varies, as the data in the lower panel of table 2.3 show, six out of ten of the sampled population in the Northeast consists of Jews by religion, compared to just under half in the South and only four in ten in the West. The relatively greater concentration of Jews by religion in the South is undoubtedly related to the heavy in-migration of older persons. Particularly significant, the West contains relatively more secular Jews than do the other regions. Except for the comparatively small percentage of Jews by descent/other religion in the Northeast, the regions seem to differ minimally in the concentrations of non-Jewish household members.

Compared to all other regions, in the Northeast fewer household members are secular, Jews by choice, switchers from Judaism, or born to Jewish parents but practicing another religion. The Northeast clearly continues to be the "major bastion" of Judaism in the United States, even as its position is diluted through the redistribution of population to other regions of the country. It is also clear that the mix of Jewish identities varies considerably from region to region, and that losses to the core Jewish population through intermarriage, conversion out, and children not raised as Jews are more prevalent outside the Northeast. Such a pattern has particular implications for the future of the national community if redistribution continues to be toward the Sunbelt areas.

Metropolitan/Nonmetropolitan Residence

Jews in the United States have historically been overwhelmingly concentrated in urban places. In 1957 about nine out of every ten Jews age 14 and over lived in urbanized areas of 250,000 or more persons, in contrast to only 37 percent of the total American population. Almost all of the remaining Jews resided in smaller urban places; only 4 percent lived in rural areas, compared to 36 percent of Americans as a whole (U.S. Bureau of the Census, 1958).

Since then, Jews have become more dispersed. An analysis of changes in geographic distribution by Newman and Halvorson (1979) covering the period 1952–1971 found that the highest growth in Jewish population occurred in counties other than those of traditional Jewish residence; many were in areas new to Jewish settlement. By contrast, areas of high concentration in 1952 had moderate or low growth. The observed changes pointed to both higher rates of dispersion and continued growth associated with urbanization and metropolitanization (cf., Fishman, 1963).

This pattern of redistribution was corroborated by Kosmin, Ritterband, and Scheckner (1987). Their analysis compared the distribution of Jewish population among the thirty largest metropolitan areas of Jewish residence in 1936 and 1986. In 1936, 90 percent of the country's Jewish population was found in the seventeen largest metropolitan areas; by 1986, the top thirty metropolitan areas had to be considered in order to encompass so high a proportion of American Jewry. As Kosmin, Ritterband, and Scheckner conclude, "there are more Jewish population centers than in the past, but with fewer Jews in each center" (173).

In 1936, only one of the thirty largest Jewish communities was further south than Washington, D.C., or St. Louis, and that was Houston with its 16,000 Jews. By 1986, the Miami/Ft. Lauderdale metropolitan area had the third largest Jewish population in the United States, with 367,000 persons, and six other southern metropolitan areas were among the leading thirty, including two more in Florida with a combined population of over 100,000 Jews. Similar developments occurred in the West. Only three of the leading communities in 1936 were west of the Rockies, and none of these exceeded 100,000 Jews. By 1986, there were six, and Los Angeles, with its 604,000 Jews, ranked as the second largest Jewish community in the United States.

Meanwhile, metropolitan communities in the East and Midwest experienced declines. The New York metropolitan area's reported Jewish population decreased from 2.6 million to 2.2 million in the fifty-year interval, and Chicago's went from 378,000 to only 254,000. Declines also characterized Philadelphia, Cleveland, Detroit, Pittsburgh, and St. Louis. While some of these changes may be an artifact of the way the basic statistics were collected and/or reported, the overall pattern suggests major changes in the patterns of Jewish population growth and distribution among metropolitan areas. The new geography has serious implications for integration and assimilation, and for other areas of social, economic, political, and religious concern.

Particularly interesting is the extent to which Jews have participated in movement to smaller locations. Such dispersion, especially when it involves movement to communities with few Jewish residents, has particular relevance for the strength of individual ties to the Jewish community. It has the potential of weakening opportunites both to interact with other Jews and to have easy access to Jewish facilities, agencies, and institutions. Much more research is needed on how the "Jewish environment," as indicated by density of Jewish population and facilities, affects individual Jewish identity and the vitality of the community.

Some insights into the impact of metropolitan/nonmetropolitan residence can be obtained from NJPS-1990. In 1990, Jews continued to be heavily concentrated in metropolitan areas: fully 95 percent of all core Jews enumerated in NJPS-1990 were living in metropolitan areas (table 2.4),[2] far more than the three-fourths of the total white population in metropolitan areas (Frey, 1993; see also O'Malley, 1994). Such high Jewish concentration in metropolitan areas reflects their very strong historical tendency to settle in America's cities, especially large ones, and then to participate in the movement to the suburbs surrounding the cities. Not only were Jews concentrated in metropolitan areas—just over half of the total adult core Jewish population lived in *central* cities, that is, the urban core. This is almost twice as high as the proportion of the American white population reported as living in cities by the U.S. census. Only 5 percent of all Jews were living in nonmetropolitan areas in 1990, that is, not only outside the central cities of the nation's 283 metropolitan areas, but also beyond their suburban areas. From other information included in NJPS, we know that about half of the nonmetropolitan core population lived in counties containing fewer than 40,000 total population.

The pattern of metropolitan residence varied significantly among the different regions of the country. The Midwest and South had the highest concentration of Jews in central cities, about 60 percent. Just half of the Jews in the Northeast also lived in central cities. By far the lowest percentage was in the West, where only four in ten adult Jews lived in central cities. This pattern contrasts with the regional variations for the white American population, among whom more of those in the West (33 percent) lived in central cities compared to the three other regions (about one-quarter).

Table 2.4
Metropolitan/Nonmetropolitan Residence, by Region:
Core Jews and Peripheral Population

Metropolitan Residence	Region of 1990 Residence				
	Northeast	Midwest	South	West	Total
Core Jews					
Metropolitan					
Central City	49.9	62.6	59.4	39.9	51.0
Central City County	14.5	20.4	10.2	47.9	21.9
Suburban County	15.3	11.4	21.8	7.9	14.7
Other*	16.9	0.3	—	—	7.3
Nonmetropolitan	3.4	5.3	8.6	4.4	5.1
Total Percent	100.0	100.0	100.0	100.0	100.0
Peripheral Population					
Metropolitan					
Central City	39.5	38.4	48.5	37.1	41.3
Central City County	9.1	20.2	10.0	45.1	21.5
Suburban County	15.9	30.5	21.6	11.3	19.2
Other*	25.3	—	—	—	6.7
Nonmetropolitan	10.3	11.0	19.9	6.4	11.4
Total Percent	100.0	100.0	100.0	100.0	100.0

*In metropolitan area with no central city.

Conversely, suburban living was most popular for core Jews in the West (almost 56 percent), followed by the Northeast (47 percent). Only in the Midwest and the South did as few as one-third of the population live in suburbs. In all four regions, nonmetropolitan residence never exceeded 10 percent, and in the West and Northeast it was below 5 percent.

Among those respondents in the sample's peripheral population, the residence patterns were quite different, both nationally and within each region, falling between the patterns characterizing the core Jewish population and the total white American population. Fewer lived in central cities and more lived either in the suburbs or outside metropolitan areas (table 2.4).

The regional variations were also quite different than those for core Jews. The South had the highest percentage—almost half—of peripheral population living in central cities; in the three other regions, the percentages varied only between 37 percent and 40 percent. More of the peripheral population in these regions lived in suburbs, a pattern that stands in clear contrast with that of the core Jews. In addition, in every region, more of the peripheral population lived in nonmetropolitan areas; this differential was especially pronounced in the South, where one in five non-Jews in the NJPS sample lived outside metropolitan areas.

The residential distribution between cities and suburbs also varies by type of Jewish identity within the core Jewish group (table 2.5). Consistent with the concentration of Jewish institutional facilities and agencies in central cities, more of the respondents classified as Jews by religion are located in central cities, and the smallest proportion live outside metropolitan areas. By contrast, a very small percentage of the Jews by religion, but 11–13 percent of secular Jews and Jews by choice lived outside metropolitan areas. Although, the proportion of each group living in the more heterogeneous suburban categories varied less, to the extent that concentration varies inversely with distance from the central city, dispersion is greater for the Jews by choice, and least for the Jews by religion; the secular Jews are intermediary.

With some exceptions, the same patterns characterize the four regions. The West is the most exceptional, with relatively more Jews by choice than Jews by religion living in central cities and far fewer in suburbs. This pattern may reflect the different ecological distribution of the population in the West, where some communities in the suburban parts of the geographically larger metropolitan areas may be more analogous in structure to central cities elsewhere. Across all regions, few Jews by religion (less than 5 percent) live in nonmetropolitan areas, but among Jews by choice as many as one-third in the Midwest and one in five in the South do so. Secular Jews in the South are also found disproportionally outside the metropolitan areas, possibly reflecting a history of settlement in small towns. These distribution patterns are largely the result of the varying mobility patterns of core Jews of varying identity and of the peripheral population.

Table 2.5
Metropolitan/Nonmetropolitan Residence, by Region and
Jewish Identity

Metropolitan Residence	Region of 1990 Residence			
	Northeast	Midwest	South	West
Jews by Religion				
Metropolitan				
Central City	51.4	64.6	61.7	38.4
Central City County	14.3	18.4	10.4	50.6
Suburban County	14.9	12.2	24.1	7.4
Other*	17.2	—	—	—
Nonmetropolitan	2.2	4.7	3.8	3.6
Total Percent	100.0	100.0	100.0	100.0
Secular Jews				
Metropolitan				
Central City	44.3	59.3	52.1	43.0
Central City County	15.9	30.3	6.4	42.6
Suburban County	15.4	8.7	17.0	9.8
Other*	14.1	—	—	—
Nonmetropolitan	10.2	1.6	24.6	4.7
Total Percent	100.0	100.0	100.0	100.0
Jews by Choice				
Metropolitan				
Central City	32.2	45.2	51.1	48.4
Central City County	19.1	—	27.9	33.6
Suburban County	26.9	15.0	—	5.1
Other*	18.2	6.7	—	—
Nonmetropolitan	3.5	33.1	21.0	12.8
Total Percent	100.0	100.0	100.0	100.0

*In metropolitan area with no central city.

MIGRATION PATTERNS

Migration is a key dynamic in helping to explain the national redistribution of the Jewish population. It is also the salient factor in the changing distribution between metropolitan and nonmetropolitan areas. NJPS-1970/71 documented the extensive mobility of American Jewry (Goldstein, 1982). At that time, only 62 percent of the Jewish population age 20 and over were "residentially stable," living in the same city or town as five years earlier. As many as 9 percent had moved to a different state in the five-year interval, and an additional one-quarter had moved within their state of residence. The information collected in NJPS-1990 suggests that this high level of mobility has continued, possibly at an accentuated level (Table 2.6). Only 57 percent of the Jews in the core population were residentially stable during 1985–90. About 10 percent had moved between states, and another third changed residence within their state, including 20 percent who made local moves. Overall, both the proportion moving and those moving a greater distance increased somewhat.

The mobility levels of Jewish Americans very closely parallel those of the total American population. Among all Americans, 53 percent had not changed their house of residence and 26 percent had made only local moves (within county) between 1985 and 1990. Ten percent had moved between states, and 10 percent had made intrastate moves beyond the local area. The virtually identical levels of Jewish and general mobility suggest that the underlying economic and social forces that account for a very mobile American population operate among Jews as well. This is not surprising, given the educational and occupational composition of Jewish Americans and their generally high degree of acculturation. Perhaps what is surprising is that Jews are not more mobile than the general population. Possibly, the stimulus for movement provided by these factors are still counterbalanced to some extent by ties to family and community.

The cumulative effect of such extensive mobility is evidenced in the proportion of Jewish adults who had moved during their lifetime (table 2.7). Just under one in five were living in the same city/town in which they were born. One-quarter of all adults had moved elsewhere in their state, and almost half were living in a different state in 1990 than their state of birth. Those who were foreign-born constituted the remaining 10 percent of the adult pop-

Table 2.6
Five-Year Migration Status, By Jewish Identity

Migration Status	Core Jewish Population				U.S. Population Mobility 1985–90*
	By Religion	Secular	By Choice	Total Jews	
Same House	60.5	44.0	52.5	57.1	53.3
Different House/Same Town	19.2	24.0	21.2	20.1	25.5**
Intrastate	9.4	18.2	13.1	11.2	9.7
Interstate	10.0	12.4	10.8	10.5	9.3
International	0.9	1.4	2.5	1.1	2.2
Total Percent	100.0	100.0	100.0	100.0	100.0
Total Number (in millions)	3.16	0.76	0.17	4.09	230.45

Peripheral Population

	Switched Religion	Jewish Background	Gentiles	Total Non-Jews
Same House	61.1	48.3	46.2	48.3
Different House/Same Town	22.2	27.8	24.2	24.8
Intrastate	11.4	9.9	15.1	13.6
Interstate	4.6	13.5	13.2	12.3
International	0.7	0.5	1.3	1.1
Total Percent	100.0	100.0	100.0	100.0
Total Number (in millions)	0.20	0.41	1.28	1.89

* Source: U.S. Bureau of the Census, 1990.
** U.S. data refer to within state, intercounty.

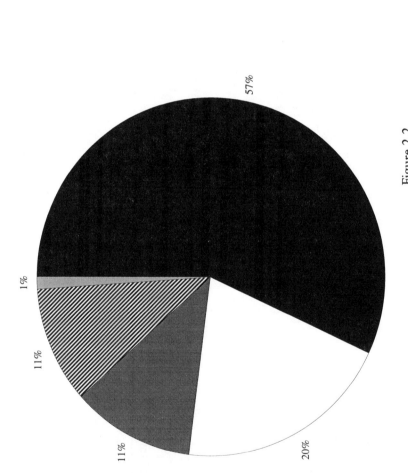

Figure 2.2
Five-Year Migration Status: Core Jews

ulation. According to this lifetime index of mobility, Jews are considerably more mobile than the general population, among whom only 29 percent had changed state of residence (cf., Hansen, 1991). That 57 percent of all Jews were living outside their country or state of birth, attests to migration's key role as a dynamic for change among America's Jewry.

That it does so for both Jews by religion and secular Jews is suggested by the comparative data. The comparison will be lim-

Table 2.7
Lifetime Migration Status, by Jewish Identity

	Core Jewish Population			
Migration Status	By Religion	Secular	By Choice	Total Jews
Same House	2.0	2.6	2.3	2.1
Different House/ Same Town	18.3	14.0	10.7	17.2
Intrastate	24.8	22.2	22.7	24.2
Interstate	44.0	51.8	58.4	46.1
International	10.9	9.4	6.0	10.4
Total Percent	100.0	100.0	100.0	100.0
Total Number (in millions)	3.18	0.77	0.17	4.12

	Peripheral Population			
	Switched Religion	Jewish Background	Gentiles	Total Non-Jews
Same House	0.5	3.3	2.9	2.7
Different House/ Same Town	19.7	10.6	13.8	13.7
Intrastate	30.1	32.8	29.5	30.2
Interstate	41.7	44.9	44.3	44.2
International	8.0	8.4	9.5	9.1
Total Percent	100.0	100.0	100.0	100.0
Total Number (in millions)	0.20	0.41	1.29	1.90

ited here to the recent migrants, that is, those who had moved in the five years before the survey. Ten percent of Jews by religion had made an interstate move between 1985 and 1990, and almost 10 percent more moved intrastate beyond their local area. Jews by choice were more mobile, and secular Jews were the most mobile of all, probably reflecting both their somewhat younger age composition and a greater willingness to leave places of concentrated Jewish settlement. In all, about one-third of all secular Jewish adults were living outside their 1985 community by 1990, in contrast to only one-fifth of the Jews by religion and about one-quarter of the Jews by choice.

Age affects the propensity to move since migration is closely linked to events in the life cycle. Thus, whereas 72 percent of Jews age 18–24 lived in the same city/town in 1990 as in 1985, this was true of only 54 percent of the 25–34 age group (table 2.8); graduate studies, marriage, and beginning a career all help explain the heightened mobility. That as many as 22 percent of the core Jews age 25–34 were *interstate* migrants further attests to the dramatic role of migration at this stage of the life cycle. Similar patterns were observed for 1970 (Goldstein, 1982).

Thereafter, increasing age is associated with greater stability: Rising proportions lived in the same house in 1985 and 1990, reaching a high of 83 percent of those age 65 and over, compared to a low of only 21 percent of those age 25–34. Conversely, the percentage who reported interstate migration dropped sharply. Nonetheless, a majority of those age 35–44 and over one-quarter of those age 45–64 changed residences during the five-year interval. Mobility is clearly not restricted to the younger segments of the population. Moreover, some of the mobility of the middle-aged and elderly represent repeat movement (see Chapter 3).

The lifetime migration data suggest that movement has a cumulative effect, but also that it tends to be initiated early in the life cycle. Even among those age 18–24, over one-third had experienced interstate mobility before 1990, perhaps as children. In fact, 21 percent of all core Jews under age 18 had migrated interstate by 1990. And an unusually high proportion of those age 25 and over, as many as 50 percent, were not living in their areas of birth by 1990. For example, almost half of those age 25–34 had made at least one interstate move and over one-quarter more had migrated intrastate; only 20 percent were still living in the same community in which they were born. The levels and types of lifetime movement are quite sim-

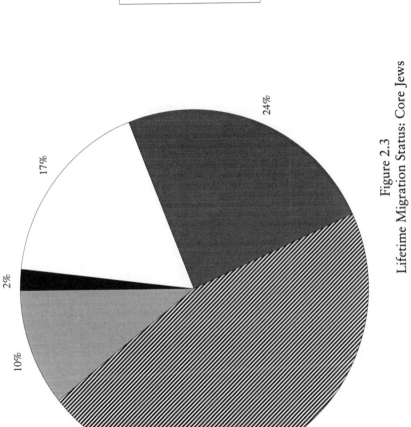

Figure 2.3
Lifetime Migration Status: Core Jews

Table 2.8
Five-Year and Lifetime Migration Status of Core Jewish Adults, by Age

Migration Status	Age Group				
	18–24	25–34	35–44	45–64	65 + over
Five-Year Migration					
Same House	54.3	21.0	48.6	73.1	82.7
Different House/ Same Town	17.3	33.0	26.9	14.3	9.1
Intrastate	16.5	21.3	12.8	5.7	3.9
Interstate	11.5	22.1	10.4	6.2	4.1
International	0.3	2.6	1.4	0.7	0.1
Total Percent	100.0	100.0	100.0	100.0	100.0
Lifetime Migration					
Same	13.4	2.3	0.1	0.2	0.8
Different House/ Same Town	16.2	17.5	12.3	19.8	19.5
Intrastate	29.0	27.5	29.7	23.5	14.0
Interstate	36.0	45.8	48.5	46.2	48.4
International	5.4	6.8	9.4	10.2	17.3
Total Percent	100.0	100.0	100.0	100.0	100.0
Total Number (in millions)	0.43	0.85	0.92	1.02	0.90

ilar for older groups, except that the proportion who reported international migration rose consistently with age to 17 percent of the elderly, reflecting the higher percentage of immigrants among older segments of the population.

The high levels of migration characterizing the core Jewish population as a whole are thus apparently set early in life. Additional moves made later, as documented by the five-year migration data, occur in conjunction with career changes, family reorganization, and retirement, but they seem often to take the form of repeat moves rather than adding significantly to the overall levels

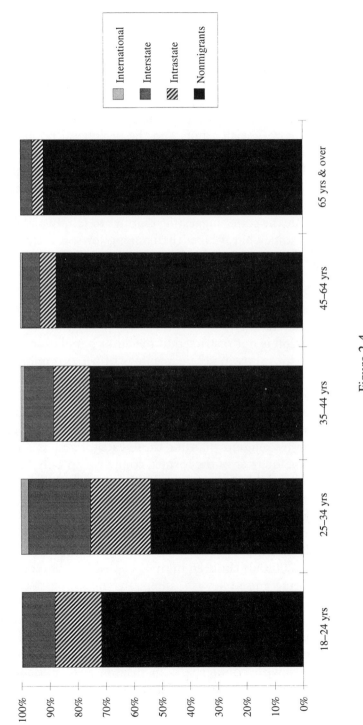

Figure 2.4
Five-Year Migration Status, by Age: Core Jews

of lifetime migration. Since our data are cross-sectional and refer to different age cohorts rather than to the same persons followed over their lifetime, such a conclusion can only be suggestive of future patterns. Whether young Jewish Americans will eventually have experienced more mobility than their parents' and grandparents' generations will only become clear in the future.

NJPS-1990 also allows comparison of the five-year mobility patterns of the core Jewish adults and the peripheral population of "Jewish" households (table 2.6). Such a comparison indicates that the core Jews as a whole are somewhat less mobile than the total peripheral population. More of the peripheral population had changed residence locally, made moves to other parts of their state, and outside the state, suggesting that ties to family and community may be somewhat weaker than among Jews. Examination of the subgroups within the peripheral population indicates, however, that greater mobility is mainly characteristic of the gentile members of the households and, to a lesser extent, those born of Jewish parents but not raised Jewish. Those who switched religion displayed greater stability.

That migration is not restricted to the adult population is evident in the statistics showing the percentage of persons under age 18 who were living in a state other than the one in which they were born (not in table). Among all the children classified as core Jews, 21 percent had made interstate moves by the time of the survey. The level of migration is considerably higher for children classified as Jewish by religion than for those categorized as secular Jews. Almost one-quarter of the former, compared to only 16 percent of the secular children, had moved interstate. The high degree of mobility among Jewish youth points to the necessity of assessing more fully the implications that such movement has on their integration into the Jewish community, and particularly into systems of Jewish education.

Among the 700,000 children in the sampled households classified as not being raised Jewish, interstate migration occurred more frequently than among the Jewish children—29 percent had made such moves. The higher migration levels of the non-Jewish children contrasts with the pattern of the parental generation, suggesting that core Jewish families with children may be less mobile than their non-Jewish counterparts in the sampled households. The underlying reasons for such a differential need in-depth evaluation.

BILOCAL RESIDENCE

The high level of mobility in the United States, as indicated by permanent changes in residence, is augmented by a considerable amount of temporary, or seasonal, movement. This reflects a variety of factors, including leisure tastes, climate and health concerns, family ties, inherited property, and retirement. A growing proportion of the American population, including Jews, maintain multiple residences in different parts of the country and sometimes overseas. Doing so, they circulate between their permanent and their second places of residence and, as a result, live only part-time in any given community. In its first effort to collect information on such nonpermanent residents, the U.S. Bureau of the Census (1982) found in April 1980 that 547,100 persons in the United States were staying in housing units occupied entirely by nonpermanent residents, that is, persons with a usual residence elsewhere. These half-million persons probably represent a minimum count for two reasons: it excludes individuals staying in hotels and motels, and the April timing of the enumeration does not coinicide with the peak period of seasonal residence. Many bilocal residents are "snowbirds," circulating between the northern and sunbelt areas of the country.

Florida alone accounted for 46 percent of all nonpermanent residents identified nationally, and almost two-thirds were encompassed by the three sunbelt states of Florida,[3] Arizona, and California. In terms of origin, New York accounted for the largest number of nonpermanent residents—11 percent of the nation's total. The four midwestern states of Michigan, Ohio, Illinois, and Indiana together accounted for one-fifth of all nonpermanent residents away from their usual residence on April 1, 1980. The kinds of persons engaged in nonpermanent mobility is suggested by the finding that their average age was 60.1 years, in contrast to 30.0 for the American population as a whole, and that 42 percent were one-person households, compared to about 22 percent nationally.

For Jews, as for others, such bilocal residence gives rise to the problem of "dual loyalty," raising questions about which community should be regarded as the "permanent" place of residence, and the extent of commitment to the original community versus the one in which the bilocal residents spend the other part of the year. To which community should charitable contributions go?

Where do such persons use services? Where do they volunteer? Is divided residency used as a way to avoid commitments to one or both communities? If they give to one community, should the part of their contributions allocated for local use be shared with the other community proportionate to length of residence? Does it call for a centralized national fundraising mechanism that supercedes, for such bilocal cases, the location-specific channels?

For example, an assessment of part-year residents (less than seven months) of Palm Beach County, Florida found that 63 percent of the bilocal residents indicated involvment in Jewish organizations in their home communities, but only 33 percent reported such involvment in Palm Beach County (Sheskin, 1987). In fact, more than half of those reporting memberships in home community were not organizationally active in Palm Beach County, and only one-sixth of those most active at usual residence were active in Florida. Sheskin (1987) suggests that the comparatively low rate of involvement in Palm Beach County of those who were members at home may stem from a desire to relax and "get away" from such responsibilities or because the type of commitment to their "home" institutions had not yet developed in Palm Beach County. Conversely, for the small proportion not active at home but involved in Florida, the availability of more leisure time or easier access to activities may account for the change. Equally significant, as many as 30 percent are not involved either at usual place of residence or in Palm Beach County.

In an attempt to gain some insight nationally on the extent of temporary mobility and bilocal residence among Jews, NJPS-1990 asked a series of questions of persons who were away from their residence for more than two months of the year. For such respondents, information was obtained on whether, during their absence, they lived mostly in one or in multiple places, in what state or country they spent most of their time, and whether they or their family owned a residence in the second location.

The Extent of Bilocal Residence

Of all Jewish respondents, 12 percent reported bilocal residence, i.e., being away from their current residence for more than two months during the year (table 2.9). They were equally divided between those who owned a second residence and those who rented. The level of bilocal residence was higher among the core

Jewish population than among those respondents in the sample who were of Jewish descent but not currently Jewish; among the latter, only 7.6 percent were away for more than two months, but most of these owned their second home.

The highest percent of bilocal residence was reported by the youngest group of the core Jewish population, those under age 25, of whom 28 percent indicated being away from their current place for more than two months per year. This finding is not surprising, since almost half of this age group were still students, some 43 percent of whom maintained a separate residence during part of the year.

Many do not return to full-time residence in their community of origin after completing their education, but move on to a third destination in conjunction with initiating a career or marriage. Such postcollege migration helps explain the high rates of mobility characterizing this age cohort. The high degree of bilocal residence that is already part of a young person's lifestyle emphasizes the

Table 2.9

Dimensions of Bilocal Residence: Core Jews and Peripheral Population

| | *Percent Bilocal Residents* | | *Ownership Status** | |
Age Group	*Core Jews*	*Peripheral Population*	*Owned*	*Rented*
18–24	28.3	15.5	47.0	53.0
25–34	8.1	6.3	49.4	50.6
35–44	6.3	9.2	42.9	57.1
45–64	15.2	2.4	58.6	41.4
65 and over	13.9	10.5	46.8	53.2
Total	12.0	7.6	44.8	50.2

| | *Percent Bilocal Residents* | | | |
| | *Lifetime Migrants* | | *Five-Year Migrants* | |
Migration Status	*Core Jews*	*Peripheral Population*	*Core Jews*	*Peripheral Population*
Nonmigrant	14.1	10.8	12.1	6.5
Intrastate	11.6	8.1	11.5	7.9
Interstate	11.5	7.8	11.5	17.2

*Core Jews only.

importance of developing appropriate mechanisms to facilitate their continued involvement in the Jewish community. Such programs may be especially important since many will face even greater disruptions as they establish new residences elsewhere after completion of their education.

The lowest rates of bilocal residence characterize those age 25 to 44—only 6 to 8 percent. For them, the economic and social restrictions imposed by early stages of career development and family formation undoubtedly explain the low level of bilocal residence. As these restrictions relax with more stable employment, higher income, the "empty nest" experience, and, for some, early retirement, the proportion of bilocal residence about doubles, for those age 45 and over. That the elderly do not have still higher levels of bilocal residence may be because upon retirement more older persons change residence completely and no longer divide their time between two locations. Nonetheless, for the 15 percent who are bilocal, involvement in community life and commitment to given locations may be weaker or at least divided compared to those who spend most of their time in a single location.

For the currently non-Jewish respondents, the pattern of bilocal residence by age is similar to that of Jews, but generally at a lower level. Only for the 35–44 age group does the percentage for non-Jews exceed that of Jews; for the 45–64 age group it is particularly low. Consistently across age groups, however, more of the non-Jews own their second home than rent, suggesting more fixed ties to the second place of residence.

Is bilocal residence in any way related to previous migration experience? For example, individuals who migrate from an area may retain a home in the original area or may inherit such a residence from parents (cf. Sheskin, 1987). While the NJPS-1990 data do not lend themselves to testing such speculations, they do allow assessment of whether persons classified as lifetime or five-year (recent) migrants have different rates of bilocal residence than those who have not migrated.

Compared to lifetime migrants, persons still living in their place of birth had slightly higher levels of bilocal residence (lower panel of table 2.9). The differences between intrastate and interstate migrants were minimal. Non-Jews show the same pattern (except for the very small percentage of international migrants), but always at a lower level than the core Jews. These small differences suggest that continued residence in a given location rather than movement to it may be conducive to more extended temporary movement away from the location. The disruptions associated with migration may lead to somewhat lower levels of prolonged absences and temporary residence elsewhere. Whether this is a function of duration of residence may be suggested by the data for five-year migration.

In fact, for the core Jewish population, the five-year migration data suggest that migration status does not affect the extent of bilocal residence. Only slightly fewer of the intrastate and interstate recent migrants than of the nonmigrants reported being away for two or more months. For the peripheral population the pattern is somewhat different. More of the interstate migrants than of either the intrastate or the nonmigrants reported bilocal residence. In this respect, the pattern for the five-year migrants among the peripheral population supports more closely our original hypothesis, and the core Jewish group contradicts it, both for lifetime and recent migrants.

For most individuals (67 percent) who reported being away for two months or more, the absent time was spent in more than one location. This suggests that the travel did not involve prolonged residence in any given community and that for such persons, it is the absence from the home community rather than the possibility of strong integration into another community that may constitute a barrier to involvement. Yet, one-third of the temporary absentees spent their time in a single community elsewhere; bilocal residence therefore has become an important factor in evaluating community loyalties and participation (Sheskin, 1987).

Location of Second Home

The South was clearly the most popular location for persons who were away from their current residence for more than two months (table 2.10). Whereas it was the region of residence of 32 percent of the population reporting temporary movement, it accounted for 43 percent of their destinations. By contrast, the Northeast was the home region of 57 percent of all temporary movers, but only 42 percent indicated they spent most of their absence from home in this region. The West and the Midwest each encompassed fewer than 10 percent of both the origin and destination categories.

A majority of bilocal residents originating in the Northeast spent most of their time away from home in that region, but two-thirds of those from the Midwest who left home for at least two months during the year went outside their region. Most of the latter (37.7 percent of all bilocals) spent their time in the West, but a substantial number (30 percent of all bilocals) went to the South. For Northeasterners who were away from home for at least two months, the South was, by far, the most popular destination outside their own region, attracting one-third of the bilocals. Southerners had the highest proportion who remained within their own region; of those who left, the Midwest was favored over the Northeast and the West. By contrast, few Westerners who were away for more than two months stayed within the West; three-quarters reported travelling to the Northeast, possibly because most originated in that region.

Overall, these data, as do those on permanent change in residence, point to streams of movement in virtually all directions, with favored orientations differing from one region to another. The bilocal patterns add weight to the conclusion that the Jewish community of the United States has, in fact, become continental in character and that programs designed to maintain the cohesiveness of the community and the strength of individual ties to it and to Judaism must operate on the continental level rather than purely in terms of local and especially single communities.

Table 2.10

Region Where Bilocals Spent Most Time When Away from Home,
by Region of Current Residence: Core Jews

| Region of Current Residence | Region Where Bilocals Spent Most Time When Away from Home | | | | Total Percent | Distribution by Current Residence |
	Northeast	Midwest	South	West		
Northeast	62.8	3.7	33.5	—	100.0	56.9
Midwest	—	32.8	29.5	37.7	100.0	5.9
South	5.9	15.0	71.1	8.0	100.0	31.7
West	75.4	—	—	24.6	100.0	5.6
Total	41.8	8.8	43.3	6.1	100.0	100.0

FUTURE MOBILITY

The importance of migration in the demographic and social experience of the American Jewish community is evidenced not only by the record of past mobility, but also by expectations of future mobility. Past research (Goldstein, 1958; Morrison, 1971; DaVanzo and Morrison, 1981) has shown that many Americans move frequently during their lifetime, and that repeated mobility likely accounts disproportionally for the total mobility of the American population. Moreover, repeated mobility is not distributed randomly across all segments of the population; rather, it tends to occur more frequently among those with higher education and in white-collar occupations. Since a high percentage of Jews are in these high socioeconomic status groups and because of opportunities for Jews to be employed in national corporations, we would expect repeat movement to be particularly characteristic of the Jewish population.

For those who do move with some frequency, questions arise about their ability to become fully involved in their community. Integration into the new Jewish community may be impeded by the comparative brevity of duration of residence, particulary if the migrant individual or family anticipates another move in the near future. Investment of efforts and finances required to become a functioning member of the community may then not be deemed worthwhile.

To allow fuller assessment of the extent of repeat and future movement, the NJPS survey included questions on expected mobility in the three years following the survey. The respondent was asked whether a move during this interval seemed very likely, somewhat likely, or not at all likely. For those respondents who indicated that they might move, the likely destination of the move was ascertained, categorized in terms of within the state, to another state, and out of the country. Only 4.7 percent either indicated that they did not know or did not answer the question. The analysis that follows refers only to those who indicated the likelihood of a move in the specified three-year period. Consideration of the information on expected mobility in conjunction with information on past movement can enhance our understanding of the extent and impact of repeated mobility.

That the answers to the question on mobility expectation are meaningful is evidenced in the results of a 1993 follow-up study to NJPS-1990 focussing on intermarriage (Phillips, n.d.). That study was able to locate and reinterview half of the original sample of intermarried couples. The nonresponse was highly correlated with mobility. Almost 56 percent of the 277 mixed-married couples in households in which, in 1990, mobility within the next three years was expected to be very likely were lost to follow-up because they had moved during the ensuing three years. This compared to only 29 percent of those who thought a move was somewhat likely and 22 percent of those who did not expect to move. Clearly, expectations were highly correlated with later mobility behavior. It seems likely therefore that expected mobility also had an impact on other behavioral traits related to involvement in community life. That twice as many of the households who rented their homes compared to those who owned homes had moved lends weight to such a thesis.

Levels of Future Mobility

Quite a high percentage of respondents anticipated future mobility. One-fourth of all core Jewish adults reported that a move in the next three years was very likely, and an additional one-fifth thought it somewhat likely (table 2.11). Thus, almost half of the adults anticipated that a move was very or somewhat likely in the near future, pointing to the dynamic role of spatial mobility in the Jewish community. The level of expected movement varied considerably by age and previous migration experience, confirming the importance of both life-cycle factors and past mobility history in affecting migration.

Anticipated mobility was highest for the youngest group, undoubtedly related to expected changes in family and employment status; almost four of every five expected to move, and over half thought such a move to be very likely. With increasing age, the percentage indicating that a move was likely declined. By age 35–44, just under a majority said that a move was either somewhat or very likely, and only one in five were in the very likely category. Among those age 65 and over, the percentage of likely movers was down to 17 pecent, and, of these, more thought the move only somewhat likely rather than very likely. The possibility of retirement migration therefore does not seem to manifest itself among a sufficiently large number of aged or near-aged to affect the pattern of declining levels of expected migration with rising age. Thus, mobility in the next three years appears about four times more likely among the youngest cohort compared to the oldest, and the certainty of such movement is also strongest among the younger groups.

The extent of mobility expectations is very much affected by prior migration experience. Among those who did not move in the five years preceding the survey, only 42 percent indicated it was either somewhat or very likely that they would move in the next three years; of these, more said it was somewhat likely rather than very likely. By contrast, among those who had moved intrastate, the level of expected movement increased to 56 percent; among previous interstate migrants, 63 percent anticipated a future move. Moreover, a relatively high percentage indicated that it was very likely they would do so. This contrasts sharply with the low level of expected mobility on the part of those who had not moved in the five years before the survey, and the disproportional number of such potential movers who regarded a move as only somewhat likely. Clearly, both level of expected mobility and the certainty of a move is positively correlated with previous migration experience.

The interaction of age and past migration experience results in particularly high levels of expected mobility for young persons. For example, only 48 percent of adults under 25 years who had not moved in the previous five years thought it very likely that they would move in the next three years. However, 79 percent of those in this age group who had experienced an interstate move between 1985 and 1990 considered it very likely that they would move again by 1993. While not all age groups displayed the same pattern, expected mobility was generally greater among those who had made an interstate move than among those not having made any recent move or only an intrastate move. Moreover, within each mobility status category, with rare exception, the level of expected mobility was greatest for the younger age groups and lowest for the aged. Additionally, the certainty of a prospective move was generally far greater among the younger groups than among the older ones.

Overall, then, these data suggest that those most likely to have experienced the greatest disruption in personal and institutional ties through mobility are the ones most likely to move again, especially interstate. This tendency is exacerbated by being younger—in those early stages of the life cycle associated with marriage, family formation, and career development. To the extent these

Table 2.11
Likelihood of Moving in the Next Three Years, by Five-Year Migration Status and Age: Core Jews

Likelihood of Moving	Age Group					
	18–24	25–34	35–44	45–64	65 and over	Total
	Total Population					
Very Likely	55.6	47.4	20.0	11.6	7.0	25.6
Somewhat Likely	23.7	24.3	27.0	19.8	10.3	21.3
Not Likely	20.6	28.3	53.0	68.6	82.7	53.2
Total Percent	100.0	100.0	100.0	100.0	100.0	100.0
	Nonmigrant					
Very Likely	47.6	49.0	17.6	11.8	6.6	21.4
Somewhat Likely	27.3	24.3	28.8	19.8	9.8	21.1
Not Likely	25.2	26.7	53.6	68.5	83.6	57.4
Total Percent	100.0	100.0	100.0	100.0	100.0	100.0

Intrastate Migrant

Very Likely	69.2	37.8	23.8	5.5	3.4	34.5
Somewhat Likely	22.3	24.2	21.8	10.4	16.7	21.5
Not Likely	8.4	38.0	54.4	84.1	80.0	44.0
Total Percent	100.0	100.0	100.0	100.0	100.0	100.0

Interstate Migrant

Very Likely	78.9	51.7	29.9	12.6	21.4	42.5
Somewhat Likely	5.7	23.9	18.8	25.9	16.4	20.7
Not Likely	15.4	24.4	51.2	61.4	62.2	36.8
Total Percent	100.0	100.0	100.0	100.0	100.0	100.0

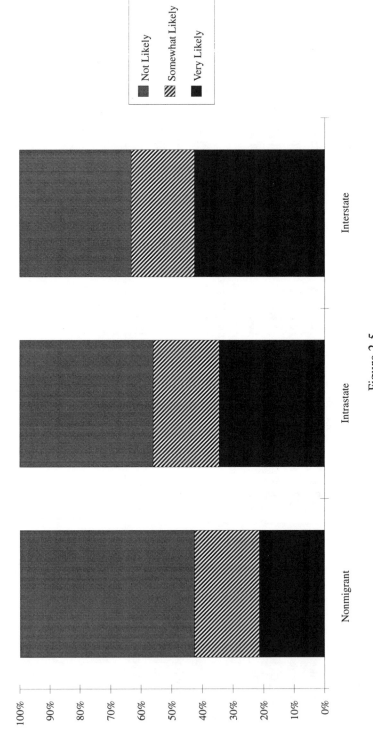

Figure 2.5
Likelihood of Moving in the Next Three Years, by Five-Year Migration Status: Core Jews

may also be the stages which are particularly critical to establishing or maintaining one's Jewish identity through interaction with other Jews, participation in Jewish activities, and affiliation with Jewish institutions, such repeat movement may be risk-laden for both the movers and the strength of community cohesion. Later assessment of the relation between repeat migration and communal affiliation may provide some indication of the degree to which this hypothesized effect is, in fact, true.

Do the relations observed for the total core Jewish population equally characterize the different categories of Jews identified by NJPS-1990. Jews by religion may be less likely to engage in repeat movement because of their greater need for integration into the Jewish community to meet such requirements as synagogue/temple affiliation, Jewish education for their children, and access (for some) to kosher foods. Selection of appropriate destinations can resolve such concerns, but the concerns themselves may serve as more of an impediment to repeated migration for Jews by religion than for secular Jews. What do the data suggest?

Overall, secular Jews were more likely to move in the next three years than were Jews by religion—one-third of all adult secular Jews indicated that they were very likely to move and an additional one-quarter said they were likely to move (table 2.12). This contrasts sharply with the 24 percent and 20 percent of all adult Jews by religion in these two expected-mobility categories. The mobility plans of Jews by choice, where comparisons are possible, more nearly resembled those of the Jews by religion than the secular Jews. These comparisons for total groups may, however, be affected by the differential age and migration-status composition of the three subsegments of the Jewish population.

Indeed, when controls are instituted for age, the pattern of differential varies. For example, among the youngest age group, secular Jews appear more likely to move in the next three years than Jews by religion. However, by age 25–34, the patterns of the two groups were quite similar, and by the next-oldest group secular Jews show greater stability. Thereafter, secular Jews anticipate greater mobility than Jews by religion. With some exceptions, especially in age groups with fewer cases, Jews by choice again tend to resemble the Jews by religion more than the secular Jews.

Overall, these data by age and Jewish identity status do not point to any consistent relation across the life cycle between identity and proclivity for future mobility. It may well be that the rela-

Table 2.12
Likelihood of Moving in the Next Three Years, by Jewish Identity and Age

Likelihood of Moving	Age Group					Total
	18–24	25–34	35–44	45–64	65 and over	
Jews by Religion						
Very Likely	50.7	47.6	20.6	10.7	6.7	23.7
Somewhat Likely	26.0	23.2	28.1	19.0	8.7	20.4
Not Likely	23.3	29.3	51.3	70.3	84.5	55.9
Total Percent	100.0	100.0	100.0	100.0	100.0	100.0
Secular Jews						
Very Likely	63.7	48.2	17.7	18.7	6.3	33.5
Somewhat Likely	20.3	25.8	23.0	23.0	25.0	23.6
Not Likely	16.0	26.0	59.3	58.4	68.6	42.9
Total Percent	100.0	100.0	100.0	100.0	100.0	100.0
Jews by Choice						
Very Likely	*	37.6	20.7	—	*	23.2
Somewhat Likely	*	36.6	25.8	20.8	*	26.0
Not Likely	*	25.8	53.5	79.2	*	50.8
Total Percent	100.0	100.0	100.0	100.0	100.0	100.0

*Fewer than 10 unweighted cases.

tion varies across the life cycle. Secular Jews seem to anticipate more mobility in the early stages of adulthood when marriage, education, and occupational concerns are primary, and in later life when the empty nest, possible retirement, and marital disruption through death of a spouse take on significance. Having less involvement with the community may facilitate greater movement at these stages. By contrast, in the 25–44 age period, other forces may be operating more strongly to minimize differences between Jews by religion and secular Jews with respect to likelihood of mobility.

Probable Destination of Future Moves

Beyond the question of whether repeat mobility is affected by previous migration experience, stage of the life cycle, and type of Jewish identity is the related question of whether, for those likely to move, these same factors affect their expected destination. Respondents who thought a move somewhat or very likely were asked whether the move would be within the state, to another state, or to another country. For those expecting an interstate or an international move, information on the specific state or country was sought. Attention here focusses on the general categories. International moves will not be assessed for specific destinations since not enough such moves are anticipated to allow detailed evaluation.

Not surprisingly, most anticipated moves (67 percent) were local in character—within the current state of residence (table 2.13). Yet, 31 percent of all adults who expected to move anticipated changing their state of residence. These data underscore migration's importance for the Jewish community, particularly in light of our earlier finding that almost half of all adults thought it somewhat or very likely that they would move in the next three years.

If intrastate movement is equated with short-distance mobility and interstate movement with long-distance migration, then it is the older rather than the younger segments of the population who seem more likely to move the greater distances (data not in table). About 70 percent of the likely movers under age 35 anticipated only an intrastate change in residence; just over one-fourth expected to make an interstate move. By contrast, the percentage of intrastate movers declines to about 60 percent of those age 45

Table 2.13
Destination of Likely Move by Five-Year Migration Status
(Core Jews Who Indicated a Move Was Likely)

Proposed Destination	Migration Status			Total Population
	Non migrants	Intrastate Migrants	Interstate Migrants	
Same State	64.6	83.5	63.4	66.9
Other State	32.9	15.5	35.9	31.0
Other Country	2.5	1.0	0.7	2.1
Total Percent	100.0	100.0	100.0	100.0

and over, and almost one out of three in the middle and older age groups anticipated an interstate move. The differential may reflect the more important role that marriage and family formation plays in the mobility decisions of the younger cohorts. Such moves are more likely to revolve about changing housing needs rather than longer-distance movement associated with changes in employment.

Previous mobility experience also seems to affect the nature of anticipated future movement, although not always consistent with the hypothesis that the greater the extent of previous movement the greater the distance the future move is likely to be. Among those who did not move between 1985 and 1990, but who anticipated making a move before 1993, 65 percent expected to remain in their 1990 state of residence and 33 percent anticipated migrating to another state. The percentage of expected intrastate movers is greater for those who previously had moved intrastate. Conversely, long-distance movement decreases, so that only about half as many past intrastate movers as nonmovers expected to make an interstate or international move between 1990 and 1993. For these groups, all of whom constitute either nonmovers or short-distance migrants, the distance moved within the state seems to operate negatively in affecting the expected distance of future movement.

For those whose previous move was interstate, however, over twice as many anticipated an interstate move as was true of the intrastate migrants. In fact, these earlier interstate migrants overall more closely resemble the nonmovers in their anticipated future movement than they do the intrastate migrants. Evidently, past mobility affects future mobility more clearly with respect to whether a move is likely to occur than its probable destination. However, the mixed patterns of differentials by type of previous movement characterizing the various age groups suggest that factors other than previous migration experience have an important impact on the likely destination of any future moves.

CHAPTER 3

The Impact of Mobility
on Regional Distribution

A major change for the Jewish American community in the last half of the century has been its development as a continental society. From a heavy concentration in the Northeast, large numbers of Jews are now found in all regions of the country. This is true of all types of Jews, even though the mix of identities varies considerably from region to region. Part of the regional dispersal has been the dramatic increase in the number of metropolitan areas where Jews live as they have responded to the economic, environmental, and leisure-time opportunities in the different areas of the country. In a number of respects, this impressive redistribution across states and regions mirrors that of the general American population.

NJPS-1990 provides information on the origin and destination of the interstate migrants, thereby permitting evaluation of their regional redistribution patterns across the country. It also allows assessment of movement to metropolitan and nonmetropolitan areas. The first part of this chapter focuses on intrastate and interstate migration to the center cities and suburbs of metropolitan areas and to nonmetropolitan areas. Attention then turns to the patterns of interregional migration and how such movement varies among the different segments of the Jewish population.

The third section of the chapter takes advantage of the information collected by NJPS on place of birth, residence five years before the 1990 survey, and residence at the time of the survey to identify different types of migration over time in relation to regional redistribution. Particular attention is given to the extent of repeat and return migration and whether recent patterns of movement differ from those that occurred before 1985. The analysis ends with attention to whether and how interregional migration affects the Jewish identity composition of the various regions of the country.

METROPOLITAN MIGRATION

As noted, Jews have been, and generally continue to be, highly concentrated in America's metropolitan areas. Nonetheless, recent decades have witnessed considerable dispersion, both within and across metropolitan areas and, to a lesser extent, to nonmetropolitan locations. The metropolitan/nonmetropolitan distribution of different migration-status groups provides further insights.

We first turn to the lifetime migration status of the population living in central cities, suburbs, and nonmetropolitan areas. The greatest stability characterizes core Jews living in central cities in 1990; just over one-quarter reported no intra- or interstate move, although they may have changed residence within cities (table 3.1). Central cities, where most Jewish immigrants initially settled, exert a considerable "holding effect." In part, the higher percentage of nonmigrants in central cities reflects the fact that fewer Jews now migrate to such cities, preferring instead to live in suburbs. Nonetheless, the substantial communities that still exist within central cities in the New York, Los Angeles, Philadelphia, Chicago, and Baltimore metropolitan areas attest to the tenacity of the relation between being Jewish and living in a central city, even as old ghetto areas are abandoned for newer, "golden" ghettos.

The 1991 New York study, for example, found that 72 percent of all Jews living in the New York study area (consisting of New York City's five boroughs plus Westchester, Nassau, and Suffolk counties) resided in the five boroughs of the city. That study collected limited information on population mobility, directly asking only in what year the respondent had moved into the borough or county of current residence. Since the survey did not ascertain origin of the move, it has very limited value for assessing migration patterns. Indirect evidence on migration is, however, available for the adults (age 18 and over) living in the sampled households through information collected on state-of-birth.[1]

For the core Jewish population, the state-of-birth question shows that 71 percent of the adults were born in New York State. This comparatively high level of stability varied minimally by age, declining by only 4 percentage points from 72 percent of those age 18–34 to 68 percent of those age 50 and over. The decline very largely reflects the high proportion of immigrants (22 percent) among the older population, compared to the youngest segment (12 percent). If the data are restricted to the native born, the proportion born within New York rises to 86 percent, but the relation to age is reversed, with 4 percentage points more in the older group (88 percent) than in the two younger ones (84 percent). Among all age groups, the most popular places of origin for those not born in New York were the nearby states of the Northeast. For the older and middle aged groups, successively fewer migrants originated in the Midwest, South, and West. However, for those between ages 18 and 34, each of these regions accounted for about the same proportion of migrants, suggesting that the growing continental character of the Jewish American community is reflected in the more recent flow of population to the New York metropolis.

The absence of any information in the New York study on persons who out-migrated from the area precludes assessment of the extent to which out-migration cancels the gains through in-movement or the ways in which out-migrants differ from the in-migrants from other states. Indirect evidence is provided by comparisons by age cohorts of the populations surveyed in 1981 and 1991. Those data point to an overall decline of 11 percent in the core Jewish population between ages 0 and 75 in 1981. Every age group except the 0–4 and 25–34 groups in 1981 experienced declines over the ten years. For example, the number of persons between ages 5 and 24 in 1981 (ages 15–34 in 1991), generally the peak migration ages, declined by 13 percent, largely because of out-migration, since death minimally affects these ages. Some attrition may also have occurred because individuals in this age group (as in others) may have opted to stop identifying as Jews during the decade. Among the older population, deaths become a more important explanation of the ten-year decline in numbers; but even with mortality taken into account, migration remains an important factor, explaining almost 80 percent of the population decline among those age 35–54 in 1981 and about half of the decline of those age 55–74.

Thus, for New York the combined insights provided by the state-of-birth data and the cohort follow-up between 1981 and 1991 point to considerable out-migration, more so for older groups than for younger ones. Typical of patterns characterizing the Northeast as a whole (discussed in detail below), New York evidently has become on balance less attractive to the core Jewish population. As a major center of concentration for such Jews, it has contributed through out-migration, including movement associated with retirement, to the much wider dispersion of core Jews

Table 3.1
Lifetime and Five-Year Migration Status, by Metropolitan/Nonmetropolitan Residence: Core Jews and Peripheral Population

Metropolitan Residence	Migration Status				
	Nonmigrant	Intrastate	Interstate	International	Total Percent
		Lifetime Migrants			
		Core Jews			
Metropolitan					
Central City	25.9	17.6	45.2	11.3	100.0
Central City County	7.8	25.9	55.7	10.6	100.0
Suburban County	7.3	32.0	55.8	4.9	100.0
Other*	10.5	54.0	30.0	5.5	100.0
Nonmetropolitan	9.1	24.3	60.1	6.4	100.0
		Peripheral Population			
Metropolitan					
Central City	20.3	21.9	42.7	15.1	100.0
Central City County	14.1	36.6	42.6	6.7	100.0
Suburban County	16.8	30.1	44.2	8.8	100.0
Other*	—	82.7	14.5	2.9	100.0
Nonmetropolitan	19.5	33.1	44.0	3.5	100.0

Five-Year Migrants

Core Jews

Metropolitan					
Central City	80.7	7.7	10.7	0.8	100.0
Central City County	72.1	17.8	8.6	1.4	100.0
Suburban County	65.9	15.2	18.2	0.7	100.0
Other*	75.2	13.4	10.7	0.7	100.0
Nonmetropolitan	70.2	17.2	12.2	0.4	100.0

Peripheral Population

Metropolitan					
Central City	80.7	5.5	13.4	0.4	100.0
Central City County	76.7	14.3	9.0	—	100.0
Suburban County	68.3	15.9	14.1	1.7	100.0
Other*	86.2	13.8	—	—	100.0
Nonmetropolitan	72.9	10.4	16.6	—	100.0

*In metropolitan area with no central city.

across the United States. At the same time, the pull factors that help explain New York's role as the leading metropolitan center for Jews continue to remain strong, especially for younger Jews from the very regions to which others have been moving. This type of turnover points to the need for fuller evaluation of the characteristics of migrants and the impact of migration on their integration into the Jewish community.

Jewish migration to and from New York City seems to parallel that of the general population. While New York has continued to be a strong magnet for immigrants, its attraction for migrants from other parts of the United States diminished sharply in the 1980s; between 1985 and 1990, nearly twice as many people left the city as moved to it (*NY Times*, 6 March 1994). A majority of out-migrants, pushed by economic factors, left the region. For example, more left the region for Florida than for the suburbs of Long Island, and most of the Florida-bound migrants were young job-seekers. Yet, migration was not unidirectional: Almost 400,000 people entered the city from elsewhere in the States and an even larger number of immigrants took up residence in it.

Despite the greater stability revealed by NJPS-1990 for central city Jews, a majority of Jews living in cities at the time of the national survey in 1990 had migrated during their lifetime. Of all the core Jews living in central cities at the time of the survey, 11 percent had moved there from overseas and close to half (45 percent) had migrated from another state in the United States.

Suburbs became popular places of residence primarily since the early 1950s, so it is not surprising that most of the current suburbanites, both within central city counties and within other counties of metropolitan areas, are migrants. Over half were lifetime interstate migrants, suggesting that even when core Jews move the longer distances represented by crossing state lines, suburbs are popular destinations. In fact, suburban movement may be interstate even when it is within a larger metropolitan region; shifts in residence from New York City to suburbs in New Jersey or Connecticut would be interstate. That many core Jews making short-distance moves opt for suburbs is evident from the substantial proportion of intrastate movers among the current residents of suburbs. Not surprisingly, since immigrants are attracted to ethnic neighborhoods in cities, more central city residents than suburban Jews originated overseas.

Among the small proportion of core Jews living outside metropolitan areas, only 9 percent were nonmigrants. Six in ten had migrated from other states, and another quarter had shifted residence within the same state. Like suburban residence, nonmetropolitan residence among the core Jewish population is apparently a more recent phenomenon than central city residence.

The peripheral population in the NJPS sample living in the varied residence categories has a different migration profile from that of the core Jews. A smaller percentage of the peripheral population in suburbs and nonmetropolitan areas were nonmigrants. Conversely, compared to the core Jews, more of the peripheral population in most residence groups were intrastate lifetime migrants and fewer had engaged in interstate movement.

Overall, these patterns suggest that a high proportion of core Jews living in central cities were persons who were lifetime residents of the cities rather than individuals attracted to these cities from other parts of the country; that core Jews are more likely than the peripheral population to have moved to the suburbs more recently; and that when Jews migrated they were more likely to move longer distances. Such differentials seem reasonable in the context of the role that a clustered residential pattern of settlement has played for Jewish communities in the United States, the progressive weakening of traditional ties to the community, and the widening of opportunities for Jews to move where they wished or where their careers led them. Whether the movement of the peripheral population to suburban and exurban locations reflects a cause or a consequence of their disrupted ties to the core Jewish population is also a question of considerable interest. The absence of longitudinal data precludes evaluation of this possible relation.

Fuller insights into the relation between city/suburban residence and migration can be gained by attention to the migration patterns in the five years immediately preceding the 1990 survey (table 3.1). Overall, one-quarter of all the core Jews had changed community of residence in this short interval. Once again, the levels of mobility varied by type of residence in 1990. Jews living in central cities were the most stable; only 19 percent had lived in a different location five years earlier. By contrast, between 28 and 34 percent of the three categories of suburban Jews had migrated between 1985 and 1990, and 30 percent of those in nonmetropolitan areas had done so. Even within this most recent period,

then, more core Jews living in central cities in 1990 had a history
of stability than those living in suburbs and nonmetropoltian
locations, confirming both the greater residential tenacity of city
Jews and the relative recency of suburbanization among Jews.

The data suggest that Jews who migrated into central cities in
the previous five years were more likely to come from other states
rather than moving within state. Many probably came from
other central cities. On the other hand, more of the migrants to
suburbs tended to come from within state rather than from other
states, suggesting that much of this movement involved changes
related to short-distance suburbanization. Yet, there was also a
substantial movement from other states (some undoubtedly from
nearby cities).

Core Jews and the peripheral population living in comparable
residential categories differ from each other only minimally in
their mobility between 1985 and 1990. The similarity suggests
considerable assimilation of mobility behavior in recent years.
This would be expected if the forces discussed earlier have, in
fact, come into play comparatively recently. The continuing
breakdown of ghetto areas and the greater freedom in choosing
both place of residence and type and place of employment would
be expected to reduce differences between core Jews and the
peripheral population in levels of migration and in type of residence, as well as between these two groups and the general population.

Comparison of the migration experience during 1985–90 of
Jews by religion and secular Jews shows that of those who moved
intrastate, more of the Jews by religion settled in central cities (37
percent) than did secular Jews (28 percent) and Jews by choice
(10 percent). By contrast, far more secular Jews moved to nonmetropolitan areas (16 percent), compared to only 3 percent of
the Jews by religion and 6 percent of Jews by choice. Suburban
destinations were the most popular locations of all three identity
types of intrastate movers, but especially of Jews by choice.
Among *interstate* migrants, however, residence in central cities
was most prominent for all three groups. Here again, more secular Jews took up residence in outlying, nonmetropolitan locations
than did either Jews by religion or Jews by choice. Thus, for both
intra- and interstate migrants among secular Jews, suburbs
tended to be less favored than among Jews by religion or by
choice.

LIFETIME REDISTRIBUTION PATTERNS

The highest lifetime migration rates characterized those core Jews born in the Northeast and Midwest; 30 percent of the former and 42 percent of the latter were living in a different region in 1990 than that in which they were born (table 3.2). By contrast, only 23 percent of those born in the South and even fewer, 13 percent, of those born in the West had changed region of residence (cf. Rebhun, 1993a, 1993b).

The direction of movement among those who moved is clearly to the Sunbelt. About half of the 838,500 persons leaving the Northeast moved to the South, and another third migrated to the West. Of the 335,860 Jews leaving the Midwest, almost one-third went to the South and just over half headed to the West. Of the much smaller numbers leaving the South and the West, almost half shifted to the Northeast; the second largest stream was the interchange between the South and the West. The direction of the overall shift is most evident in the streams for the Northeast and Midwest: These two regions were the origin for a large share of all interregional migrants, but the destination by 1990 of only a very small proportion. The opposite situation held for the South and West. Relatively few of all interregional migrants were born in the South and the West, but a large percentage resided in these regions by 1990. On balance, this redistribution resulted in a net loss of almost 677,000 Jews to the Northeast and 219,000 to the Midwest. By contrast, the South gained 485,000, and the West netted 411,000. Clearly, migration has produced a massive redistribution of Jews among the major regions of the United States.

The movement of the non-Jewish members of the surveyed households closely parallels that of the Jews, with a net shift from the Northeast and the Midwest to the South and the West. The Northeast experienced a lifetime loss of 115,000 persons and the Midwest lost 113,000 persons, while the South gained 84,000 and the West 143,000. With the exception of the small gain of non-Jews by the Northeast from the Midwest, the overall direction of interregional migration patterns of Jewish and non-Jewish household members were similar; however, the shift of the Jewish members to the South and West was more pronounced, reflecting the fact that fewer of the non-Jews originated in the Northeast.

Earlier analysis demonstrated that Jews by religion had a different national distribution than did those classified as secular

Table 3.2
Region of 1990 Residence, by Region of Birth and Interregional Lifetime Migration, U.S.-Born Population: Core Jews and Peripheral Population

Region of Birth	Region of Residence, 1990				Total Percent	Distribution by Region of Birth
	Northeast	Midwest	South	West		
	Core Jewish Population					
	Percent Distribution of Total Population					
Northeast	69.7	2.9	17.2	10.2	100.0	57.3
Midwest	6.9	57.6	13.3	22.2	100.0	16.4
South	11.5	4.0	76.8	7.7	100.0	11.9
West	5.9	1.8	5.4	86.9	100.0	14.4
Total	43.3	11.8	22.0	22.9	100.0	100.0
	Percent Distribution of Out-Migrants					
Northeast	—	9.7	56.7	33.6	100.0	59.9
Midwest	16.2	—	31.4	52.4	100.0	24.0
South	49.5	17.2	—	33.3	100.0	9.6
West	45.3	13.6	41.1	—	100.0	6.5
Total	11.6	8.4	44.2	35.8	100.0	100.0

Interregional Lifetime Migration

Total In-Migration	+161,930	+116,970	+618,330	+501,860
Total Out-Migration	−838,500	−335,860	−133,570	−91,160
Net Migration	−676,570	−218,890	+484,760	+410,700

Net Interregional Flows

Northeast		+27,040	+409,310	+240,220
Midwest	−27,040		+82,440	+163,490
South	−409,310	−82,440		+ 6,990
West	−240,220	−163,490	− 6,990	

Peripheral Population

Percent Distribution of Total Population

Northeast	76.1	3.7	15.2	5.0	100.0	36.7
Midwest	7.3	57.2	15.5	19.9	100.0	20.1
South	7.6	8.8	71.7	12.0	100.0	23.3
West	4.1	3.0	6.8	86.1	100.0	19.9
Total	32.0	15.5	26.8	25.7	100.0	100.0

Table 3.2 (continued)

Region of Birth	Region of Residence, 1990				Total Percent	Distribution by Region of Birth
	Northeast	Midwest	South	West		
	Percent Distribution of Out-Migrants					
Northeast	—	15.3	63.7	21.0	100.0	32.7
Midwest	17.1	—	36.4	46.5	100.0	32.2
South	26.7	31.1	—	42.2	100.0	24.7
West	29.6	21.5	48.9	—	100.0	10.4
Total	15.2	14.9	37.6	32.3	100.0	100.0
	Interregional Lifetime Migration					
Total In-Migration	+ 99,070	+ 97,630	+245,840	+211,010		
Total Out-Migration	−213,970	−210,220	−161,660	− 67,700		
Net Migration	−114,900	−112,590	+ 84,180	+143,310		
	Net Interregional Flows					
Northeast	—	− 3,150	+ 93,160	+ 24,890		
Midwest	+ 3,150	—	+ 26,110	+ 83,330		
South	− 93,160	− 26,110	—	+ 35,090		
West	− 24,890	− 83,330	− 35,090	—		

Note: In this and subsequent tables, the columns may not always add exactly to the totals indicated because of computer rounding.

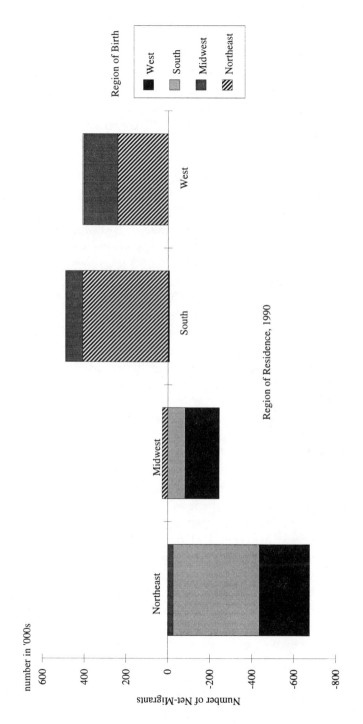

Figure 3.1
Net Interregional Lifetime Redistribution of Core Jewish Population

Jews. To what extent is this differential associated with variations in migration patterns among these two major segments of the core Jewish American population? Is the West attracting relatively more secular Jews than other parts of the country? The data on lifetime redistribution of adults who, in 1990, were classified either as Jews by religion or as secular Jews provide some insights on this. The absence of information on "Jewish type" at earlier stages of the life cycle and especially at time of migration necessarily restricts the assessment to current differentials.

Based on lifetime migration (table 3.3), almost 700,000 Jews by religion left the Northeast—the major bastion of this segment of the population—to move to other regions of the country. The Midwest lost about 226,000 Jews by religion. By contrast, reflecting generally lower overall Jewish population density, the South experienced an out-migration of only 76,000 Jews by religion and the West of 58,000. Both these regions greatly benefited from the outflow of Jews by religion from the Northeast and the Midwest. The South gained almost 500,000 Jews by religion through in-migration and the West 361,000, whereas far fewer migrated to the Northeast and Midwest. On balance, therefore, for the South and the West lifetime migration significantly increased their number of Jews by religion at the expense of the Northeast and Midwest.

The overall redistribution of the Jewish population becomes clear if viewed from the perspective of region of birth compared to region of 1990 residence. Of all persons classified as Jews by religion in 1990, 64 percent had been born in the Northeast and 15 percent in the Midwest. The remaining one-fifth were equally divided between the South and the West. By 1990, this distribution had changed substantially. Just under half of all Jews by religion lived in the Northeast, and 11 percent were in the Midwest; by contrast, 22 percent were in the South and 19 percent in the West. Clearly, Jews by religion participated substantially in the movement to the southern and western regions of the United States. That the shift to the South was even greater than that to the West undoubtedly reflects the higher concentration in this particular migration stream of older persons who are more likely to be Jews by religion.

The relation is made even more explicit by examination of the distribution of the in- and out-migration flows. Whereas two-thirds of the Jews by religion who migrated left the Northeast and 21 percent moved out of the Midwest, only 7 percent originated in the South and 6 percent in the West. By contrast, only 10 percent of the interregional in-migrants took up residence in the Northeast, and even fewer did so in the Midwest. By far, the largest proportion settled in the South (47 percent) and the West (34 percent). Clearly, a major redistribution had taken place across regions over the lifetime of the 1990 population of Jews by religion.

Secular Jews both resemble and differ from the Jews by religion in their redistribution patterns. Of the 278,000 mobile secular Jews who changed region of residence over their lifetime, almost half left the Northeast and 75,000 migrated from the Midwest. Far fewer out-migrated from the South or the West, partly reflecting the smaller size of the total population in these regions in earlier decades. These general patterns parallel those of the Jews by religion, but, as later assessment will document more fully, the comparative differences in the size of the flows were not as great as for the Jews by religion.

Like Jews by religion, secular Jews moved most heavily to the South and the West, although they were more likely to move to the West, whereas Jews by religion went more to the South. These patterns partly reflect the differential age composition of the respective streams. The Northeast lost secular Jews to all regions of the country, but especially to the South and West. The West gained from all regions, but especially from the Northeast and the Midwest. On balance, the South also gained from the Northeast and the Midwest, but at levels below the West, and it lost a small number to the West. Clearly, a selective process was operating in choice of destination.

The overall effect of the redistribution of secular Jews can again be summarized best by comparing their regional distributions at time of birth and in 1990. At birth, just over one-third of the secular Jews lived in the Northeast, and 19 percent in the Midwest. In sharp contrast to the Jews by religion, 16 percent of the secular Jews were born in the South and 28 percent in the West. Although the data on region of birth do not refer to a fixed point in time, they do suggest that in earlier decades proportionally more of the secular Jews than Jews by religion lived in the South and especially the West. Migration has reinforced these regional differentials. By 1990, as a result of the population shifts, the Northeast's share of secular Jews had declined to 29 percent and the Midwest's to 13 percent, whereas the South increased its share

Table 3.3

Interregional Lifetime Migration Flows of Jews by Religion and Secular Jews
(U.S.-Born Only)

Region of Birth	Region of Residence, 1990					
	Northeast	Midwest	South	West	Total Percent	Distribution by Region of Birth
	Jews by Religion					
	Percent Distribution of Total Population					
Northeast	70.2	2.9	17.4	9.4	100.0	64.0
Midwest	6.8	58.8	11.8	22.6	100.0	15.0
South	11.4	4.0	80.3	4.3	100.0	10.5
West	7.4	1.6	6.0	85.0	100.0	10.5
Total	47.9	11.3	22.0	18.8	100.0	100.0
	Percent Distribution of Regional Out-Migrants					
Northeast	—	9.9	58.4	31.7	100.0	65.9
Midwest	16.5	—	28.7	54.8	100.0	21.4
South	57.8	20.3	—	21.9	100.0	7.2
West	49.6	10.4	40.0	—	100.0	5.5
Total	10.4	8.6	46.8	34.2	100.0	100.0

Interregional Lifetime Migration

Total In-Migration	+109,880	+ 90,240	+493,960	+360,930
Total Out-Migration	−695,580	−225,680	− 76,020	− 57,730
Net Migration	−585,700	−135,440	+417,940	+303,190

Net Interregional Flows

Northeast	—	+ 31,460	+362,310	+191,930
Midwest	− 31,460	—	+49,200	+117,700
South	−362,310	−49,200	—	− 6,440
West	−191,930	−117,700	+ 6,440	—

Percent Distribution of Total Population

				Secular Jews		
Northeast	66.8	2.8	14.9	15.5	100.0	37.1
Midwest	4.7	60.2	13.5	21.7	100.0	18.6
South	11.0	3.9	71.7	13.4	100.0	16.1
West	4.5	2.3	5.1	88.2	100.0	28.2
Total	28.7	13.5	21.0	36.8	100.0	100.0

Table 3.3 (continued)

Region of Birth	Region of Residence, 1990				Total Percent	Distribution by Region of Birth
	Northeast	Midwest	South	West		
	Percent Distribution of Regional Out-Migrants					
Northeast	—	8.6	44.8	46.6	100.0	44.6
Midwest	11.8	—	33.8	54.4	100.0	26.9
South	38.8	13.7	—	47.5	100.0	16.5
West	37.9	19.1	43.0	—	100.0	12.0
Total	14.1	8.4	34.3	43.2	100.0	100.0
	Interregional Lifetime Migration					
Total In-Migration	+ 39,260	+ 23,330	+ 95,350	+ 120,340		
Total Out-Migration	−124,190	− 74,830	− 45,810	− 33,440		
Net Migration	− 84,930	− 51,500	+ 49,540	+ 86,900		
	Net Interregional Flows					
Northeast	—	+ 1,820	+ 37,920	+ 45,200		
Midwest	− 1,820	—	+ 19,010	+ 34,330		
South	− 37,920	− 19,010	—	+ 7,390		
West	− 45,200	− 34,330	− 7,390	—		

to 21 percent, and the West reached 37 percent, replacing the Northeast as the major region where secular Jews were concentrated.

The extent of redistribution can be understood more clearly if the analysis is limited to those secular Jews who changed region of residence between birth and 1990. The regional origins of the secular Jews indicates that 45 percent were born in the Northeast and just over one-fourth in the Midwest; only 16 percent of all migrating secular Jews came from the South, as did 12 percent from the West. By 1990 the Northeast had attracted only 14 percent of secular Jews, and the Midwest 8 percent. Over one-third of all migrating secular Jews settled in the South, and 43 percent moved to the West.

Both secular Jews and Jews by religion have left the Northeast and the Midwest in substantial numbers, and the South and the West have gained very considerably from the exchange. Comparatively, however, the West has gained more secular Jews, and the South has netted relatively more Jews by religion. In part, this difference reflects the older age composition of migrants to the South. The greater movement of secular Jews to the West has reinforced this region's predominance as a place of residence for secular Jews; by 1990 it encompassed more secular Jews than any other region. Nonetheless, the West also gained Jews by religion. As a result of all the redistribution, by 1990 in both the West and the South, Jews by religion constituted the single largest subtype of core Jews (see table 2.3), although they were a relatively smaller group than in the Northeast.

The situation is neatly illustrated by the experience of Corvallis, Oregon (Plotnick, 1994). First established in the mid-nineteenth century by Jewish merchants who served the local farmers, the Jewish community of Corvallis declined in succeeding generations. It was revitalized in the 1940s when Oregon State University located there. The in-migrants in the 1940s and 1950s were typical of the larger movement to the West—Jews seeking greater freedom "from the constraints of traditional Jewish communities"—and included many who were intermarried. By the 1990s, much greater diversity had come to characterize the community, still made up largely of migrants, but ranging from the traditionally observant to the secular and "just Jewish."

A summary measure which indicates the overall impact of lifetime migration on the national distribution of Jews by religion and secular Jews is the index of dissimilarity. The index indicates the percent of the migrants in specific religious-identity groups who would have to be redistributed for the migrant distributions at destination to match those at origin (Shryock, Siegel, and Associates, 1976:131–132). The index can thus provide insights into which group is more regionally concentrated.

The index suggests that the redistribution process has resulted in somewhat greater realignment of the Jews by religion than the secular Jews. Just over two-thirds of the Jews by religion and 59 percent of the secular Jews would have to be redistributed by region to have their postmigration patterns of settlement resemble their regional patterns at time of birth. This differential reflects the heavy migration of Jews by religion into regions where relatively few of them had lived at time of birth—the South and the West. The movement of secular Jews into these regions was to a greater extent matched by the out-migration of other secular Jews, who had been more concentrated in these two regions at earlier times.

The impact of migration is emphasized further by the index of dissimilarity comparing the regional distribution of in-migrants with the 1990 regional distribution of Jews by religion and of secular Jews. Forty percent of in-migrant Jews by religion would have to be redistributed among the regions for their destinations to resemble the regional distribution of all Jews by religion. For the secular Jews, the index of dissimilarity is only half as large—20 percent—because they moved to regions where there were already comparatively high concentrations of secular Jews. These indices therefore suggest that migration has served to bring about a greater "nationalization" of the Jews by religion. At the same time, the disproportional movement of secular Jews to the West has helped to maintain this region's distinctively higher proportion of secular Jews. This may in turn help to explain the regional differences in levels of organizational participation, ritual behavior, and intermarriage.

FIVE-YEAR REGIONAL FLOWS

Lifetime migration measures provide insights on the cumulative effect of population redistribution, but they do not allow insights into recent patterns of movement. The former are of particular interest for historical perspectives on the redistribution process, but concern with current issues requires attention to more recent migration patterns. This is made possible by use of the information from NJPS on place of residence five years before the survey, in May 1985. These data show that about 430,000 adults in the core Jewish population changed state of residence between 1985 and 1990 and that, of these, 250,000 migrated between the four major regions of the United States.

As in the case of lifetime migration, both the Northeast and the Midwest lost population in the five-year interregional redistribution process (table 3.4). A net of some 35,000 core Jews left the Northeast and 24,000 moved away from the Midwest, but both of these net losses represent the balance between much larger out-migrations partially compensated by fairly substantial in-migrations. Both the South and the West gained through the regional redistribution process, continuing the pattern shown by the lifetime data. In the five-year period, however, the South gained over twice as many core Jews as did the West, whereas the lifetime redistribution pointed to much closer similarity. This change suggests that the southern states have become by far the preferred region of destination. Both the South and the West also were characterized by compensating movements; the net gains from in-migration were reduced by at least 60 percent through out-movement.

The net effect of the exchanges can best be summarized by comparing the regional distribution of the core Jewish interregional migrants in 1985 with that in 1990 (table 3.4). Whereas in 1985 four of every ten lived in the Northeast and 22 percent in the Midwest, by 1990 only one-fourth of the interregional migrants still lived in the Northeast and only 13 percent in the Midwest. By contrast, the number in the South increased from 26 percent of all interregional migrants to 42 percent at the time of the survey. Similarly, the West's share rose from only 13 percent of the out-migrants to one-in-five of the in-migrants. An impressive redistribution has resulted for those changing region of residence.

This is further demonstrated by comparison of the regions of residence of all interstate migrants, both between and within regions (table 3.4). Five-year regional movement was much stronger to the South than to the West, in contrast to the more equal gains resulting from lifetime migration (which also favored the South). The more recent movement was also characterized by a considerable narrowing in the differences between the regions of res-

Table 3.4
Interregional Five-Year Migration Flows:
Core Jews (U.S.-Born Only)

Region of Residence, 1985	Region of Residence, 1990					Distribution by Region of Residence in 1985
	Northeast	Midwest	South	West	Total Percent	
	Percent Distribution of Interstate Migrants					
Northeast	41.1	8.1	39.7	11.2	100.0	39.9
Midwest	27.6	26.3	26.7	19.4	100.0	17.9
South	31.0	10.3	45.4	13.3	100.0	27.8
West	10.7	10.4	30.6	48.3	100.0	14.4
Total	31.5	12.3	37.6	18.6	100.0	100.0
	Percent Distribution of Regional Out-Migrants					
Northeast	—	13.7	67.3	19.0	100.0	39.5
Midwest	37.4	—	36.3	26.3	100.0	22.3
South	56.8	18.9	—	24.3	100.0	25.6
West	20.6	20.1	59.3	—	100.0	12.6
Total	25.4	12.8	42.2	19.6	100.0	100.0

Interregional Five-Year Migration

	Northeast	Midwest	South	West
Total In-Migration	+ 63,640	+ 32,000	+105,400	+ 49,010
Total Out-Migration	– 98,900	– 55,750	– 64,020	– 31,380
Net Migration	– 35,260	– 23,750	+ 41,380	+ 17,630
Net Interregional Flows				
Northeast	—	– 7,270	+ 30,270	+ 12,260
Midwest	+ 7,270	—	+ 8,100	+ 8,380
South	– 30,270	– 8,100	—	– 3,010
West	– 12,260	– 8,380	+ 3,010	—

idence in the size of the in- and out-migration streams. Again, the index of dissimilarity (not in table) can be used as a summary measure. The index indicates that only 24 percent of the recent migrants would have had to shift their regions of destination to have their regional distribution match that at origin. By contrast, the index of dissimilarity for all core Jewish lifetime migrants is 64.

This change is largely due to the much larger proportions of recent migrants than of lifetime migrants who moved out of both the South and the West (compare tables 3.2 and 3.4). Such a pattern became possible because by 1985 both regions had increased their density of Jewish population; when many of the lifetime migrants first settled in these regions they were still outposts of Jewish life. The increase of Jewish populations in these regions in recent years means that many born in them or moving to them will in turn migrate elsewhere when better opportunities arise or when personal/family needs change. The lower index for the recent migrants is also affected by the lower proportion of all recent migrants settling in the West (20 percent), compared to the proportion of lifetime migrants who did so (36 percent). By contrast, the proportion settling in the South among both lifetime and recent migrants was virtually identical (44 and 42 percent).

The other sharp change between lifetime and recent migrants was the reduction in the proportion leaving the Northeast (from 60 percent to 40 percent) and the increase in the proportion moving to this region (from 12 percent to 25 percent). The massive exodus from this older region of Jewish settlement appears to have slowed, and the region may, in fact, have become somewhat more attractive in recent years to migrants from other parts of the country. Thus, even while the Jewish populations in the South and the West continue to grow through the redistribution process, the complementarity of the in- and out-migration streams that characterize all regions reinforces the argument that the American Jewish community has indeed become a national (continental) one.

Five-Year Regional Interchanges

The redistribution process can also be viewed from the perspective of the interchange between specific regions (table 3.4). Between 1985 and 1990, the Northeast, on balance, lost to both the West and the South, but especially to the latter. It gained from the Midwest, in contrast to the net loss shown by lifetime migration. The

Midwest lost core Jews to each of the other three regions between 1985 and 1990, in almost equal numbers. Only the South gained from all three regions, but the largest net movement by far was from the Northeast. That the South gained even a small number from the West between 1985 and 1990 contrasts with the loss to the West from lifetime movement and points to the changing attractiveness of these two sunbelt areas to interregional migrants. The West's largest net gains were also from the Northeast, followed by the Midwest. Again, with the exception of the net movement from the Midwest to the Northeast and from the West to the South, these data suggest the continuation in recent years of the same patterns of national redistribution identified by the lifetime migration statistics (see table 3.2). What has changed most is the comparative magnitude of the different streams and the diminution of the losses to the Northeast and the gains by the West.

Still another perspective for gaining insights on whether regional patterns of migration of core Jews may be changing is to compare the regional origins and destinations of the younger and older segments of the population (table 3.5). Such comparisons in general suggest much less diversity between the opposing streams among younger persons than among older ones. For example, the index of dissimilarity between the regional distributions of the 25–34-year-old out- and in-migrants is only 4.4, indicating the close similarity in the regional origins and destinations of migrants in this age range. The index increases to 13.7 for those age 35–44, and to 17.0 for those age 45–64. It then jumps to 59.0 for the aged. The oldest segment of the population thus is making very distinct choices of destination, whereas the younger segments of the population have a near balance in moves out of and in to particular regions. Evidently, migration associated with retirement and the needs of the elderly is more regionally selective than is migration associated with economic and family-related factors.

This pattern is clarified by attention to the magnitude of the various streams for different age groups. One-quarter of the aged migrants moved to the West, but only 10 percent originated in this region. The contrast is even sharper for the South, to which 58 percent moved but from which only 14 percent came. The Sunbelt has obvious strong attraction for older core Jews who migrate interregionally. The Northeast contributed most heavily to the out-migrant streams but drew only a small percentage of all eld-

Table 3.5
Distribution of Five-Year Interregional Migrants, by Regions of Origin and Destination, by Age:
Core Jews

Region	25–34		35–44		45–64		65 and over	
	Out-Migrants	In-Migrants	Out-Migrants	In-Migrants	Out-Migrants	In-Migrants	Out-Migrants	In-Migrants
Northeast	37.4	36.8	41.6	32.1	32.2	19.1	59.7	14.4
Midwest	20.8	19.3	15.9	11.7	9.2	5.8	16.2	2.2
South	27.8	32.2	27.5	33.0	37.2	54.3	13.9	57.9
West	14.0	11.7	15.0	23.2	21.4	20.9	10.2	25.5
Total Percent	100.0	100.0	100.0	100.0	100.0	100.0	100.0	100.0
Index of Dissimilarity	4.4		13.7		17.0		59.0	

erly interregional migrants. The Midwest notably attracted only a token percentage of elderly.

Elderly Jewish migration is thus quite similar to that of the elderly population as a whole. For the United States, despite the image of retirement being highly associated with migration, in 1990 older persons migrated interstate at only half the rate (4.5 percent) as did the general population (9 percent). In fact, the vast majority of older persons preferred not to move, wanting to stay in their own home (Longino, 1994). For those who did move, older migrants were very selective in their choice of destination, with Florida and California rating first and second. Concurrently, and indicative of the complexity of migration, Florida and California were also, after New York, among the top three sending states. Some of the movement from Florida and California was undoubtedly return migration, when health, social, and/or economic considerations argued for a return to places nearer to family and friends.

In contrast to the mobility of elderly Jews is the experience of those 25–34 years of age. More migrated out of the West than entered it, and almost as many left the South as moved to it. The most popular single region of destination for the age 25–34 interregional migrants group was the Northeast; they virtually cancelled out the number leaving there. While less popular as both origin and destination, the one-in-five leaving the Midwest were also matched by the proportion moving there. The intermediate age groups had more diverse patterns, but their streams of regional in- and out-migration were still more balanced than among the aged. Whether these age comparisons have any predictive value cannot be ascertained here, but they strongly suggest that stage of the life cycle must be considered in assessing the impact of migration on both who moves and where they move.

Five-Year Migration Flows by Jewish Identity

Given the considerable regional variation in the concentration of Jews by religion and of secular Jews, does recent migration help to account for these differentials? This possibility can be explored by comparing the 1985–1990 interregional flows of Jews by religion with those of secular Jews. (Jews by choice are omitted in this discussion because of their small numbers when subdivided by migration status and region.) For such purposes we assume that type of Jewish identity was the same in 1985 as in 1990, since no information on type of identity was collected specific to 1985. The data point to substantial and quite different patterns of regional redistribution among the migrants in these two major subgroups (table 3.6).

Among Jews by religion, the largest proportion moved out of the Northeast (44 percent), reflecting the density of Jews by reli-

Table 3.6
Interregional Five-Year Migration Flows, by Jewish Identity
(U.S.-Born Only)

| Region | Percent Distribution | | Number | | |
	In-Migrants	Out-Migrants	In-Migrants	Out-Migrants	Net-Migrants
	Jews by Religion				
Northeast	25.0	43.9	47,630	83,470	−35,840
Midwest	13.8	19.9	26,210	37,860	−11,650
South	44.9	24.1	85,390	45,960	+39,430
West	16.3	12.1	31,090	23,030	+ 8,060
Total	100.0	100.0	190,320	190,320	—
	Secular Jews				
Northeast	26.6	27.3	12,530	12,840	− 310
Midwest	10.5	33.1	4,930	15,620	−10,690
South	24.9	31.2	11,750	14,700	− 2,950
West	38.0	8.4	17,910	3,960	+13,950
Total	100.0	100.0	47,120	47,120	—
	Peripheral Population				
Northeast	20.5	29.7	27,570	39,810	−12,240
Midwest	14.0	19.5	18,720	26,230	− 7,510
South	41.8	33.1	56,080	44,400	+11,680
West	23.7	17.7	31,830	23,760	+ 8,070
Total	100.0	100.0	134,200	134,200	—

gion in this region. By contrast, only one-quarter of the interregional migrants who were Jews by religion came to the Northeast. Reflecting this sharp difference, this region lost a net of 36,000 Jews by religion to other parts of the country. The Midwest also lost substantially, accounting for one-in-five of all regional out-migrants but gaining only 14 percent of the in-migrants by 1990. The result was a net loss of almost 12,000 Jews by religion in this five-year period.

By contrast, both the South and the West gained Jews by religion, with the South gaining the most. It was the region of origin of one-quarter of all such out-migrants but the destination of 45 percent of the in-migrants, resulting in a net gain of just under 40,000 persons between 1985 and 1990. During this same interval, the West gained only 8,000 Jews by religion; its share of all such interregional in-migrants was only slightly above its contribution of out-migrants. These data therefore point to major outflows of Jews by religion from the Northeast and the Midwest, important gains by the South, and little effect on the number living in the West.

The patterns for secular Jews are different. Almost equal numbers left and moved into the Northeast, resulting in a net loss of only 300 secular Jews over the five years. By contrast, the Midwest continued as a major "supplier" of such migrants for the other regions. It accounted for one-third of all secular Jewish interregional out-migrants, but was the destination of only 11 percent. As a result, it lost on balance almost 11,000 adult secular Jews, almost identical to the loss sustained by Jews by religion. A sharp distinction characterized the migration of secular Jews to and from the South between 1985 and 1990, in comparison to its strong attraction to Jews by religion. More moved out than settled there. Just over 31 percent of all interregional migrants originated in the South, but only 25 percent chose it as their destination. The net loss of 3,000 secular Jews contrasts dramatically with the region's net gain of over 39,000 Jews by religion. While this partly reflects differentials in the age compostion of the two groups of migrants, the magnitude of the differential suggests that other factors must also be affecting the direction of movement.

Particularly striking is the pattern for the West. Only 8 percent of all interregional out-migrants in this five-year interval originated in the West despite the substantial number who lived in the region by this time. On the other hand, 38 percent of all secular

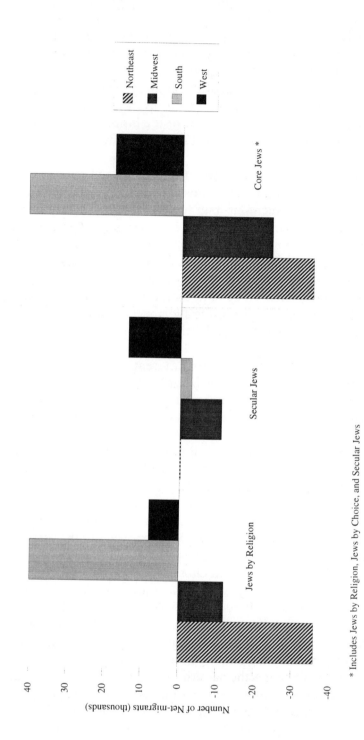

Figure 3.2
Net Interregional Five-Year Migration Flows: Core Jews and by Jewish Identity (U.S.-Born Only)

* Includes Jews by Religion, Jews by Choice, and Secular Jews

Jewish migrants crossing regional boundaries moved to the West, well above the one-quarter who chose the Northeast and the South. Thus, some 18,000 secular Jews shifted to the West, whereas only 4,000 left it. The net gain of almost 14,000 was greater than the net change in any other region and exceeded the number of Jews by religion moving into the region by almost 6,000.

In sum, the differential patterns of redistribution in the last half of the 1980s resulted in net losses in the number of Jews by religion living in the Northeast and the Midwest as well as losses of secular Jews in the Midwest. The South benefited most from the redistribution of Jews by religion, but lost secular Jews. Finally, the West was the major benefactor of the redistribution of secular Jews, but it also gained some Jews by religion.

A major finding of this analysis is the very large number of both Jews by religion and secular Jews involved in the regional redistribution process in the relatively short period of five years. For example, the net loss of 36,000 Jews by religion in the Northeast involved some 131,000 persons moving into or out of the region. And the number was equally high for the South. Even for the West, which had the lowest gross movement, it took a turnover of 54,000 persons to produce the net change of 8,000. Similarly, for secular Jews, the very small loss of about 300 adults in the Northeast resulted from a combined in-and out-migration of over 25,000 persons. Clearly, substantial numbers coming and going across regions, augmented by the intraregional migrants moving both interstate and intrastate, makes migration a major dynamic on the American Jewish scene.

Does the currently peripheral-population portion of the surveyed population differ from the Jewish core in its migration patterns? The peripheral population consist of adults who were born of Jewish parents or raised Jewish but did not identify themselves as Jewish at the time of the survey, and gentile members of households containing a person who was either currently Jewish or of Jewish background.

The interregional migrants in the peripheral population differ from the core group in having had fewer persons living in the Northeast and in the Midwest and more in the South and West in 1985. Only three out of every ten migrants in the peripheral population originated in the Northeast (table 3.6) compared to four in ten of the core Jews (table 3.4). The differential was not as great for the Midwest. Whereas one-quarter of all interregional migrants among core Jews moved from the South, as many as one-third of the peripheral population originated in this region. The differential was as sharp for the West, where 13 percent of the core Jewish migrants but 18 percent of the peripheral population lived in 1985.

Overall, the pattern of redistribution of the core and peripheral groups were more similar than their original patterns of residence. Among both, most moved to the South. For the peripheral population, the second most popular region of destination was the West, whereas for the core migrants it was the Northeast. The order was reversed for the third most popular destination. The Midwest was the least popular for both core and peripheral-population migrants, and far fewer in both groups moved there compared to the percentage who left.

The factors leading to regional movement among both core Jews and adults in the peripheral population thus seem quite similar. The redistribution among both segments of the sample population has resulted in a net loss for the Northeast and Midwest, and gains for the West and South. In these respects, both groups seem to be part of a larger nationwide pattern of redistribution. By the same token, Jews can also be expected to deviate from established trends when social and economic conditions lead to alterations in the general population's patterns of movement. The net exodus from California in the early 1990s, reflecting the loss of almost 600,000 jobs in the first three years of the decade (*New York Times*, 19 December 1993), undoubtedly affected the Jewish population as it did the non-Jewish. Whether these out-migrants will return when economic conditions improve remains to be seen. Other conditions, including wildfires, riots, earthquakes, and landslides, that have plagued California during these years may also exacerbate out-migration and reduce the attractiveness of the state for migrants from elsewhere. Exit polls taken in Los Angeles in 1992, for example, indicated that as many as 35 pecent of the Jewish voters were either definitely planning to leave Los Angeles by 1997 or were contemplating such a move (Fisher, 1994).

Whether Jews leaving California have joined the flow to such other western states as Idaho, Nevada, Colorado, Washington, and Oregon, or are moving to the East and South remains to be ascertained through future studies. Boise, Idaho, for example, is one of the fastest growing cities in the nation (*New York Times*, 14

November 1993). In 1991 it had only 220 Jews in its population, and Idaho as a whole encompassed only 500 Jews (Kosmin and Scheckner, 1992:264, 269). Whether its attraction for migrants will lead to expansion of the Jewish community deserves monitoring, as do the experiences of other such growing communities, for the insights they may provide on the extent of participation of Jews in general population redistribution trends and the ways in which such redistribution may lead to new concentrations of Jewish populations in locations that previously contained few Jews.

DIFFERING FORMS OF MOBILITY

Integrated use of the information on place of birth and place of residence five years preceding the survey (1985) in conjunction with residence at the time of the survey (1990) allows some attention to repeat movement during the lifetime of respondents. For such an evaluation, a modification of the framework first suggested by Hope Eldridge (1965) is used. Initially the framework will be used to provide an overview of the extent of different forms of mobility in the lifetime of the respondents and how these vary by age for core Jews and the peripheral population in the sampled households. This overview will use the state as the unit of analyis for measuring migration; it is the smallest spatial unit to which this approach can be applied using the NJPS data. The analysis is restricted to those born in the United States.

Five migration-status categories are identified:

1. Primary migrants: those persons who were living in the same state in 1985 as that in which they were born but who changed state of residence between 1985 and 1990

2. Early migrants: those movers who were living in a different state in 1985 than that in which they were born and who were in that same state in 1985 and at the time of the survey in 1990

3. Repeat migrants: persons who resided in different states at all three reference points—birth, 1985, and 1990

4. Return migrants: movers who reported living in the same state in 1990 as that in which they were born but who had a different state of residence in 1985

5. The residue category of nonmigrants: respondents who reported themselves as residing in the same state at all three reference points

This typology is not sensitive to additional moves made during the intervals between birth and 1985 and between 1985 and 1990. In the absence of a complete migration history, a typology based on three reference points therefore allows for only partial evaluation of lifetime movement. To the extent, however, that most persons do not reside in more than three states over the course of their lifetime, the coverage is relatively complete. For purposes of simplifying the discussion that follows, the observed changes in state of residence are treated as if they were the only moves made. Following the review of interstate movement, attention will turn to the relation between different types of migration and the regional redistribution of the population.

Types of Mobility

Among the core Jewish population, over half of all adults had made some interstate move between birth and 1990 (table 3.7). The greatest number (40 percent) did so between birth and 1985, and then remained settled until 1990. Another 10 percent of the population who also moved during the period between birth and 1985, made an additional interstate move in the next five years: 7 percent of all respondents went on to live in a third state and almost 3 percent returned to their state of birth during the post–1985 period. The remaining 4 percent of the population who qualified as migrants made their first and only recorded interstate move between 1985 and 1990. Together with the 10 percent who either moved on to a third state or returned to their state of birth during this interval, about 15 percent of the population moved interstate during 1985–1990. The overall mobility patterns of the non-Jewish respondents in the sampled households did not differ substantially from those of the core Jews.

Both the extent and the type of migration vary considerably by age. With only one small exception among the five age groups compared, increasing age is associated with more lifetime migration. Whereas 56 percent of those under age 25 in the core Jewish population had not yet made any interstate move, this was true of only 42 percent of the aged. The increase in migration with rising

Table 3.7
Distribution of Interstate Migration Type, by Age:
Core Jews and Peripheral Population (U.S.-Born Only)

Age Group	Non-migrant	Early Migrant	Primary Migrant	Repeat Migrant	Return Migrant	Total Percent
			Migration Type			
			Core Jews			
18–24	55.9	28.0	6.9	4.3	4.9	100.0
25–34	47.2	28.0	8.8	11.7	4.2	100.0
35–44	44.9	41.8	2.8	8.4	2.1	100.0
45–64	47.8	43.6	1.5	5.4	1.7	100.0
65 and over	41.7	52.2	1.2	3.5	1.3	100.0
Total	46.5	40.1	3.9	7.0	2.6	100.0
			Peripheral Population			
18–24	57.6	19.4	11.0	7.0	5.0	100.0
25–34	49.9	26.7	8.0	9.4	6.0	100.0
35–44	49.3	40.3	3.3	4.4	2.7	100.0
45–64	41.1	45.5	2.1	6.9	4.3	100.0
65 and over	40.9	49.1	—	7.7	2.3	100.0
Total	47.9	36.0	5.0	6.9	4.2	100.0

age is most evident among those who were early migrants, reflecting its cumulative character between birth and 1985. Compared to the 28 percent of those under age 35 who had migrated interstate between birth and 1985, over half of the aged had done so. This pattern probably largely reflects the greater length of time that older persons have had to make a move, but it also attests to the extent to which interstate migration becomes a part of the lifetime experience of so many Jews.

Migration actually occurs most often at an early stage of the life cycle, as is evidenced in the differences by age in the proportion classified as primary migrants (i.e., having made their first interstate move during 1985–1990). The proportion is highest in the two youngest age groups. Almost 7 percent of those under age

25 and 9 percent of those age 25–34 migrated interstate between 1985 and 1990, undoubtedly reflecting the migration impact of enrollment for higher education and employment. Thereafter, the proportion declines regulary with rising age to less than 2 percent of those age 45 and over, suggesting that most interstate moves are made early in the life cycle and that older persons who had not moved interstate earlier in their lifetime were unlikely to do so later.

In fact, for every age group but the very youngest, more persons made repeat moves across state lines than made a first move in the period 1985–1990, and the differential was especially strong for those over age 35. Among those age groups 45 and over, return migration to state of birth in this five-year period also occurred more frequently than a primary move. Evidently, an interstate move early in the life cycle is more conducive to another interstate move in midlife or old age than is a record of residential stability in the earlier years. This finding is consistent with evidence from other studies that a disproportionate amount of total movement is attributable to the repeat moves of the same persons rather than to more widespread movement by different persons. It also reinforces the findings in chapter 2 showing that more of those who had moved in the past expected to make another move in the next three years.

Repeat migration is highest for those age 25–34: almost 12 percent changed state of residence for at least the second time. For many, such moves may have been in conjunction with completing education and taking up employment; for others, the moves may have involved sequential shifts related to education and marriage or to marriage and changes in employment. The level of repeat migration was also comparatively high for the 35–44 year age group (8 percent), but it declined with rising age to a low of 3.5 percent for the aged.

For all age groups except those age 18–24, return movement occurred less frequently than repeat interstate migration and the differentials were substantial. The higher level of return migration for the youngest group most likely is related to a return home by those who obtained their higher education out of state. Among persons age 45 and over the level of return is low compared to younger age groups. Yet, more of these older persons returned to their state of birth than moved away from it as primary migrants, suggesting that for some older persons migration may be motivated by a desire to return to areas of origin to be closer to family. Overall, these data by age suggest that mobility patterns are very much affected by stage of the life cycle. A substantial proportion of the population did not change state of residence, and many of those who did made only one such move before "settling down" in their state of destination. Respondents in the younger age groups especially, however, experienced a considerable rate of recent interstate migration, much of it repeat or return movement. Such mobility at these early stages of the life cycle takes on special significance for the integration of the migrants into the Jewish community, since most are at critical transitions in family formation and career development.

With some exceptions, the age-selective patterns noted for the core Jewish population operated as well for the peripheral population in the sample. The proportion of nonmigrants declined from a high of 58 percent of the youngest group to a low of 41 percent of the aged. On the other hand, the proportion of early migrants rose from only 19 percent of those under age 25 to almost half (49 percent) of the aged, a pattern paralleling that of the core Jews but with relatively less such migration in the youngest group. By contrast, primary migration occurred at a higher level for the peripheral population in the youngest group, but was quite similar at older ages. Repeat migration for the peripheral population, as for core Jews, was highest for those age 25–34. However, persons in the peripheral population, both under age 25 and 45 and older, had higher levels of repeat migration than the core Jews. Return migration levels were higher for the peripheral population at all ages. Overall, somewhat more of the migration of the peripheral population at most ages seems to have been recent and to have consisted of repeat and return movement. However, the general impression conveyed by these comparisons is that both the Jewish and the peripheral-population members of the sample households experienced the same underlying patterns of interstate migration.

Within the core population, do the patterns for Jews by religion, secular Jews, and Jews by choice differ? On the assumption that ties to the organized Jewish community and to Jewish facilities serve as a deterrent to mobility, we expect Jews by religion to be more stable. Either as cause or effect, secular Jews and Jews by choice might be more mobile and to engage in more repeat movement. Because of data limitations, for this analysis, no account is taken of changes in self-identity. Identity at birth and in 1985 are assumed to be the same as that in 1990. The data for all ages combined generally support such expectations.

Secular Jews are more mobile than Jews by religion, and Jews by choice are more migratory still (table 3.8). The proportion classified as early migrants rises from 39 percent of the Jews by religion to half of the Jews by choice. Also, more of the secular Jews than of the Jews by religion engaged in primary migration, but fewer of the Jews by choice did so. The level of repeat migration is highest for the Jews by choice, suggesting somewhat greater residential instability. By contrast, Jews by choice displayed the lowest level of return migration, possibly reflecting their greater break with place and family of origin. Again the level for the secular Jews was above that of the Jews by religion.

Overall, therefore, these patterns conform to the expectation that Jews by religion are characterized by comparatively lower levels of interstate migration, and, conversely, that secular Jews will have higher rates of movement, both in earlier times and more recently. They also point to a high degree of mobility, including repeat movement, among Jews by choice. These patterns suggest that mobility may operate quite differently as cause and effect of integration for the various subdivisions of the Jewish population. However, to the extent that age itself has an important effect on migration and because the age composition of the various Jewish subgroups differs, some attention must be given to how patterns by migration types differ for these groups. For such purposes, the 25–34-year age group is used since it has the highest level of recent mobility.

Even for this age cohort, greater stability characterizes Jews by religion than either secular Jews or Jews by choice (table 3.8). More of the secular Jews (38 percent) than of the Jews by religion (one-quarter) were early migrants. Jews by choice had relatively fewer persons in this category. More of them were primary movers, having made their first interstate move between 1985 and 1990. Moreover, more of the Jews by choice than either Jews by religion or secular Jews had made repeat interstate moves and return moves.

The patterns for this age cohort suggest, therefore, that factors associated with type of Jewish identification are related to the extent and character of mobility behavior. Whether these differen-

Table 3.8

Distribution of Interstate Migration Type, by Jewish Identity: Total Core Jews and Those Age 25–34 (U.S.-Born Only)

			Migration Type			
Jewish Identity	Nonmigrant	Early Migrant	Primary Migrant	Repeat Migrant	Return Migrant	Total Percent
			All Ages			
Jews by Religion	48.7	38.9	3.5	6.7	2.3	100.0
Secular Jews	40.2	42.6	5.7	7.5	4.0	100.0
Jews by Choice	37.0	49.6	2.3	9.6	1.4	100.0
			Age 25–34			
Jews by Religion	51.0	24.5	8.8	11.6	4.2	100.0
Secular Jews	38.1	38.0	8.5	11.5	3.9	100.0
Jews by Choice	35.8	28.1	12.3	16.1	7.7	100.0

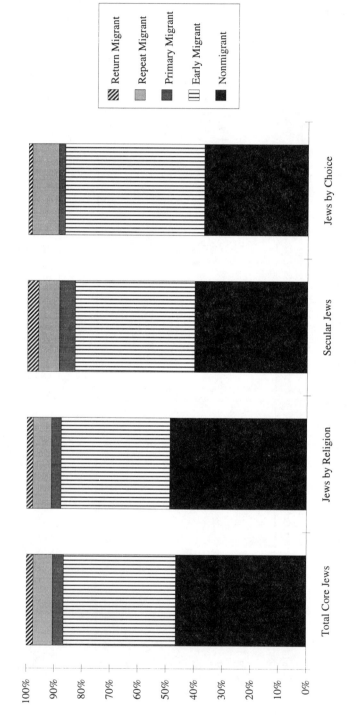

Figure 3.3
Distribution of Interstate Migration Type: Core Jews and by Jewish Identity

tials will persist throughout their lifetime remains to be assessed through follow-up studies and longitudinal analysis. Cross-sectional comparisons for older age groups (not presented here) suggest that the observed differences between Jews by religion and secular Jews decline, but those between Jews by choice and the other two groups are accentuated. Since occupational and educational factors vary among the different cohorts, such cross-sectional comparisons are not likely to reflect the future mobility behavior of the younger cohorts.

Regional Variations in Mobility Types

Attention turns next to the extent to which these different forms of migration vary among the different regions of the country and the ways in which they affect the regional redistribution of the Jewish population. For such purposes, region of residence, rather than state, becomes the defining unit. Under this definition, individuals may have moved intrastate or even between states within a given region during the specified intervals, but they would not be considered migrants. Use of the five categories allows insights into lifetime regional migration patterns and limited insights into when, in the course of a lifetime, movement across regions occurred.

Attesting to the extensive movement that has characterized the core Jewish population, 37 percent had made at least one interregional move during the course of their lifetime, including almost 3 percent who had changed region of residence at least twice (table 3.9). The largest single proportion of mobile adults (30 percent) moved before 1985 and made only one regional change in residence. Another 4 percent made their interregional move between 1985 and 1990. Among the 3 percent who made at least two interregional moves, somewhat more returned to their region of origin than moved on to a third region of the country. Yet, despite the relatively high levels of movement, over six of every ten core Jews had never changed region of residence, suggesting that both stability and mobility are features of the American Jewish scene.

For core Jews, the extent of movement varies considerably by region of birth. The highest stability, by far, characterizes those born in the West. Over eight of every ten were living in the West at all three reference points. This contrasts with a low of 48 percent for those born in the Midwest. Those born in the Northeast and the South were almost equally stable; just under two-thirds made no change in region of residence. For all four regions, most migrants had changed region of residence only once—before 1985—suggesting that for most the type of long-distance movement represented by an interrregional move occurs at fairly early stages of the life cycle. For each of the regions, 5 percent or fewer of adults had made their one interregional move in the 1985–1990 period. Repeat movement either to a third region or back to region of birth characterized the mobility history of only a small minority of the population.

Interestingly, as the comparative data in table 3.9 suggest, the lifetime migration patterns of the core Jews did not differ much from those of the peripheral population in the sample. The core Jews tended to be slightly more mobile, but most of their additional movement took the form of early migration. Even the regional pat-

Table 3.9
Distribution of Interregional Migration Type, by Region of Birth:
Core Jews/Peripheral Population and Jewish Identity
(U.S.-Born Only)

Region of Birth	Migration Type					
	Non-migrant	Early Migrant	Primary Migrant	Repeat Migrant	Return Migrant	Total Percent
Core Jews						
Northeast	63.8	30.1	3.5	1.0	1.6	100.0
Midwest	48.5	42.6	5.4	1.6	1.9	100.0
South	65.4	26.5	4.6	0.7	2.9	100.0
West	82.2	14.2	2.2	1.1	0.3	100.0
Total	63.4	30.1	3.8	1.1	1.6	100.0
Peripheral Population						
Northeast	69.9	22.5	4.7	1.4	1.4	100.0
Midwest	55.4	37.2	5.5	—	1.9	100.0
South	60.7	28.6	6.5	0.7	3.4	100.0
West	83.0	12.4	2.9	0.4	1.4	100.0
Total	67.2	25.1	4.9	0.8	1.9	100.0

Table 3.9 *(continued)*

	Migration Type					
Region of Birth	*Non-migrant*	*Early Migrant*	*Primary Migrant*	*Repeat Migrant*	*Return Migrant*	*Total Percent*
			Jews by Religion			
Northeast	64.5	29.4	3.0	0.9	1.6	100.0
Midwest	50.6	41.7	4.4	0.8	2.4	100.0
South	70.1	20.7	4.8	0.4	4.0	100.0
West	79.2	16.7	2.9	1.2	—	100.0
Total	63.9	29.6	3.8	0.9	1.8	100.0
			Secular Jews			
Northeast	59.1	35.7	2.7	1.0	1.5	100.0
Midwest	43.9	43.2	10.4	1.7	0.8	100.0
South	58.2	35.1	5.3	1.3	—	100.0
West	83.9	12.8	1.4	1.0	0.9	100.0
Total	62.1	31.5	4.2	1.2	1.0	100.0
			Jews by Choice			
Northeast	70.5	21.2	5.6	1.3	1.4	100.0
Midwest	50.2	41.0	6.9	—	1.9	100.0
South	58.0	32.2	9.1	—	0.7	100.0
West	83.1	12.6	2.0	—	2.2	100.0
Total	66.4	25.6	5.9	0.6	1.5	100.0

terns were quite similar, with the highest mobility characterizing those born in the Midwest and the least typifying those born in the West. Compared to core Jews, more of the peripheral population born in the South were mobile and fewer of those from the Northeast were. Small proportions from all regions were repeat or return migrants, although for both the core and peripheral populations, somewhat more of those born in the South who had moved away from it before 1985 tended to return thereafter.

Within the core Jewish group, the general patterns for Jews by religion, secular Jews, and Jews by choice also tend to closely parallel one another. Apparently, the underlying forces affecting interregional migration have not varied significantly among the subsegments of the core Jewish population.

The analysis of migration type by interstate movement indicated that levels and types of mobility are associated with stages of the life cycle. Similar relations characterize interregional movement (table 3.10). Among core Jewish adults under age 25, almost three-fourths have never migrated beyond their region of birth, and most who had made an interregional move were early migrants, suggesting that their move occurred while they were children as part of family mobility. However, 5 percent of all young adults made a primary move, probably in conjunction with enrollment in college, marriage, or employment. In the 25–64 age groups, the proportion

Table 3.10
Distribution of Interregional Migration Type, by Age:
Core Jews and Peripheral Population
(U.S.-Born Only)

Age Group	Migration Type					Total Percent
	Non-migrant	Early Migrant	Primary Migrant	Repeat Migrant	Return Migrant	
Core Jews						
18–24	72.9	19.7	4.9	0.7	1.7	100.0
25–34	64.8	21.8	7.9	1.6	3.9	100.0
35–44	63.7	30.5	2.6	1.5	1.7	100.0
45–64	65.2	31.3	1.8	0.8	0.9	100.0
65 and over	54.5	42.5	2.6	0.3	0.2	100.0
Total	63.4	30.1	3.8	1.1	1.6	100.0
Peripheral Population						
18–24	72.4	17.0	8.9	—	1.8	100.0
25–34	68.8	17.4	9.4	1.2	3.1	100.0
35–44	71.0	24.6	2.5	0.6	1.2	100.0
45–64	59.0	37.1	2.1	1.2	0.7	100.0
65 and over	60.9	34.9	—	—	4.2	100.0
Total	67.2	25.1	4.9	0.8	1.9	100.0

of nonmigrants varies minimally, at just under two-thirds, pointing to a high degree of regional stability among a substantial segment of the population.

The types of regional moves do, however, vary by age. More of those age 25–34 were primary migrants, reflecting the higher proportion of persons in this younger age group who have just completed higher education, are marrying, and are beginning their careers. By age 35, most have already undergone these key life-cycle events and have less incentive to undertake a long-distance move. The higher proportion in the early category, having moved before 1985, attests to this greater recent stability. Also reflecting the greater mobility in the 25–34 age period, more in this cohort engaged in both return and repeat mobility than was true of any other age group. This, too, may be associated with the completion of education.

The aged had the lowest proportion of nonmigrants; only 55 percent were living in the same region at all three reference points. Their high mobility level reflects the cumulative effect of lifetime migration, most of which involved moves made before 1985. These may include moves made in conjunction with retirement. Somewhat surprisingly, few were classified as primary migrants, and this age group had the lowest proportion of both repeat and return migrants. Evidently, once they changed region of residence, they had no strong tendency to move interregionally again in old age.

A different perspective for examining the lifetime regional mobility experience of the core Jewish population is in terms of current region of residence rather than region of birth. Not surprisingly, such data portray a very different picture (table 3.11). The Northeast, reflecting its lesser popularity as a destination, consists very heavily (89 percent) of persons who were born in the region and also lived there in 1985 and 1990 (i.e., nonmigrants). Most of the in-migrants had come to the region before 1985. The Midwest, too, consisted largely (72 percent) of nonmigrants, and a vast majority of the others had lived there since before 1985. By contrast, only 29 percent of the South's adult core Jewish population was born and had always lived in the South. Almost six of ten moved there from another region before 1985, and almost 10 percent did so during 1985–1990. The West, too, was composed of a majority of in-migrants from other regions, but not as heavily as the South. Moreover, relatively more of the total movement to the West occurred before 1985, suggesting that during 1985–1990 it did not have as strong an attraction for migrants from other regions as did the South.

Repeat and return migration constituted only a small proportion of current residents in each region, lending weight to earlier conclusions that core Jews do not engage in repeated interregional migration with any frequency. Changes in residence are more likely to involve intraregional movement. The major regional shifts that have occurred therefore appear to stem largely from a decision made fairly early in the life cycle to move cross-regionally in conjunction with completion of education, initiation of a career, and/or marriage. Only a much smaller proportion undertake later moves involving great distances, and a disproportional number of these seem to be associated with retirement.

Jewish identity is related to type of mobility differently in the various regions. In the Northeast, probably reflecting its position as "stronghold" of Jews by religion, 91 percent of all Jews by reli-

Table 3.11

Distribution of Interregional Migration Type, by Current Region of Residence: Core Jews/Peripheral Population and Jewish Identity (U.S.-Born Only)

Region of Current Residence	Non-migrant	Early Migrant	Primary Migrant	Repeat Migrant	Return Migrant	Total Percent
			Migration Type			
			Core Jews			
Northeast	89.3	6.7	1.4	0.3	2.2	100.0
Midwest	72.3	20.1	2.5	2.2	2.9	100.0
South	29.2	58.9	9.3	1.3	1.3	100.0
West	41.4	53.1	3.6	1.8	0.2	100.0
Total	63.4	30.1	3.8	1.1	1.6	100.0
			Peripheral Population			
Northeast	84.4	10.7	2.9	0.2	1.7	100.0
Midwest	70.4	23.1	2.4	1.7	2.4	100.0
South	50.9	36.5	9.4	0.4	2.8	100.0
West	59.2	33.8	4.8	1.2	1.0	100.0
Total	67.2	25.1	4.9	0.8	1.9	100.0

Table 3.11 *(continued)*

Region of Current Residence	Non- migrant	Early Migrant	Primary Migrant	Repeat Migrant	Return Migrant	Total Percent
			Migration Type			
			Jews by Religion			
Northeast	91.2	5.2	1.0	0.3	2.2	100.0
Midwest	72.0	19.8	2.5	2.2	3.5	100.0
South	25.6	61.9	10.3	0.7	1.5	100.0
West	33.9	60.3	3.8	2.0	—	100.0
Total	63.9	29.6	3.8	0.9	1.8	100.0
			Secular Jews			
Northeast	81.3	12.7	3.5	0.4	2.1	100.0
Midwest	69.3	24.2	3.0	2.2	1.3	100.0
South	43.3	49.1	6.4	1.2	—	100.0
West	54.4	39.6	3.9	1.6	0.6	100.0
Total	62.1	31.5	4.2	1.2	1.0	100.0
			Jews by Choice			
Northeast	71.6	21.6	1.9	1.8	3.1	100.0
Midwest	86.0	10.5	—	3.5	—	100.0
South	36.0	47.3	3.1	10.5	3.1	100.0
West	56.9	43.1	—	—	—	100.0
Total	60.6	32.3	1.4	3.9	1.8	100.0

gion living there in 1990 were born in the region and always lived there. This declines to 81 percent of the secular Jews and to only 72 percent of the Jews by choice. Conversely the proportion of early migrants to this region rises from only 5 percent of the Jews by religion to 22 percent of Jews by choice. By contrast, in the West, which has the greatest concentration of secular Jews and Jews by choice, these two groups display much greater stability; a majority are nonmigrants in contrast to only 34 percent of the Jews by religion. In fact, six of every ten Jews by religion in the West were early migrants to the region (i.e., before 1985), compared to only four in ten of the secular Jews and Jews by choice.

Thus, although nationwide the three identity groups have similar patterns by type of migration, these patterns vary considerably by region of current residence and tend to reflect the differential identity composition of the regions and the more frequent movement to them of Jews of different identity.

Mobility Types and Interregional Distribution

What effect does the migration experience between birth and 1985 and, in turn, between 1985 and 1990 have on the regional distribution of the Jewish population in the United States? The overall net consequences, assessed earlier, clearly pointed to substantial shifts from the Northeast and the Midwest to the South and the West. Evaluation of migration between birth, 1985, and 1990 suggests that recent net movement represents a continuation of the patterns characterizing earlier decades (table 3.12).

Table 3.12
Distribution of Interregional Migration at Birth, in 1985, and in 1990, by Region, and Net Regional Change:
Core Jews/Peripheral Population and Jewish Identity
(U.S.-Born Only)

Region of Residence	Percent Distribution			Net Change, Birth to 1990	Net Change, 1985 to 1990
	Birth	1985	1990		
Core Jews					
Northeast	61.9	45.0	44.2	−640,240	−27,570
Midwest	17.1	12.0	11.4	−204,350	−19,930
South	9.9	21.3	22.3	+445,820	+32,950
West	11.1	21.7	22.1	+98,800	+14,550
Total Percent	100.0	100.0	100.0		
Peripheral Population					
Northeast	39.3	33.2	32.6	−113,900	−11,540
Midwest	21.6	17.4	17.1	−77,620	− 5,860
South	21.1	24.6	25.2	+69,770	+11,320
West	18.0	24.8	25.1	+121,770	+6,100
Total Percent	100.0	100.0	100.0		

Table 3.12 *(continued)*

Region of Residence	Percent Distribution			Net Change, Birth to 1990	Net Change, 1985 to 1990
	Birth	1985	1990		
	Jews by Religion				
Northeast	68.0	49.1	48.0	−557,620	−30,500
Midwest	16.0	11.7	11.3	−132,810	−10,850
South	8.1	21.1	22.3	+395,800	+33,340
West	7.9	18.1	18.4	+294,630	+8,010
Total Percent	100.0	100.0	100.0		
	Secular Jews				
Northeast	42.7	31.3	31.5	−78,530	+740
Midwest	18.0	12.4	11.3	−44,390	−7,660
South	15.6	21.5	20.9	+36,300	−4,000
West	23.7	34.7	36.3	+86,610	+10,920
Total Percent	100.0	100.0	100.0		
	Jews by Choice				
Northeast	34.7	30.7	32.1	−4,120	+2,180
Midwest	32.7	16.4	15.5	−27,140	−1,400
South	17.8	24.3	26.6	+13,720	+3,630
West	14.7	28.7	25.9	+17,560	−4,380
Total	100.0	100.0	100.0		

If judged by residence at time of birth (a point which does not refer to a fixed date since it varies depending on the ages of the individuals in the sample), 62 percent of the core Jewish population were born in the Northeast and another 17 percent in the Midwest. Only 10 percent reported the South as their birth region, and only slightly more (11 percent) the West. The distribution for 1985, however, shows that only 45 percent of the core Jews lived in the Northeast, pointing to a major exodus from this region of the United States. The Midwest's portion of the total also declined substantially, to only 12 percent. By contrast, both the South and the West just about doubled their share of the core Jewish population. Movement before 1985 had thus led to a major redistribution of the Jewish population to the South and West, a pattern consistent with that characterizing the American population generally.

In the comparatively short interval between 1985 and 1990, the volume of movement was obviously less than during the much longer period encompassed by birth to 1985. Nonetheless, the patterns set in these earlier years continued. The Northeast and the Midwest both lost core Jews in this interval—about 27,600 and 19,900, respectively. The South and West both gained—32,950 and 14,550, respectively. The net result was further redistribution of the population among regions, although the changes were proportionally small. Thus, whereas the South and West together accounted for only one-third as many core Jews as the Northeast, if judged by birthplace, by 1990 the proportion of core Jews in these two regions slightly exceeded that of the Northeast. Unless major changes in redistribution patterns occur, it is easy to envisage a majority of America's Jews living in the South and West by the early decades of the twenty-first century.

The changes characterizing the peripheral population were in the same direction as those of the core Jews, but they were far less dramatic. Fewer of the peripheral population were born in the Northeast, only 39 percent. This proportion declined to 33 percent by 1985 and to slightly less by 1990. The percentage living in the Midwest also declined. Like the core Jews, the percentage of the peripheral population living in the sunbelt regions rose between birth and 1985 and again slightly in the next five years, but the changes were not as sharp. The overall lifetime regional shifts for the peripheral population, continuing into the recent past, have also resulted in a redistribution of population away from the former heavy concentrations in the Northeast and the Midwest to the South and the West.

Variations by Jewish Identity Categories

The long- and short-term impact of migration on the regional redistribution of Jews by religion, secular Jews, and Jews by choice is also evidenced in the information available on lifetime and recent migration (table 3.12). Reflecting the strong long-term shift of Jews by religion out of the Northeast and Midwest, these regions in 1990 contained 30 percent fewer Jews by religion than the proportion who reported being born there. On the other hand, by 1990 the proportion of Jews by religion living in the South and West was 2.7 and 2.3 times greater than the number of such Jews born in the respective regions. Clearly, lifetime regional migration has produced a major shift in the region of residence of Jews by religion.

The redistribution process has continued in recent years: 6 percent of all the lifetime interregional migrants lost by the Northeast and 8 percent of those lost by the Midwest had left these regions betwen 1985 and 1990. The comparative attraction of the South over the West to Jews by religion is shown in the South's 8 percent of total net lifetime gains that occurred in the five years before 1990 compared to only 3 percent in the West.

As a result, in comparing the distribution of the proportion of the nation's total native-born Jews by religion measured at time of birth with that in 1990, we find the Northeast's share reduced from 68 percent to 48 percent. For the Midwest, the reduction was from 16 percent to 11 percent. By contrast, the South and West increased their share from 8 percent each to 22 percent for the South and 18 percent for the West.

The patterns of lifetime and recent migration were different for secular Jews. Their net lifetime exodus from the Northeast was almost as great, relatively, as that of Jews by religion, but the movement of secular Jews from the Midwest was even greater. On balance, over one-third of all those born in the Midwest had moved away by 1990. Yet, the net impact on the regions of gain, the South and West, was far less than for the Jews by religion. Net lifetime migration increased the number of native-born secular Jews in these two regions by only one-third and one-half, respectively, probably reflecting the comparatively greater number of secular Jews born and still living in these regions. Moreover, in contrast to the Jews by religion, the gains through migration of secular Jews were relatively greater in the West than the South; this result may be related to the greater initial concentration of secular Jews in the West and the attraction that the more secular character of the Jewish community in the West held for those leaving the Northeast and Midwest.

Secular Jews also differed from Jews by religion in the relation of net recent migration (1985–1990) to net lifetime migration. Whereas the net redistribution of Jews by religion during 1985–1990 constituted 6 percent of all their lifetime redistribution, for secular Jews the recent net changes accounted for almost 10 percent of lifetime redistribution. This suggests an increased pace of redistribution among secular Jews. Some change in the direction of regional shifts is also evident. During 1985–1990, in contrast to substantial lifetime losses, the in- and out-streams of secular Jews in the Northeast were virtually balanced, resulting in a very small net gain. The Midwest continued to lose secular Jews between 1985 and 1990; in fact, the net out-migration in these five years accounted for 17 percent of the aggreagate lost through lifetime out-migration, a rate twice as high as that for Jews by religion.

Differentials also characterized the South and West. Whereas the former had gained secular Jews through migration over the period between birth and 1985, it lost secular Jews between 1985 and 1990. This loss in recent years contrasts with the substantial gain to the South of Jews by religion. The different pattern may reflect the inflow of older persons through retirement migration and the out-migration of younger persons because of occupational mobility. Unlike the South, the West continued to gain secular Jews during 1985–1990, accounting for almost 13 percent of the aggregate gain from lifetime migration, a level far above the recent movement of Jews by religion.

These varying patterns result in a redistribution of secular Jews across the regions. Judged by time of birth (which does not represent a fixed point in time), 43 percent of all native-born secular Jews lived in the Northeast; by 1985, this had declined to only 31 percent, and it remained at about this level in 1990. The Midwest, by contrast, experienced continuous decline in its percentage of the total national secular Jewish population, from 18 percent at time of birth to 11 percent in 1990. The South was characterized by a variable pattern: Its secular Jews, who accounted for only 16 percent of the total at time of birth, increased to over 21 percent by 1985, but then declined slightly to just under 21 percent by 1990. The West reinforced its position as having a large regional concentration of secular Jews: It had the second largest regional concentration when judged by region of residence at birth; by 1985, it had moved into first place with almost 35 percent, and strengthened its position by accounting for over 36 percent by 1990. This increasing concentration of secular Jews in the West helps to explain the generally lower Jewish identification profile of Jews in this region.

Thus, for secular Jews, as for Jews by religion, migration contributed to significant regional redistribution of the population, yet the index of dissimilarity shows that the extent of change was not as great as for Jews by religion. The 1990 regional distribution of Jews by religion differed from that at time of their birth by 25 percentage points; the differential for secular Jews was only 18 percentage points. The difference possibly reflects the heavy movement from the Northeast where the population initially consisted disproportionally of Jews by religion. More of these Jews shifted to other regions, leading, in turn, to a substantial growth in the number of Jews by religion in the South and the West.

Intrinsic to Jews by choice is a change in their religious identity at some earlier time. The data do not allow assessment of when this occurred in relation to migration. All we can determine is whether their lifetime migration patterns differed from persons classified as Jews by religion or as secular Jews and speculate whether any observed differences are a function of their special Jewish identity. Over the course of their lifetime, Jews by choice conform to the same general pattern noted for the other two groups—a net exodus from the Northeast and Midwest and net in-migration to the South and West. This pattern is also consistent with the general redistribution patterns characterizing the American population as a whole.

Compared to the patterns of Jews by religion and secular Jews, the extent of redistribution among Jews by choice is at a lower level. The percentage of Jews by choice living in the Northeast in 1990 was only slightly below the percentage born there, suggesting a low rate of exodus from this region. In part this results from a reversal in migration patterns; during 1985–1990, the region gained about 2,000 Jews by choice, compensating some for a loss of over 6,000 in prior years. By contrast, for the Midwest, the number of Jews by choice in the region in 1990 was under half the number born there, and net out-migration characterized both the long-term and short-term periods.

The relative gains of Jews by choice in the South (50 percent) and West (76 percent) were greater than those of the secular Jews but less than the increase of Jews by religion. Again, the data suggest a change in pattern. Between 1985 and 1990, the South continued to add Jews by choice through migration; in fact, about one-quarter of all lifetime movement to the region by Jews by choice occurred in this five-year interval. By contrast, more Jews by choice left the West between 1985 and 1990 than moved there, making Jews by choice the only identity category to experience net out-migration from the West in recent years.

What has been the effect of lifetime and recent migration on the distribution of Jews by choice across the country? The sharpest change characterized the proportion in the Midwest, which declined by half, from 33 to 16 percent of the national total. Both the South and the West benefited by the redistribution, raising their proportions of the total by almost 50 percent each. Minimal change characterized the Northeast. Overall, the result was a more balanced distribution of Jews by choice among the four regions.

THE IMPACT OF REDISTRIBUTION
FOR JEWISH AMERICANS

The foregoing two chapters have shown the dramatic redistribution of the Jewish American population across the United States. From being mainly concentrated in the Northeast and the Midwest at the beginning of the twentieth century, by 1990 large segments of American Jewry were living in the South and the West. In this respect, Jewish migration patterns have paralleled those of the general American population. The result has been the creation of a truly national Jewish population.

Migration levels have been high for Jews. Only one in five had never made a move since birth, and 30 percent had moved either within state of residence or between states in the five years preceding the survey. Many of these moves were closely related to the life cycle, occurring during periods of change in employment and marital status, primarily at the younger ages, but also among the elderly. The young are also most likely to make another move in the future; they are prominent among the almost half of all respondents who said it was very likely or somewhat likely that they would move within three years. Since the times of establishing an independent household and forming a family are critical stages for identification with a given community, such high levels of mobility may hamper the establishment of roots in any one place and may promote a pattern of nonaffiliation. Once such a pattern is established, active involvement in a community may be less likely, and strong identification may suffer.

The redistribution of the Jewish population has occurred not only across regions, but also across metropolitan areas. Many more metropolitan areas now encompass Jewish populations, and within them, Jews are more widespread. Particularly notable is the movement to the suburbs and away from concentrations in the central cities. Again, this trend is like that characterizing the general American population. For the Jewish community, it raises serious questions about the location of institutions and the provision of services.

Underlying the broad changes in the heavy turnover among Jews are the differentials by religious identification. Jews by religion have been heavily concentrated in the Northeast, but because of migration, by 1990 they had become much more evenly spread across regions. In the process, the South and the West both gained substantially, especially when lifetime migration is considered, and the Northeast in particular lost Jews by religion even while remaining the region of heaviest concentration. The movement of secular Jews reinforced their relatively heavy concentrations in the South and West; they are most concentrated in the latter. During 1985–1990, lifetime patterns of redistribution continued, but the exodus from the Northeast abated somewhat and the streams out of the South and West increased.

High population turnover and migration across metropolitan areas, states, and regions have thus radically changed the distribution of American Jewry. While the Northeast continues to be a strong center of Jewish life, with a disproportionate number of Jews by religion, other regions now claim more equitable shares of all segments of the Jewish population. Such dispersion may have both positive and negative consequences. On the one hand, it can be an important factor in invigorating Jewish life in areas that were quite marginal in the past. On the other hand, it can substantially weaken locations by drawing off a critical segment of the community's Jews. This may be especially serious if the Jews who leave are those most strongly identified with the Jewish community. At the individual level, mobility may seriously disrupt ties with the Jewish community both because it takes time to integrate into a new community of residence and because movement may often be to locations with no or weak Jewish institutions. Such barriers to integration Jewishly may be exacerbated if movement occurs primarily in response to economic or life-style factors that have little to do with being Jewish.

CHAPTER 4

Socioeconomic Differentials

We have seen that the migration of Jewish Americans is affected by age and gender as well as by the nature of Jewish identity. Many other factors also affect who moves and the type of move made. Migrants, whether Jewish or not, respond differentially to conditions influencing the decision to migrate and to the comparative attractions of different types of locations. Decisions on migration depend to some degree on an individual's socioeconomic characteristics as well as on the characteristics of the places of origin and of potential destination. As a result, migrants tend to be differentially concentrated in selected socioeconomic segments of the population.

The high educational and occupational levels of Jewish Americans means that for many Jews full realization of their goals and potential requires movement into labor markets other than those in which they were raised or where their families live. Moreover, for many, job advancement may require additional moves, especially if they are employed by national firms with multiple plants and offices. Futhermore, because Jews are concentrated in those high educational and occupational categories characterized by high migration rates (U.S. Bureau of the Census, 1991), we would expect high mobility for the Jewish population as a whole even while mobility levels and type of movement will differ from the general patterns for those Jews who are of somewhat lower socioeconomic status.

Stages of the life cycle may also affect mobility, but in ways quite different from education and occupation. Formation of a new household, changes in housing needs as a family grows and declines in size, divorce and widowhood, as well as retirement may all lead to changes in residence. Since marital status change as well as educational achievement and occupational affiliation may affect the volume and type of migration, we must consider all three variables in analyzing migration differentials among the Jewish population and in assessing what implications differentials may have for involvement in the Jewish community and for Jewish identity.

The analyses that follow use the NJPS-1990 data to assess migration differentials by education, occupation, and marital status. In doing so, we will focus most heavily on internal migration during 1985–1990, because the socioeconomic characteristics refer to status at the time of the survey in 1990. To the extent that lifetime migration could have occurred at any time between birth and the survey, the relation between a 1990 characteristic and an early move is quite tenuous. The ideal data set would have information on characteristics both preceding and following the move to allow fuller evaluation of whether the move itself was associated with a change in the characteristic. However, such detailed information is beyond the scope of an omnibus survey such as NJPS-1990.

The focus on differentials is restricted to the core Jewish population. This approach will allow greater consistency with the attention given in subsequent chapters to the relation between migration and a series of variables indicative of Jewish practices and identity, all of which are restricted to the core Jewish population. Moreover, the heterogeneous character of the peripheral population makes subdivision into its varied socioeconomic segments statistically tenuous, since the number of cases in some subcategories will not be adequate for analyzing migration. For this reason, the various subtypes of the core Jewish group also are generally not treated separately in this assessment of the relation between migration and socioeconomic variables. Proceeding in this way allows more detailed attention to the impact of age and gender, both of which must be considered for fuller understanding of the relation between migration and the socioeconomic factors.

EDUCATION DIFFERENTIALS

The Bureau of the Census has found a complex relation between population movement and education (U.S. Bureau of the Census, 1991). As expected, persons with at least some college education had higher mobility rates than those with only a high school education, and the latter moved more than those with only an elementary education. This pattern applied only to individuals moving long distances, however, supporting our earlier thesis that higher education often leads to migration across labor market areas. The Census found that among local movers, those with only elementary education were also less likely to move, but that having a high school or college education made little difference. Part of the explanation for the lower mobility of the least educated was their heavier concentration in the older ages.

In the United States, for both men and women, after age, education is the characteristic that is most likely to determine migration (Long, 1988:40). For many, the very act of obtaining higher education involves a geographic move, since the college of choice may be some distance from home. After graduation, a substantial proportion may not return to community of origin because their specialized training may dictate where occupational opportunities are located. Some may remain in the vicinity of the college/university to maintain ties to that location; many others will move to still a third location. To the extent that education and eventual occupation are closely related, specialized training often may entail repeated migration. Moreover, the conditions conducive to migration may be compounded for those couples with both spouses holding higher degrees, so that both careers may be best served by migration, but not necessarily in the same location.

To the extent that Jews are highly concentrated at those educational levels most prone to higher rates of migration, we would expect the overall migration rates of Jews to exceed those of the general population. This may be especially true as Jews enter professions that are not tied to family businesses. On the other hand, if Jews prefer to live in areas of high Jewish concentration and in places with Jewish institutions and facilities, then Jewish migration may be reduced by the limited number of locations that can satisfy these noneconomic considerations.

An analysis of males included in the 1970/71 National Jewish Population Survey found that education affected mobility (Goldstein, 1982). Whereas 72 percent of the Jews with less than a secondary education were living in 1970 in the same city as in 1965, that was true of only 57 percent of those with a post-graduate education. More of those with higher education were involved in all kinds of movement—local, intrastate, and interstate—than were those with less education, and the differentials were greatest for destinations involving longer distances. These data thus support the thesis that higher education serves to stimulate moves that are job-related and therefore leads to more moves that are between labor markets and involve greater distances.

The 1970/71 data also attest to the important relation between age and mobility, and the differing importance of education by age. For example, only 1.3 percent of the aged with a postgraduate degree moved interstate, but about 18 percent of those age 20 through 39 did so. Among those under age 40, only 7 percent with a high school education and none with less than a high school education migrated interstate. Interestingly, for the aged, the proportion moving interstate varied inversely with level of education, from a high of 7 percent of those with less than high school experience to just over one percent of those with postgraduate degrees. This pattern may reflect a greater tendency among older, more educated persons to remain in the labor force longer and therefore not to engage in postretirement migration as much as those who retired earlier.

Assessment of the educational achievements of the Jewish population, based on the NJPS-1990 data, confirmed the very high proportion of Jewish men and women, especially among the younger segments of the population, who not only attend and graduate from college, but who also undertake graduate or professional studies (Goldstein, 1992). Attention turns now to the relation between migration and education, focusing first on lifetime migration and then in more detail on recent movement.

At least half of all males in every educational group lived outside the state or country of their birth, testifying to the high incidence of migration among Jews. Yet for males, level of education clearly affects lifetime migration, especially interstate movement. With age controlled through standardization,[1] interstate migration characterized only 39 percent of those with a high school education or less; 45 percent of those who attended college; and 53 percent of those who had some graduate education (table 4.1). By contrast, the percent living in the same locality or elsewhere in their state of birth is quite similar (45–49 percent) for those with less than graduate studies but declines to 38 percent of those who undertook graduate/professional work. Because so many younger Jews now engage in graduate studies, we can expect that migration will be a particularly important factor in their lives. It will therefore also have great significance for the community as a whole.

The patterns of lifetime migration in relation to education are not as clear or consistent for women. As for males, the percentage reporting interstate migration was lowest for those with high school education or less (39 percent), but the highest level characterized those with some college education (57 percent) rather than those who had undertaken graduate studies (49 percent). This "irregularity" may reflect the fact that many women, especially older ones, may have migrated because of marriage and family considerations. Better insights into the effects of education on female migration may be provided by the data on recent migration and by the data for women in younger age groups. Attention turns next to such data sets.

In contrast to lifetime migration, which includes the movement to the United States of earlier waves of immigrants, recent migration encompasses relatively little international movement. For both men and women in the core Jewish population, with age controlled, recent interstate migration varies directly with educational level. About twice as many of those with graduate training migrated across states than did those with less than a college education. Since this interstate movement occurred in the short space of five years, the high levels for those who at least completed college, and especially for those with graduate studies, attests to the important impact which migration may have on a substantial segment of the community and on the community itself.

Such a conclusion is reinforced by our finding that only about half of the men and women in each of the groups with college or graduate studies lived in the same house in 1990 as in 1985. Only for those with high school education or less did residential stability exceed 60 percent. Of those who moved within a state, more (usually many more) did so within the same locality (i.e. to a different house) rather than across city or town boundaries, and no clear education differentials appear. Most such movement was undoubtedly related to changing residential needs and preferences rather than job changes, and, as such, may have been less disruptive of ties to the community. Yet, that at least 30 percent or more of the population in all educational groups moved within states (including intralocal movement) over the course of only five years points to the importance of taking mobility into account in planning location of facilities and integration of the population into the larger social and religious life of the community.

Table 4.1

Distribution by Lifetime and Five-Year Migration Status, by Education and Sex, Age Standardized: Core Jews

Sex and Education	Nonmigrant	Migration Status			
		Intrastate	Interstate	International	Total Percent
		Lifetime Migrants			
Males					
High School or Less	20.2	26.3	39.3	14.1	100.0
Some College	21.5	27.2	46.8	4.5	100.0
Completed College	17.4	27.5	44.9	10.1	100.0
Graduate School	17.0	20.8	52.9	9.3	100.0
Females					
High School or Less	19.4	25.9	39.0	15.7	100.0
Some College	19.1	19.3	56.7	4.9	100.0
Completed College	15.9	26.3	49.3	8.5	100.0
Graduate School	18.3	22.1	48.5	11.1	100.0

Five-Year Migrants

Males					
High School or Less	84.2	8.6	7.1	0.1	100.0
Some College	79.9	7.2	10.5	2.5	100.0
Completed College	75.6	11.0	12.2	1.2	100.0
Graduate School	75.8	9.9	13.4	0.9	100.0
Females					
High School or Less	85.2	8.6	6.2	—	100.0
Some College	74.9	17.6	7.3	0.2	100.0
Completed College	71.4	14.3	12.3	2.0	100.0
Graduate School	75.0	9.5	13.7	1.8	100.0

Focusing on the migration levels of the total population, even with age controlled, masks the much higher levels of mobility that characterize selected age segments of the population and the especially high levels of those who also have high levels of education. We focus here on the 25–34 age group; its peak levels of mobility are associated with completion of graduate studies, entrance into the labor force, and marriage (table 4.2). For males age 25–34, the percentage of interstate migrants at each educational level was about twice as high as for the total males in all age groups. Higher levels of interstate migration also characterized each educational category of women age 25–34 compared to women in all age groups combined, but the differences were as sharp as those for men only for the college graduates and those with some graduate education. Moreover, for the latter two groups, the levels of interstate migration were about as high as for men.

These data for those age 25–34 reveal a clear and sharp differential in the extent of interstate migration by educational level. That as many as 16 percent of the men with a high school education or less migrated across state lines between 1985 and 1990 is impressive. Much more so is the fact that one-quarter of the college graduates and slightly more of those with graduate education made an interstate move during these five years. The differential is even sharper for women; three times as many of those with graduate studies were interstate migrants as were those with no more than a high school education. Educational achievement clearly constitutes a major factor in determining longer-distance movement among Jews, just as it does in the general population. To the extent that the proportion of Jews with more education will increase as younger cohorts age and become an increasing proportion of the total, we can expect that in the years ahead migration will become an even more prevalent feature in the Jewish community.

The pattern of higher migration levels for the 25–34 age group compared to the total Jewish population was not restricted to interstate migration. It also held for intrastate and local mobility, and did so for both men and women. However, the direct relation to educational level was not as consistent; for shorter-distance movement, education apparently played a less crucial role in influencing the extent of mobility. This is understandable since a higher proportion of such moves were probably undertaken for noneconomic reasons.

Table 4.2

Distribution by Five-Year Migration Status, by Education and Sex, Persons Age 25–34: Core Jews

Education	Migration Status				
	Nonmigrant	Intrastate	Interstate	International	Total Percent
Males, 25–34 Years					
High School or Less	70.9	13.1	15.9	—	100.0
Some College	64.8	8.0	20.2	6.9	100.0
Completed College	50.4	22.4	25.4	1.8	100.0
Graduate School	51.7	20.7	27.1	0.5	100.0
Females, 25–34 Years					
High School or Less	70.0	20.6	9.4	—	100.0
Some College	52.3	35.8	11.9	—	100.0
Completed College	45.2	24.4	23.8	6.6	100.0
Graduate School	55.4	15.7	26.6	2.4	100.0

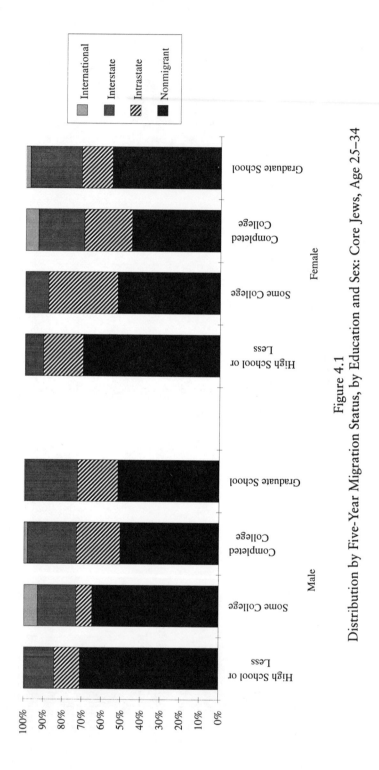

Figure 4.1
Distribution by Five-Year Migration Status, by Education and Sex: Core Jews, Age 25–34

As a net result, residential stability over the short span of five years characterized comparatively few persons age 25–34. These overall low levels of residential stability, and especially the high levels of mobility among the more educated, point to the great importance of education in influencing movement, and the serious implications it may have in affecting the socioeconomic structure of the population at places of origin and destination. Areas experiencing high out-migration could readily lose a substantial proportion of the best-trained segments of their population; conversely, those areas experiencing high rates of gain through migration could attract such persons disproportionally. Whether this would strengthen or weaken Jewish life in the respective communities would, of course, depend on the nature of the Jewish identity of those with more education and the way migration itself affects such identity and ties to the community. That such migration is especially frequent among those in the age group 25–34, an age range that coincides for many with family formation, career development, and initiation of new social linkages, gives added weight to the significance of the process for both individuals and the community at large.

OCCUPATIONAL DIFFERENTIALS

Many surveys have shown economic motives are primarily responsible for longer-distance movement. Long (1988:235), for example, found that, during 1979–1981, 22 percent of American households (defined as "household reference persons") who relocated interstate did so because of job transfers and 19 percent to assume new jobs. Just over 6 percent moved in quest of employment and 3 percent for unspecified reasons related to employment. In all, therefore, almost half of all household moves were work-related.

Not surprisingly, the motivation for interstate migration varied by age. Work-related reasons were cited by only 46 percent of interstate migrants under age 25, but by 60 percent of the migrants between ages 35 and 39. Among older age groups, the percentage declined as family reasons, concern for climate, and retirement assumed increased importance. However, for all groups between ages 25 and 44, at least half of the reasons given were related to employment, attesting to the key role that economic factors play in the redistribution of the American population among the states.

Despite the overall importance of economic considerations, they do not operate uniformly across all occupational groups. Movement, especially across greater distances, is influenced by the differential opportunities in various locations to use skills and to obtain greater rewards, in terms of remuneration, job security, and advancement. Employment by national firms may also necessitate movement, as staff is transferred among branches or in conjunction with relocation of activities. Dual careers among couples and partners compound the impact that employment concerns and specific occupational affiliations may have on migration, both as spur and as deterrent.

For Americans as a whole, migration rates differ by occupational group. For example, of the U.S. workers surveyed in 1990 (U.S. Bureau of the Census, 1991), high white collar workers were the most mobile compared to sales workers and manual laborers. Both the high correlation between education and occupation and the differential distribution of employment opportunities contributed to such differentials.

These patterns have special significance for Jews since such a high percentage are concentrated in the higher white collar occupations (56 percent of employed Jewish males are in professional and managerial positions compared to only 30 percent of the employed U.S. white males; the parallel percentages for women are 49 percent and 31 percent). Moreover, to the extent that increasing proportions of Jews engaged in work for others rather than being self-employed (Cohen, 1983: 86–87 and Goldscheider, 1986: 137–143), we would expect greater mobility; realization of occupational aspirations may require movement to where opportunities exist, rather than settlement in home communities and employment in family firms.

In 1970/71, the occupational differentials in mobility observed for Jewish males[2] closely paralleled those noted for education (Goldstein, 1982). For all age groups combined, the level of mobility among males varied substantially, from a low of 28 percent of those in manual work to a high of 45 percent of professionals. Professionals were found more frequently in each of the internal migration categories than were those in managerial, clerical/sales, and manual work. Among manual workers, a considerably lower proportion were interstate migrants or moved intra-state beyond their metropolitan area of origin.

During 1965–1970, white collar employees, especially professionals, were most prominent among Jewish males who migrated longer distances. A somewhat lower proportion of managers moved between states, possibly because of their stronger ties to a particular business because of involvement in family establishments. As Jewish men take more appointments as employed managers, their participation in interstate movement can be expected to rise. This possibility was already supported by the 1970/71 age-specific data.

For occupation, as for education, general residential stability in 1965–1970 was much higher for all occupational categories within the older population than within younger groups; in the younger population, the general patterns noted above for the male population as a whole obtained. For the 30–39 year age group, for example, the level of stability was much greater among the blue collar workers than among the white collar males. The differentials were particularly sharp for migration between states; almost 14 percent of the professionals and over 20 percent of managers made an interstate move during the five-year interval, compared to only 5 percent of the clerical/sales workers and less than 2 percent of those in blue collar work. For those age 50 and over, however, the relation between occupation and movement became less distinct. For all occupational groups, the majority continued to live within the same city; most movement was local. Clearly, for 1965–1970, occupational affiliation in conjunction with stage of the life cycle accounted for a considerable difference in levels of geographic mobility for Jewish males.

The data from NJPS-1990 provide an interesting contrast. To determine the impact of occupation on migration as directly as possible, we have restricted the population under consideration to those who were in the labor force at the time of the survey. We are thereby replicating the procedure followed in the analyses of NJPS-1970/71 and the U.S. census. Elimination of retired persons from consideration removes any confounding effects that retirement *per se* may have had on migration patterns.

The data for employed males indicate that managers and service personnel were the least residentially stable during 1985–1990 (table 4.3). About 60 percent of the service workers and 69 percent of the managers made no moves, compared to 75 percent to 80 percent of those in the other occupational categories. Moreover, managers and service workers had about equally high levels of intra- and interstate migration. During the period under consideration, men in each of these occupations may have found it both necessary and somewhat easier to move in order to maintain employment.

The patterns differed for women, with operatives having the lowest level of stability and managers the highest; between 59 percent to 83 percent in all occupational groups were nonmigrants. Despite their low level of stability, operatives generally moved only short distances—that is, intrastate. By contrast, women professionals had by far the highest rate of interstate migration and also had relatively high levels of intrastate movement. The contrast of the male and female patterns suggests that mobility meets

Table 4.3
Distribution by Five-Year Migration Status,
by Major Occupation and Sex, Employed Persons Only:
Core Jews

| Occupation | Migration Status | | | | |
	Non-migrant	Intra-state	Inter-state	Inter-national	Total Percent
Males					
Professional	74.6	12.5	11.8	1.1	100.0
Manager	68.5	14.8	16.4	0.2	100.0
Clerical/Sales	77.2	9.2	11.4	2.3	100.0
Crafts	77.5	12.4	10.0	—	100.0
Operatives	79.9	12.0	8.2	—	100.0
Service	59.6	17.8	15.5	7.1	100.0
Females					
Professional	70.0	14.5	13.6	1.9	100.0
Manager	83.1	9.7	7.2	—	100.0
Clerical/Sales	77.1	12.3	9.0	1.7	100.0
Crafts	82.0	9.5	8.5	—	100.0
Operatives	58.9	41.1	—	—	100.0
Service	77.2	11.9	10.8	—	100.0

very different needs and is constrained by quite different forces for men and women.

The age-aggregated data for five-year migration by occupation masks important differences by age. To obtain further understanding of these relations, we turn next to examination of the patterns for men and women age 25–34 and 35–44, age periods that are, respectively, at the beginning of career and family building and then at much more stable life-cycle situations.

For both men and women, migration levels are considerably higher at the younger ages for most occupational categories (table 4.4). Moreover, men age 25–34 with white collar occupations are much more likely to move, especially interstate, than are men with lower status occupations. For example, only half of the managers age 25–34 were identified as nonmigrants, while one-quarter had

Table 4.4
Distribution by Five-Year Migration Status, by Major Occupation and Sex, for Ages 25–34 and 35–44, Employed Persons Only:
Core Jews

| | Migration Status | | | | |
Occupation	Non-migrant	Intra-state	Inter-state	Inter-national	Total Percent
		Males, Age 25–34			
Professional	54.5	21.9	21.1	2.5	100.0
Manager	50.5	23.9	24.9	0.7	100.0
Clerical/Sales	52.5	12.7	28.4	6.4	100.0
Crafts	66.1	19.3	14.5	—	100.0
Operatives	72.1	27.9	—	—	100.0
Service	62.4	31.0	6.6	—	100.0
		Females, Age 25–34			
Professional	49.1	23.2	24.3	3.5	100.0
Manager	69.7	22.5	7.9	—	100.0
Clerical/Sales	50.9	28.1	16.2	4.7	100.0
Crafts	*	*	*	*	*
Operatives	*	*	*	*	*
Service	74.3	13.0	12.8	—	100.0

Table 4.4 *(continued)*

| | Migration Status | | | | |
Occupation	Non-migrant	Intra-state	Inter-state	Inter-national	Total Percent
	Males, Age 35–44				
Professional	73.3	14.5	10.9	1.2	100.0
Manager	77.2	11.9	10.8	—	100.0
Clerical/Sales	75.4	17.1	6.3	1.1	100.0
Crafts	82.6	1.8	15.6	—	100.0
Operatives	69.0	15.4	15.5	—	100.0
Service	56.0	14.5	4.3	25.2	100.0
	Females, Age 35–44				
Professional	73.1	13.1	12.3	1.4	100.0
Manager	82.7	6.2	11.1	—	100.0
Clerical/Sales	84.5	5.1	10.4	—	100.0
Crafts	*	*	*	*	*
Operatives	*	*	*	*	*
Service	84.0	7.6	8.4	—	100.0

*Fewer than 10 unweighted cases in category.

moved interstate. By contrast, two-thirds of the operatives in this age group were nonmigrants and only 15 percent interstate migrants. Among the 35–44 age cohort, overall levels of stability were higher, and the relation between occupation and mobility was quite mixed.

Not enough women reported being either crafts workers or operatives to allow their separate inclusion in the analysis, but within the constraints imposed by the data, the patterns for women were quite similar to those for men. Overall stability levels were lower in the younger age group than in the older one, and highest levels of interstate migration for 25–34 year old women were reported by professionals. No clear pattern appears for women age 35–44. Apparently, for both men and women, only at the beginning years of career building do higher white collar occupations lead to higher levels of mobility. Especially for those who are self-employed, as, for example, doctors, lawyers, and accountants, an established practice serves as a stabilizing factor. Once careers have been established, migration is motivated by other considerations.

Data not shown in the tables for men and women who were retired at the time of the survey indicate extremely low levels of five-year migration, with only about 10 percent at most in any occupational group identified as migrants.[3] Among those who did move, the tendency was to move longer distances rather than just intrastate. Furthermore, retirees in the lower status occupations were more likely to make interstate moves than those who had been white collar.

Contrary to expectations, the data from NJPS-1990 do not point to clear patterns of occupational differentials in the overall extent of recent mobility or in the proportion migrating across states. This does not, however, detract from the fact that a high percentage of the members in most occupational groups were mobile in the five years before the survey, and that a substantial number of them moved considerable distances.

Migration differentials by occupation may have changed in the twenty years since 1970 and not in the hypothesized direction. Larry Long (1988:40–46) has suggested that over time the high returns to schooling (and being high white collar) may have declined as more persons reach higher rungs of the educational and occupational ladders. If so, he suggests that persons in these high status categories may be less willing to invest in interstate migration. On the other hand, those with less education and in lower level occupations may be more willing to do so. Dual careers, especially involving two professionals, may also serve as a barrier to mobility.

The key point Long (1988:45) stresses is that migration differentials in highly industrialized societies represent responses to age, period, and cohort effects and their interaction with broader social and economic conditions and trends. The declining economic conditions characterizing many areas of the United States in the waning years of the 1980s may especially have affected migration patterns. As Gober (1993) has pointed out, declining mobility in the United States in the late 1980s and into the early 1990s suggests a return to the longer-term trend of decreasing annual mobility rates.

For Jews, the factors contributing to migration may be even more complex since the role of Jewish identity and of accessibility to Jewish facilities and institutions must also be taken into account. These factors may often override the strictly economic considerations that affect migration decisions (cf. Kritz and Nogle, 1994). Only a full understanding of how all these changing conditions impinge on individual migration decision-making can clarify both the changes in patterns over time and the differentials noted at particular points in time. Later attention to the impact of Jewish identity on migration may provide insights into these relations.

EMPLOYMENT STATUS

Self-employment, as opposed to working for others, can be hypothesized to reduce the extent of longer-distance migration. While decisions related to careers involving self-employment may initially involve movement to what are perceived as "best locations," the likelihood seems greater that, once such a choice is made, development of a career (as in medicine or law) is likely to occur in the same general area; residential mobility is more likely to be dictated by housing preferences and needs rather than occupational demands. The availability in NJPS-1990 of information on employment status allows testing whether the self-employed did, in fact, have a different level of migration than those who were employed by others. As for the analysis by occupation, the detailed consideration of the interrelations of five-year migration and employment status is restricted to those who were in the labor force at the time of the survey.

Levels of self-employment vary widely by age and especially by gender. For both men and women, those in the youngest age group have the lowest level of self-employment—under 10 percent. For men, self-employment rises steadily with age, to one-fourth of those age 65 and over. Women's level of self-employment plateaus at about 15 percent by the 25–34 age groups and remains at that level until age 65. In no age group is women's self-employment level as high as that of men of comparable age, and the differential widens with increasing age.

The data on the relation of five-year migration and employment status support our hypothesis that the self-employed are more stable than employees (table 4.5). For example, 82 percent

Table 4.5
Distribution by Five-Year Migration Status, by Employment Status and
Sex, for Ages 25–34 and 35–44, Employed Persons Only:
Core Jews

	Migration Status				
Employment Status	Non-migrant	Intra-state	Inter-state	Inter-national	Total Percent
All Males					
Employee	70.4	13.7	14.3	1.6	100.0
Self-employed	82.0	9.4	7.4	1.2	100.0
All Females					
Employee	74.6	12.8	10.9	1.7	100.0
Self-employed	75.3	17.0	7.7	—	100.0
Males, Age 25–34					
Employee	54.1	21.1	22.1	2.8	100.0
Self-employed	61.4	16.9	19.3	2.4	100.0
Females, Age 25–34					
Employee	52.5	24.6	19.1	3.8	100.0
Self-employed	63.3	22.8	13.9	—	100.0
Males, Age 35–44					
Employee	69.4	15.2	13.5	1.9	100.0
Self-employed	84.3	9.4	4.0	2.4	100.0
Females, Age 35–44					
Employee	78.2	10.3	10.6	0.9	100.0
Self-employed	78.6	11.2	10.2	—	100.0

of self-employed men were nonmigrants, compared to only 70 percent of the male employees. This relation is particularly strong for men and for women in the younger ages (25–34 years) and for men age 35–44. Little difference characterized the stability levels of self-employed and other-employed women, except for the 25–34 age group, among whom the employees were more mobile, especially intrastate. Intrastate movement was generally more common than interstate migration, but in most cases, employees had a higher percentage of longer-distance moves than the self-

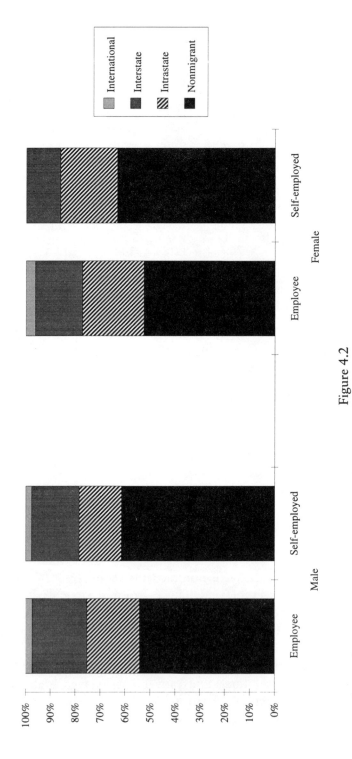

Figure 4.2

Distribution by Five-Year Migration Status, by Employment Status and Sex, Employed Persons Only: Core Jews, Age 25–34

employed. These data thus complement and corroborate the findings on the relations between occupation and migration. It must be stressed, however, that some migration classified as interstate is, in fact, only movement within large metropolitan areas that cut across state boundaries, as in the case of movement from New York City to nearby areas of New Jersey or Connecticut.

The extent to which Jews are increasingly entering occupations involving employment for others may well help explain the comparatively high levels of overall Jewish migration. It also suggests that if shifts away from self-employment persist in conjunction with continued high levels of education, then the levels of migration, especially interstate movement, may be heightened in the future.

MARITAL STATUS

Stage of the life cycle can affect the volume and distance of movement. If movement is job related, it is likely to involve distances greater than movement resulting from housing needs associated with marriage or changes in family size. Similarly, the end of a marriage through either divorce or death may result in a change of residence and may account for patterns of movement for divorced and widowed persons which differ from the patterns of those still married.

In a 1990 survey, the United States Bureau of the Census (1991) found considerable variation in the extent of both inter-county and interstate migration during the preceding year. The highest level of both kinds of movement characterized married persons living apart from spouse. Over 5 percent made an interstate move, and an additional 6 percent moved between counties in the same state. Evidently, spousal separation is conducive to extensive mobility. On the other hand, being married with spouse present has the reverse effect, as does widowhood, although the latter is largely a function of age. Divorced and single persons are even more mobile, as we might expect, because of both their weaker ties to family units and their younger age composition. More of the moves of divorced persons were short distance, probably because many had children. Clearly, marital status has an impact on both the overall level of movement and the type of move undertaken. Are the relations the same for Jews?

The 1970/71 National Jewish Population Survey found that stability was to a great extent associated with being single (Goldstein, 1982). Of single males age 20–29, 62 percent were in 1970 living in the same city as in 1965, in contrast to only 42 percent of married males of similar age. This finding may, however, reflect the fact that, in contrast to both the United States census and NJPS-1990, NJPS-1970/71 counted students living in group quarters at colleges and universities as members of their parental households unless an independent household had been established by the student. Since a large proportion of men age 20–29 are still enrolled in higher education, the comparatively high level of stability is understandable. It also helps to explain why, among this age group of males, only 7.5 percent of the singles were interstate migrants in contrast to 18 percent of married males. Undoubtedly, the high mobility of the latter is related to completion of education, entry into the labor force, and marriage.

These life-cycle factors continued to affect the mobility of those in their thirties, but married men age 40 and over tended to become much more stable, and more of the movement that did take place occurred within the same metropolitan area. In the very oldest age group, over three-quarters of the married males and just over 70 percent of the widowers had not changed their city of residence in the previous five years. For males, therefore, only among the younger groups did marital status have a significant impact on mobility behavior.

For females as for males, those who were single and in their twenties in 1970/71 had the highest geographic stability. Married women moved more, and a considerable part of the movement involved a change in state of residence: one in five of all 20–29-year-old married women had moved to another state, compared to only 7 percent of single women. Married women age 30–39 experienced almost as high a level of movement, but more of it was over shorter distances. Among older married women, as among men, the levels of stability rose considerably: only 5 to 7 percent had engaged in interstate migration in the previous five years.

The differences in mobility patterns between married and widowed women in the 50–64 age group were small. Women age 65 and over, however, experienced marked differences: married women were quite stable, mostly moving within the same metropolitan area. By contrast, over one-third of the widows moved during the interval, and a considerable proportion migrated interstate or within the state but beyond the metropolitan area. Widowhood may thus lead to movement across considerable distances. Overall, for women, as for men, marital status was strongly related to both the level of stability and the type of move made among those who changed residence, but the extent of differentials varied by age. We turn next to whether the same patterns characterize migration in the period covered by NJPS-1990.

Within the 1990 core Jewish population, virtually all males (96 percent) age 18–24, and half of those age 25–34 were still single (Goldstein, 1992). In the next several age groups, the large majority were married. For women, the proportion who were single was lower at each age, declining from 85 percent of those age 18–24 to just under one-third of those 25–34 years. Under 5 percent of those age 45 years and over were single. In contrast to men, age did not bear a consistently positive relation to the percent of women currently married. The proportion currently married reached a high of 74 percent of those age 35–44, and then declined to a low of 57 percent of those 65 years old and over, reflecting the rising percentage of widowed or divorced women. For both men and women, but especially the latter, being divorced or separated was most common between ages 35 and 64. For both gender groups, the proportion divorced/separated exceeded the proportion widowed for all age groups but the oldest. The higher proportion of women 65 years and over who were widowed (almost one in four) compared to men (only 11 percent) reflects the longer life expectancy of women and the greater propensity of elderly widowers to remarry.

Given these differences in marital status by age and gender, migration patterns can be expected to vary as well. With age controlled, the NJPS data suggest that, contrary to expectations, being male and single is associated with a high degree of residential stability (table 4.6). This finding is similar to that based on NJPS-1970/71, despite a difference in where people at college were counted. In 1990, 58 percent of the single men were living in the same house as five years earlier, and another quarter were in the same locality even though they had changed residence. Only 8 percent had moved intrastate, and 10 percent interstate. The high level of stability of the single population during 1985–1990 is attributable to the high proportion of singles who are under age 25, and to a lesser extent singles age 25–34.

Since a high proportion of Jewish males in these age groups are still completing their higher education, some may have been

Table 4.6

Distribution by Five-Year Migration Status, by Marital Status and Sex, Age Standardized: Core Jews

Marital Status	Same House	Different House, Same Locality	Intrastate	Interstate	International	Total Percent
			Males			
Never Married	57.5	23.5	8.3	9.5	1.2	100.0
Married	47.2	24.9	12.4	14.5	1.0	100.0
Divorced or Separated	42.5	34.2	8.1	11.3	4.0	100.0
Widowed	53.3	15.2	26.6	4.3	0.6	100.0
			Females			
Never Married	51.1	29.4	9.5	9.3	0.7	100.0
Married	53.2	20.5	14.8	10.5	1.1	100.0
Divorced or Separated	44.4	39.2	9.1	5.4	1.9	100.0
Widowed	57.3	18.3	3.0	21.4	—	100.0

Migration Status

living in parental homes at the time of the survey, while attending institutions in the general vicinity. More important, even though NJPS-1990 followed census procedures and enumerated students living at colleges and universities as residents of that location, because the survey was conducted in May–July, many students may have been home for summer vacation. As a result, many young persons would have been enumerated as members of their parental households because they were present there at the time of the survey. The high level of bilocalism identified earlier among students supports this interpretation.

In contrast to the singles, fewer of the married men were residentially stable, and considerably more (12 and 14 percent) had moved intra- and interstate, respectively. These much higher rates of both interstate and intrastate migration suggest that, for more of the married, entry into the labor force serves as major stimulus to longer-distance movement. Being married and perhaps having dependents does not seem to deter migration.

Divorced men were the least stable of all; only 42 percent were in the same house as five years earlier. Compared to the currently married, however, more of their mobility involved changes within their locality of residence rather than between areas. Their rate of intrastate migration is quite similar to single men and their interstate migration rate only slightly exceeds that of the singles. Breakup of a marriage for men does not seem to lead to unusually high rates of longer-distance movement.

Interestingly, almost as many widowers as single men were living in the same house in 1990 as in 1985. Far fewer, however, had moved within the same locality. Movement was most likely to have occurred between areas outside the locality but within the same state, possibly reflecting a shift nearer to other relatives or even to live with them. This pattern for widowers differed from that of widows (see below). Many fewer widowers than any other marital status group of men migrated interstate, suggesting that, for men, widowhood is strongly conducive to either residential stability or movement over relatively short distances.

In contrast to men, single women do not have the highest rate of continued residence in the same house compared to all other marital status groups—widows do. Somewhat more of the single women than men moved within the same locality. They differ minimally from men, however, in their proportion of intra- and interstate migrants, suggesting that basically the same forces determining short versus longer-distance movement affect single men and women.

A slightly higher percentage of married than of single women were in the same house in 1990 as in 1985, but far fewer had moved within the same locality. Like men, higher percentages of the married than of singles had made intra- and interstate moves, but, different from men, the intrastate moves were more numerous. For women, migration may have more likely been family-related rather than tied to changes in employment. As was the case for men, divorced and separated women had the lowest proportion living in the same house over the five-year period, and they were also characterized by low rates of intra- and interstate migration. Movement within the same locality was far more common for this marital status group than for any other.

That divorced men and women are characterized by low levels of residential stability and high rates of movement within the same locality strongly suggests a special linkage between broken marriage and mobility patterns. While some movement is inevitable with the break-up of a household, the separated parties apparently prefer to continue living in the same location. Such preference has the advantage of avoiding disruption in employment, in ties to children and other relatives, and in social networks.

Widows, like widowers, have high levels of continued residence in the same house, suggesting a tendency to remain residentially stable following loss of a spouse. However, if widows move, they are more likely to go longer distances than to remain within the same locality. One in five widows moved interstate, compared to only 3 percent who made an intrastate move; for widowers, the pattern was reversed. For women, the disruption caused by the death of a spouse generally occurs at a stage of the life cycle when they are likely to be out of the labor force, so that longer-distance movement is easier.

Fuller insights into the relation between marital status and migration can be gained from the age-specific data (table 4.7). We use only those marital status categories with adequate numbers—e.g., the never married in the younger groups and the widowed in the older ones. The married serve as a reference group for all ages except the youngest. Since such a high percentage of those under age 25 have never been married, the analysis for that age group is restricted to single persons.

The patterns for single men and women under age 25 were virtually identical, with high levels continuing to live in the same
house (59 percent) or a different house in the same locality (about
14 percent); about one-quarter of both groups moved outside
their locality, but many more of the men than women migrated
interstate. Male college students may have a greater tendency to
enroll in institutions further from families than do young women;
single, young men may also feel freer to take jobs at greater distances.

For those age 25–34, single males are clearly much less mobile
than married ones, most likely because the married men in this age
group married during the age interval and changed residence in
conjunction with marriage (Goldstein, 1992). That twice as many
married than single men were in a different house in the same general locality supports such a conclusion. Of those who moved
beyond the local area, more single men undertook interstate
migration. This differential is consistent with the assumption that
being unattached facilitates longer-distance movement.

Women age 25–34 display a somewhat different pattern. Married women were more likely than single women to be living in the
same house, and fewer changed residence within the same locality.
Since women, on average, marry at younger ages than men,
women may have engaged in marriage-related mobility before age
25. Like men, more married women have made intrastate moves
and fewer have migrated interstate, but the differences between
singles and married are not as sharp for women as for men. The
reasons for these differences in distance moved by marital status
are probably similar for men and women.

The 35–44-year-old group provides an opportunity to compare the mobility patterns of the single, the married, and the
divorced/separated. Both the never married and the married men
are characterized by much higher levels of residential stability
than the divorced, yet the divorced are similar to the never married in levels of movement within the same locality. This finding
suggests that divorce for men leads to local mobility: many prefer
not to or cannot remain in their marital home but still wish to
remain in the same location. Singles are most likely among the
three marital status groups to remain within their locality; if they
move, they tend to make shorter-distance moves. By contrast, a
much higher proportion of married men and an even higher percentage among the divorced were interstate migrants. Evidently,

Table 4.7
Distribution by Five-Year Migration Status, by Marital Status and Sex, Selected Age Groups:
Core Jews

		Migration Status				
Marital Status	Same House	Different House, Same Locality	Intrastate	Interstate	International	Total Percent
		Males, Age 18–24				
Never Married	58.7	13.7	13.9	13.7	—	100.0
		Females, Age 18–24				
Never Married	59.4	14.8	17.1	7.9	—	100.0
		Males, Age 25–34				
Never Married	31.7	21.6	16.7	28.2	1.8	100.0
Married	12.4	42.7	21.9	21.5	1.5	100.0
		Females, Age 25–34				
Never Married	15.1	37.7	21.2	23.2	2.8	100.0
Married	20.3	31.0	26.2	20.0	2.5	100.0

Males, Age 35–44						
Never Married	47.9	35.2	12.3	4.5	—	100.0
Married	47.0	26.3	13.6	10.5	2.5	100.0
Divorced or Separated	32.7	38.3	9.2	18.7	1.1	100.0
Females, Age 35–44						
Never Married	42.5	40.1	3.8	13.6	—	100.0
Married	53.8	22.3	12.4	10.3	1.1	100.0
Divorced or Separated	47.3	26.0	18.5	8.2	—	100.0
Males, Age 65 and over						
Married	83.7	9.2	3.1	4.1	—	100.0
Widowed	82.3	5.4	7.3	2.7	2.3	100.0
Females, Age 65 and over						
Married	87.6	5.9	3.3	3.3	—	100.0
Widowed	77.0	10.5	5.5	7.0	—	100.0

those men who are still single by age 35–44 have stronger ties to their areas of residence than do married or divorced men. In this respect, they differ from younger single men.

For women age 35–44, as for those 25–34 years old, the married more frequently continued to live in the same house and less frequently moved within the local area. Like men, single women engaged more than married women in local mobility. Divorced women, however, tended to be more residentially stable. Unlike men, more of the single women than of the married and divorced were involved in interstate migration. The reverse was true for intrastate movement. Divorced women may find it more important to remain closer to locations where family and friendship ties as well as support services exist, particularly since they are more likely to have custody of children; some, however, may move to be nearer relatives who can assist in child care (Sheskin, 1992, 1987). That the mobility patterns and levels of the married women age 35–44 closely resemble those of the married men suggests that movement involves households as a whole rather than just one spouse. The absence of such parallels between men and women in the 25–34-year-old group probably reflects the later ages at which men marry and the resultant moves associated with change in marital status.

Compared to younger persons, a much higher proportion of aged are residentially stable, regardless of marital status. Over four of five married and widowed men were in the same house as that in which they lived five years earlier, and fewer than 10 percent had changed residence within the local area. Of the small proportion who had moved a greater distance, about equal percentages of the married made an intra- or interstate move; more of the widowed migrated intrastate. As suggested earlier, the latter difference may reflect a greater tendency of widowers to adjust to the death of their spouse by moving nearer other relatives in the area.

Elderly married women showed somewhat greater residential stability than men. More remained in the same house and fewer moved within the same community. Like married men, only a small proportion of aged married women moved beyond the local area, and those who did so migrated intra- and interstate about equally. In contrast to both widowed men and married women, older widows moved with greater frequency to other residences in the same locality.

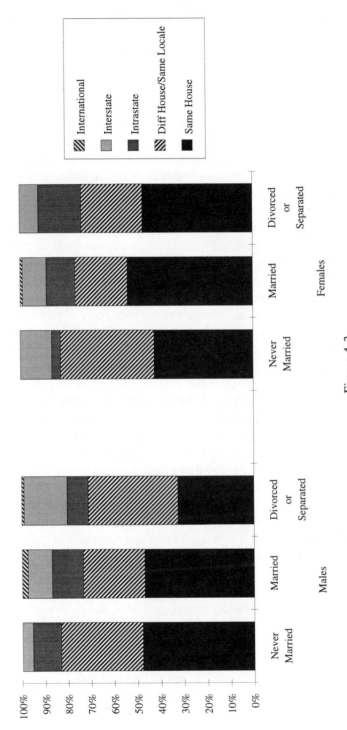

Figure 4.3

Distribution by Five-Year Migration Status, by Marital Status and Sex: Core Jews, Age 35–44

Evidently for widows, breakup of a marriage was more frequently associated with residential adjustments, although most
often within the same general area. For some, however, it took the
form of interstate migration and this, too, seemed to happen more
frequently for elderly widows than for older widowers. Widows
apparently find it easier than widowers to live some distance from
their original homes and possibly from relatives. Among elderly
women, widows were more mobile than married women and
turned to all types of mobility, whereas widowers engaged more
frequently than elderly married men only in intrastate movement.
Aged men and women clearly differ in their migration response to
disrupted marriages.

These data by age confirm that for both women and men marital status has a substantial impact both on the level of stability
and on the type of move made when there is a change of residence.
Furthermore, the age-specific evaluation indicates that the impact
of marital status varies by stage of the life cycle. Therefore, in
assessing who moves and where the movers go, and in evaluating
the impact of migration on both the individual and the community, consideration needs to be given to marital status, while also
taking account of other basic characteristics.

Additional insights into the relation between migration and
marital status can be gained by determining whether marriage
occurred before a move, in the same year as a move, or after migration. In a similar way, we can relate migration to the break-up of
marriage through divorce or death of a spouse. We consider only
the most current marriage, and migration refers to the most recent
move to current place of residence. Because marriage occurs most
frequently in the 25–44 age period, our analysis of the timing of
marriage in relation to migration will concentrate on that age
group. No controls for age are instituted for the analysis of the
break-up of marriage, which is distributed across the age categories.

For both men and women, interstate migration is more likely
if marriage and migration occur in the same year than if migration
occurs either before or after marriage (table 4.8). This relation is
especially strong for women, among whom half of those who married and migrated in the same year made an interstate move. By
contrast, women are much less likely to make such a long-distance
move before their marriage: only about one in five did so, compared
to one-third of the men. Women's migration, not surprisingly, seems
to be much more closely related to marriage than that of men.

When the break-up of marriage is considered, the patterns are quite similar for men and women. With the exception of men whose marriage termination and migration occurred in the same year, more of the movement is intrastate than longer distance. This pattern is especially pronounced for men and women who migrated before the dissolution of the marriage: for example, 61 percent of the men moved intrastate, while only 38 percent were

Table 4.8

The Timing of Marital Status Change in Relation to Migration, by Sex: Core Jews

Changing Marital Status in Relation to Migration	Migration Status			
	Intra-state	Inter-state	Inter-national	Total Percent
Males, Age 25–44				
Marriage before migration	61.8	31.0	7.2	100.0
Marriage/migration same year	56.2	39.0	4.8	100.0
Marriage after migration	64.3	31.4	4.3	100.0
Females, Age 25–44				
Marriage before migration	63.5	31.1	5.4	100.0
Marriage/migration same year	44.8	49.7	5.4	100.0
Marriage after migration	76.8	21.6	1.5	100.0
Males, All Ages				
Dissolution before migration	53.6	47.4	—	100.0
Dissolution/migration same year	39.3	51.5	9.2	100.0
Dissolution after migration	61.0	37.9	1.1	100.0
Females, All Ages				
Dissolution before migration	49.5	44.0	6.4	100.0
Dissolution/migration same year	47.2	37.4	15.5	100.0
Dissolution after migration	56.5	41.3	2.2	100.0

interstate migrants. Although international movement is uncommon at any time, it takes on some importance among those for whom the end of marriage and migration occurred in the same year, reaching as high as 16 percent of the women in this marital status/migration category.

These patterns suggest that interstate migration is somewhat more likely to be undertaken some time after the end of marriage than it is before marital dissolution. Given the rising rates of divorce and the aging of the Jewish population, we can expect increasing proportions of the population to experience marital dissolution. If the patterns discerned from the NJPS-1990 data continue in the future, we can also expect higher rates of mobility, although much of it may be relatively short distance. Even such moves, however, have serious implications for local Jewish communities in terms of service delivery, size of catchment areas, and general cohesion.

OVERVIEW: SOCIOECONOMIC DIFFERENTIALS

The foregoing assessment of the migration levels and patterns of the Jewish American population has given sequential attention to the extent and nature of the association between migration and several basic sociodemographic variables. These characteristics—age and gender, education, occupation, and marital status—do not operate independently of each other. Education and occupation, for example, are closely linked, and both vary by age and gender. Therefore, assessment of the impact of these characteristics on migration behavior also requires that they be considered jointly to allow determination of the effect on migration of each variable, net of the effect of the other variables. We do so through multinomial logit modeling.

This procedure allows us to calculate the expected proportions in each migration status category while each of the other variables under consideration is set at its mean.[4] The model, with five-year migration status as the dependent variable, has been calculated for the total adult sample including the core Jewish and the peripheral population, thereby allowing for controls for these two subgroups (table 4.9). The tabulations are restricted to persons in the labor force at the time of the survey, since earlier analysis has shown that those no longer in the labor force have distinctively different patterns from persons who are not yet retired.

Table 4.9
Expected Proportions in Each Five-Year Migration Status Category,
by Selected Characteristics
(A Multinominal Logit Model)

	Non-migrant	Intrastate Migrant	Interstate Migrant
Sample as a Whole	.7619	.1301	.1080
Sex			
Male	.7704	.1098	.1198
Female	.7497	.1535	.0968
Age			
18–44	.6131	.1955	.1914
45–64	.7552	.1079	.1369
65 and over	.8624	.0943	.0434
Marital Status			
Single	.7576	.1341	.1084
Married	.7662	.1263	.1075
Education (years completed)			
Less than 16	.7830	.1591	.0579
16–18	.7152	.1795	.1053
19 and over	.7359	.0719	.1922
Occupation			
Professional/Managerial	.7499	.1262	.1239
Other White Collar	.7822	.1398	.0779
Blue Collar	.7471	.1237	.1291
Current Jewish Identity			
Core Jews	.7492	.1641	.0866
Peripheral Population	.7652	.1019	.1329

With all other variables controlled, gender has little relation to level of interstate mobility, but women can be expected to make intrastate moves more than men. As a result, women have a somewhat lower level of residential stability, while at the same time making shorter-distance moves.

Of all the variables considered here, age has the strongest relation to predicted mobility. Those age 18–44 are far more likely to make either an intra- or interstate move, with as many as one in four expected to do so in each migration status category. Since these ages encompass the end of schooling, marriage and family formation, and career development, these patterns are not surprising. They are characteristic of people in many parts of the world, not just of Jewish Americans. By contrast, persons age 65 and over can be expected to be the most residentially stable of any group. Fewer than 15 percent made any kind of move.

Only those who had never married and the married are considered in this analysis.[5] They show few differences in expected mobility levels with all other characteristics controlled. Apparently, other factors, including age and education, override any impact that marital status per se may have on mobility.

Education, on the other hand, is a strong differentiator of mobility levels. Long-distance migration can be expected to be over three times more characteristic of those with postgraduate/professional training (19 percent) than those who do not hold a college degree (6 percent). Intrastate movement has exactly the obverse relation to level of education, with the least educated the most likely to make a shorter-distance move. Thus, while educational level does not discriminate strongly in terms of level of stability, it does bear an important relation to the kind of move that is undertaken. The more educated can be expected to move further in search of career opportunities. With such a high proportion of the Jewish American population at these very highly educated levels, interstate migration becomes a key dynamic in shaping both the local and national Jewish communities.

Occupational affiliation has quite a different relation to mobility than does education. The expected level of intrastate migration is almost the same for each of the three occupational groups considered here—varying only between 12 percent and 14 percent. Interstate migration patterns are quite different, however: both the professional/managerial group and the blue collar workers have equally high expected levels of interstate migration (12–

13 percent), while other white collar workers are much less likely to make such a long-distance move (8 percent). As suggested in the earlier analysis, a complex set of factors—including labor markets, career expectations, and ties to local communities—operate to affect the mobility of various occupational groups.

Finally, our data allow us to distinguish between core Jews (who have been the focus of the preceding analysis) and the peripheral population. Our analysis indicates that when all other socioeconomic characteristics are held constant, the peripheral population included in NJPS can be expected to make more interstate, but fewer intrastate moves. All other things being equal, therefore, the Jewish population can be expected to remain within a closer distance to place of origin than the peripheral population. Distributions of core Jews and the peripheral population are not similar, however. It is the very skewed concentration of Jews in those educational and occupational categories that are particularly associated with heightened levels of mobility that account for the importance of mobility in understanding the evolving nature of American Jewry.

In sum, age has the clearest relation to mobility, with Jews behaving very much like the general population: younger ages are most associated with high levels of mobility. At the same time, higher education intensifies this pattern, especially for the younger segment of the population. Occupation seems to have little direct relation to mobility levels; the effects of age and social/economic conditions override any occupational differentials.

The relation between age and mobility, especially long-distance movement, is also intensified by marital status, because migration is often associated with marriage and the establishment of an independent household. Those married at the time of the survey were therefore more mobile than singles, but the differences are closely associated with other changes in the life course. In a parallel relation, the dissolution of marriage is also associated with higher mobility levels, although much of it is short distance. All of these patterns point to at least the maintenance and probably an increase in mobility as Jews almost uniformly obtain high levels of education, fully participate in and are therefore affected by the general social and economic trends, and are subject to more marital dissolution because of rising divorce rates and the aging of the Jewish population.

CHAPTER 5

Differentials in Jewish Identification

The previous analyses have focussed on the extent to which and how the geographic mobility of Jews is affected by a range of demographic and socioeconomic factors, including age, gender, marital status, education, and occupation. These factors also affect the migration of the American population generally. Their relevance for Jewish mobility lies largely in whether changes in the way Jews are distributed among the various subcategories of these key explanatory variables help us to understand the levels of Jewish mobility; in whether the disproportional concentration of Jews in any particular subcategory helps account for the overall levels of Jewish population movement; and how the interactions be-tween selected socioeconomic and demographic characteristics and the Jewish identificational variables jointly lead to differential patterns of population movement among Jews. The latter relation has particular relevance for the implications of population movement for Jewish continuity in the United States.

Some attention has already been given to this question in our analyses focussing on the mobility patterns of different categories of Jews—Jews by religion, secular Jews, and Jews by choice. We turn now to the more specific variables that index intensity of Jewish identity to ascertain whether mobile Jews differ from nonmigrants on these dimensions. In particular, we focus on the relation between migration status on the one hand and such features of Jewish identity as denominational affiliation, Jewish education, intermarriage, Jewish ritual practices, and visits to Israel on the other. Chapter 6 will then focus on the relation between migration and integration into the Jewish community as indexed by a variety of indicators of participatory behavior.

As Goldscheider (1986:50–51) has pointed out, the potential impact of migration on the Jewishness of individuals can be viewed from several perspectives. On the one hand, migration is assumed to be associated with detachment from the community, from individual Jews, and from networks of Jews; it therefore constitutes a threat to Jewish continuity. The other view, which Gold-scheider holds, is that migration represents a new challenge, not a new threat; that it has the potential of facilitating the development of a wide range of new networks and institutions; and that it may thereby lead to renewed vitality of the community.

To test either view requires information on the levels and type of Jewish identity both before and after migration. This would allow in-depth evaluation of whether migration was selective of individuals with particular premigration characteristics. It would also allow determination of the impact of migration itself on manifestations of Jewish identity. With the 1990 National Jewish Population Survey (NJPS-1990) data largely restricted to individual characteristics at the time of the survey, we can, at best, only ascertain whether mobile and nonmobile persons differed in 1990. We can therefore make only tentative inferences about whether migration was the cause or the effect of the observed differences. This limitation of the data must be kept in mind, even when the observed relations are interpreted in causal terms.

DENOMINATIONAL IDENTIFICATION

If denominational affiliation is correlated with a range of socioeconomic variables as well as with the extent of observance of a variety of religious practices, we can expect denominational affiliation to be differentially associated with migration behavior. Observance of Kashrut, sending children to religious school (especially a day school), having access to a *mikveh*,[1] and having access to an appropriate synagogue could all affect decisions about where to live, which locations might be considered as possible residences, and whether to migrate. Other things being equal, Orthodox families and individuals may be the most stable, since their choice of locations is most restricted; Conservative[2] and Reform Jews as well as those who regard themselves as just Jewish may be more mobile because they have fewer observance-related constraints affecting their choice of residence.

Recent Movement

Within limits, the data support the thesis that denominational affiliation affects migration (table 5.1). For the total adult population, only one out of every ten Orthodox respondents reported a move in the previous five years. This contrasts with the much higher mobility of individuals affiliated with each of the other denominational groups. Just over 21 percent of the Conservative, and about one-quarter of the Reform and just Jewish indicated that they had been living in a different community five years earlier. The differentials generally manifest themselves as well in the percentage who were involved in interstate migration during the five-year interval, movement that is most likely to disrupt community ties. This percentage rises from only 4 percent of the Orthodox to 11 percent of Conservative and 13 percent of the Reform. The just Jewish seem to have resorted much more to intrastate movement than to interstate migration. Very small proportions of all groups had moved internationally, but this was most common among the Orthodox.

Even within the most mobile age cohort—those age 18 to 44—the Orthodox were noticeably more stable. Only 14 percent of them migrated, about equally divided among intrastate, interstate, and international moves. By contrast, over one-third of all the other denominational groups had changed community of residence in the five-year interval. Most striking are the differentials in interstate migration: whereas only 5 percent of the Orthodox age 18–44 moved interstate between 1985 and 1990, almost one in five of the Conservative and Reform did so. These patterns for the 18–44 age group clearly support the thesis that more traditional levels of observance, as indexed by denominational affiliation, are associated with greater residential stability.

The middle-aged group display higher levels of stability than do those under age 45 and also show less patterned differences by denomination. Only 8–16 percent migrated between 1985 and 1990. The highest stability characterized the Conservative, followed by the Orthodox and Reform, whose levels were quite similar. Nor did a clear pattern characterize the distribution between intra- and interstate movement. For the middle-aged group, then, denomination does not seem to be meaningfully associated with level or distance of recent movement. Whether it will be when the younger cohort shifts into middle age needs to be monitored.

The aged are even less mobile than the middle-aged, and this is true for all denominations but the Conservative; the elderly Conservative have a migration level similar to the middle-aged. The elderly Orthodox and Reform are more stable than the Con-

Table 5.1
Distribution by Five-Year Migration Status, by Denomination and Age:
Core Jews

Denomination	Migration Status				
	Non-migrant	Intra-state	Inter-state	Inter-national	Total Percent
	Total Aduls				
Orthodox	90.3	3.3	3.7	2.7	100.0
Conservative*	78.4	10.2	11.0	0.4	100.0
Reform	75.5	10.5	13.3	0.7	100.0
Just Jewish	73.5	16.7	9.6	0.1	100.0
Total	76.7	11.6	11.0	0.7	100.0
	18–44 Years				
Orthodox	86.1	4.5	5.2	4.2	100.0
Conservative*	64.2	17.6	17.4	0.8	100.0
Reform	65.4	14.5	19.5	0.6	100.0
Just Jewish	64.2	22.5	13.0	0.2	100.0
Total	65.7	17.5	15.9	1.0	100.0
	45–64 Years				
Orthodox	87.9	5.9	1.6	4.7	100.0
Conservative*	91.5	2.5	6.0	—	100.0
Reform	86.7	7.3	4.6	1.4	100.0
Just Jewish	83.5	12.2	4.2	—	100.0
Total	88.0	5.6	5.7	0.7	100.0
	65 Years and Over				
Orthodox	96.7	0.6	2.7	—	100.0
Conservative*	91.9	4.0	4.1	—	100.0
Reform	96.5	0.7	2.9	—	100.0
Just Jewish	88.6	5.4	6.1	—	100.0
Total	93.7	2.6	3.7	—	100.0

*Includes Reconstructionist.

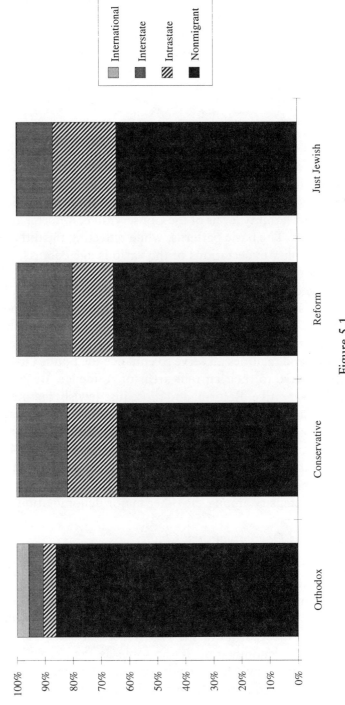

Figure 5.1
Distribution by Five-Year Migration Status, by Denomination: Core Jews, Age 18–44

servative aged and are approximately ten percentage points more stable than their counterparts in the middle-aged groups. The just Jewish are somewhat more mobile than the elderly in specific denominations, but also less so than their younger counterparts. As distinct from the middle-aged, however, among those aged who migrated, consistently more moved interstate than intrastate.

Future Mobility

When asked to consider future mobility, the Orthodox again had the greatest tendency toward residential stability (table 5.2). Just over two-thirds of all Orthodox adults reported they were not likely to move in the next three years, well above the 53–55 percent expected stability levels of the Conservative, Reform, and just Jewish groups. The basic patterns, while reflecting the differential levels of mobility expectations of the various age cohorts, persist across the three major age groups.

As judged by both past and anticipated future mobility, being Orthodox is associated with a considerably greater tendency toward stability, especially for those under age 45. This finding suggests that ties to family and friends, to neighborhood, and to institutions and facilities all serve to enhance the bonds Orthodox individuals have to their current areas of residence. By contrast, among Conservative, Reform, and those just Jewish, factors other than those associated with their religious outlook and practices have greater impact on mobility decisions; overall, these groups are characterized by more past migration and anticipate higher levels of future mobility. Evidently, whatever religious factors serve to impede movement apply more to the Orthodox and do not vary in intensity among the other major denominations.

Migration and Denominational Change

Is there any evidence that those who have changed denominational identification during the course of their lifetime are more migratory than those whose denomination in 1990 was the same as the one in which they reported being raised? To answer this question, for the U.S.-born, the experiences of "stayers" (those whose current denomination is the same as that in which they were raised) and "switchers" (those whose 1990 denominational identification was different from that in which they were raised)

Table 5.2
Likelihood of Moving in Next Three Years, by Denomination and Age:
Core Jews

Denomination	Not Likely	Somewhat Likely	Very Likely	Total Percent
	Total Adults			
Orthodox	67.7	13.9	18.4	100.0
Conservative*	55.2	23.1	21.7	100.0
Reform	53.1	20.3	26.6	100.0
Just Jewish	53.2	18.4	28.4	100.0
	18–44 Years			
Orthodox	46.8	24.6	28.6	100.0
Conservative*	34.1	31.9	34.0	100.0
Reform	39.5	23.4	37.2	100.0
Just Jewish	36.9	18.8	44.3	100.0
	45–64 Years			
Orthodox	83.2	3.2	13.5	100.0
Conservative*	71.4	18.0	10.6	100.0
Reform	68.5	19.2	12.3	100.0
Just Jewish	74.7	20.6	4.7	100.0
	65 Years and Over			
Orthodox	88.8	4.5	6.7	100.0
Conservative*	82.9	9.7	7.4	100.0
Reform	83.3	9.9	6.8	100.0
Just Jewish	77.4	14.7	7.9	100.0

*Includes Reconstructionist.

are compared. Considerable evidence supports the thesis that change in denomination is associated with geographic movement, especially when distance of move is taken into account (table 5.3).

Among the Orthodox stayers, only 53 percent had migrated in their lifetime compared to seven in ten of those who switched from Orthodox to Conservative or to just Jewish, and to 85 per-

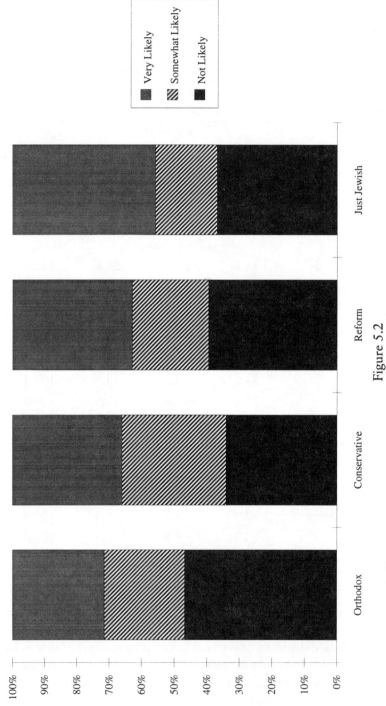

Figure 5.2
Likelihood of Moving in Next Three Years, by Denomination: Core Jews, Age 18–44

Table 5.3
Percentage of Lifetime Migrants among Native-Born Core Jews,
by Denomination Raised Compared to Current Denomination

Denomination Raised	Current Denomination			
	Orthodox	Conservative*	Reform	Just Jewish
Percent Who Migrated				
Orthodox	53.2	71.1	85.4	72.7
Conservative*	—	84.4	80.2	87.5
Reform	—	98.3	77.8	89.5
Just Jewish	—	—	81.8	78.6
Percent Who Migrated Interstate				
Orthodox	27.5	56.5	66.3	63.3
Conservative*	—	53.8	52.5	56.2
Reform	—	23.2	52.0	59.9
Just Jewish	—	—	61.7	38.4
Percent Who Migrated Interregionally				
Orthodox	15.2	46.3	50.6	36.3
Conservative*	—	36.8	40.7	43.2
Reform	—	56.2	34.9	46.1
Just Jewish	—	—	41.1	24.8

*Includes Reconstructionist.

cent of those who switched to Reform. For both the Conservative and Reform stayers, the levels of migration were much higher than for the Orthodox stayers, probably reflecting the stronger ties of the Orthodox to their community of origin. However, the level of migration of the Reform stayers was below that of those who had switched from Reform to either Conservative or just Jewish; by contrast, among those raised as Conservative, slightly more of the stayers had migrated than was true of those who had switched to Reform.

Among the interstate migrants, the pattern for stayers and switchers in the various denominations is quite mixed, although the Orthodox stayers continue to have a low level of migration.

When interregional movement is considered, the stayers in each denomination reported lower migration rates than the switchers, but the difference is not great for the Conservative. Overall, several patterns emerge. Although not with total consistency, switching denomination is associated with both higher levels of migration and greater involvement in interstate and interregional movement. The most marked differential characterizes those raised Orthodox.

Orthodox stayers reported sharply less migration than either Orthodox who switched to other denominations or to persons in other denominations who retained their denominational identity. The differential extends to both interstate and interregional migration. Especially for the Orthodox, therefore, continuous adherence to that denomination is associated with lower levels of geographic movement. The socioreligious ties within the Orthodox community coupled with the infrastructure (synagogues, kosher butchers, day schools, and *mikveh*) needed for Orthodox observance evidently leads those who adhere to such an ideology to be more residentially stable. While these infrastructural requirements are, judging by reported practices, less essential for those raised and living as Conservative, Reform, and just Jewish, persistent adherence to any denomination also seems to reduce the tendency to migrate.

Such an interpretation does not rule out the possibility that it is migration itself which contributes to a change in denomination. Marriage, higher education, the nature of the community of destination, and a host of other variables associated with mobility could contribute to such an impact. In fact, the same underlying factors that lead to migration—such as enrollment for higher education and occupational change—could also account for denominational switching; that is, the changes could be part of a larger social mobility complex involving alterations in an array of social, economic, residential, and religious characteristics.

RITUAL PRACTICES

Denominational affiliation and the extent of conformity to traditional ritual practices are correlated (Goldscheider and Goldstein, 1988; Israel, 1987). The denominations tend to form a continuum, from Orthodox to Conservative to Reform to just Jewish, paralleling their theological positions and ideologies. The Orthodox tend to adhere most strictly to a variety of practices, such as observance of Shabbat, maintenance of Kashrut, and celebration of holidays. Those reporting themselves as just Jewish, probably being more secular in orientation, very largely restrict their observances to such holidays as Chanukah and Passover, reflecting the secular messages that these holidays are seen to convey and their family significance. Given the correlation between denomination and ritual practice, we expect the degree of ritual practice to be related to migration patterns in about the same way as denominational affiliation. We hypothesize that those who are more ritually observant have had lower rates of migration and anticipate less mobility in the future.

NJPS-1990 collected information on an extensive range of ritual practices. To assess the relation between ritual practice and migration, use is made of a "sample" of ritual practices—lighting of Shabbat candles, fasting on Yom Kippur, attendance at a Seder, observance of Chanukah, and maintenance of Kashrut in the home (buying kosher meat *and* using separate dishes for meat and dairy products).[3] These are combined into a single index of ritual practice with a resultant scale of 0–16. Observance of Kashrut and lighting of Shabbat candles carry more weight as distinguishing components than attendance at a Seder, lighting of Chanukah candles, or fasting on Yom Kippur. In turn, the scale was collapsed into four categories: zero (0), low (1–4), medium (5–8), and high (9–16) levels of observance.[4]

Consistent with expectations, the level of ritual observance generally correlates with rate of migration (table 5.4). Whereas 72–73 percent of those who scored zero or low on the ritual scale were nonmigrants, this migration status characterized 78 percent of those with a medium score and almost 83 percent of those scoring high. The percentage migrating interstate showed the reverse relation, declining from 12 percent of the zero scorers to 9 percent of the high level observers. Intrastate migration also decreased consistently from 15 percent of the nonobservant to only half as many of the high level observers.

The relation between level of ritual observance and migration rates holds for both the young and the middle-aged segments of the population, but not as consistently in terms of distance. For the 18–44-year age group, the migration rate varies from a high of 41 percent of the nonobservant to a low of only 28 percent of the

Table 5.4
Distribution by Five-Year Migration Status,
by Level of Ritual Practice and Age:
Core Jews

| | Migration Status | | | | |
| | Non-
migrant | Intra-
state | Inter-
state | Inter-
national | Total
Percent |
Ritual Level					
	Total Adults				
None	71.6	15.4	12.2	0.8	100.0
Low	73.0	14.3	11.7	1.0	100.0
Medium	78.3	10.7	10.7	0.2	100.0
High	82.5	7.4	8.8	1.3	100.0
	18–44 Years				
None	59.4	22.9	16.4	1.3	100.0
Low	65.4	19.5	14.1	1.1	100.0
Medium	68.4	15.1	16.4	0.1	100.0
High	71.6	12.6	13.1	2.7	100.0
	45–64 Years				
None	85.8	1.6	12.6	—	100.0
Low	85.3	6.3	7.2	1.3	100.0
Medium	89.7	6.7	2.8	0.8	100.0
High	92.3	3.4	4.3	—	100.0
	65 Years and Over				
None	94.9	5.1	—	—	100.0
Low	84.0	6.5	9.5	—	100.0
Medium	95.9	1.6	2.5	—	100.0
High	93.5	1.5	5.0	—	100.0

Note: Construction of the Ritual Index is described in Appendix D.

highly observant. The proportion migrating across state lines shows a less regular pattern in relation to ritual observance, although the highly observant do have the lowest proportion of interstate movers. Intrastate migration is, however, strongly related to ritual observance, ranging from a high of 22 percent of the nonobservant to only 13 percent of the highly observant.

For the middle-aged, for whom the overall level of migration is lower than for the young, it nonetheless varies by level of ritual observance: 14 percent of the nonobservant moved between 1985 and 1990, compared to only 8 percent of the highly observant. For this age group, the nonobservant migrated between states at a substantially higher rate than the more observant, but the proportion of intrastate movers did not change as consistently in relation to ritual observance.

Undoubtedly related to the overall high level of stability of the aged and the different motives that account for their mobility, the elderly display less variation overall and less consistent variation in relation to ritual observance than do the two younger segments of the population. The non-, medium, and highly observant closely resemble one another, with only about 5 percent having migrated in the previous five years. Only the low level ritual observers showed a higher rate of migration, about 16 percent. More of them, too, migrated interstate, but as a proportion of all migrants more of the highly observant did so, possibly reflecting movement to such locations as Florida where continued ritual observance is likely facilitated by the high concentration of older, more observant Jews and the appropriate institutions (cf. Sheskin, 1993).

The "holding" power of traditionalism as documented by ritual observance is further evidenced in the relation between the level of the index and the likelihood of future mobility (table 5.5). The two tend to be inversely related. Among those characterized by low or no reported observance, half indicated they were not likely to move in the next three years; this contrasts with the 62 percent of the highly observant who expected to remain stable. At the other extreme, whereas 29 percent of the low observant group thought it very likely that a move would occur, only 16 percent of the highly observant did so. Clearly, the life styles and attitudes indexed by greater ritual observance are associated with a stronger tendency to remain geographically stable. In turn, either as cause or effect, this suggests that greater mobility is associated with weaker ties to Judaism.

This holds as well for the young segment of the population. Even for this very mobile age group, the ties that bind to tradition seem to be meaningfully linked to the ties that bind to location.

Table 5.5
Likelihood of Moving in Next Three Years,
by Level of Ritual Practice and Age:
Core Jews

	Likelihood of Move			
Ritual Level	Not Likely	Somewhat Likely	Very Likely	Total Percent
Total Adults				
None	52.1	18.8	29.1	100.0
Low	47.6	23.0	29.4	100.0
Medium	54.0	21.4	24.6	100.0
High	62.2	21.9	16.0	100.0
18–44 Years				
None	40.1	18.3	41.6	100.0
Low	31.7	25.7	42.6	100.0
Medium	39.7	25.4	34.9	100.0
High	48.1	31.5	20.4	100.0
45–64 Years				
None	52.8	28.5	18.6	100.0
Low	68.2	22.7	9.1	100.0
Medium	69.0	19.5	11.6	100.0
High	73.1	12.3	14.6	100.0
65 Years and Over				
None	85.3	12.8	1.9	100.0
Low	81.2	12.4	6.4	100.0
Medium	82.5	9.9	7.6	100.0
High	85.5	7.8	6.7	100.0

The existence of such a relation and evidence (Goldstein, Gold-scheider, and Goldstein, 1988; Fowler, 1977; Israel, 1987) that an increasing proportion of Jews may be shifting from being more to being less traditional, suggests that the ties that bind may in fact be becoming weaker in both spheres. If so, increasing mobility

may be a by-product. Although much greater stability characterizes the mobility intentions of the middle-aged, it nonetheless
remains true that the most traditional segment of the population
shows by far the least propensity to move.

For the aged as a whole, a high proportion did not expect to
move, and this varied minimally among the more and the less
observant, only by about four percentage points. This lack of substantial variation and the absence of a clear pattern of differences
among the observance categories resembles the situation for
denominational groups; this again suggests that reasons for movement of the elderly differ sufficiently from those of groups at earlier stages of the life cycle to result in a less clear relation between
observance and mobility. Considerations of health, retirement,
and family ties and choices of residence for noneconomic considerations may affect the probability of future moves by the aged.

INTERMARRIAGE

Either as cause or as effect, we expect intermarriage to be related
differentially to migration status. Whether a born Jew eventually
marries another born Jew depends to a considerable degree on
opportunities to meet and interact with other Jews. Such opportunities are obviously greatly influenced by the Jewish density of
the social circles within which individuals operate, particularly at
that stage in the life cycle when they are in the "marriage market"
(Waite and Sheps, 1994). Since for most Jews, as for the larger
population, this occurs during ages 20–35, it coincides closely
with the time when young adults are completing their undergrad-
uate education, engaged in graduate or professional studies, and
beginning a career. For large numbers, pursuing education, taking
a job, or establishing a profession or business requires moving.
For many, moving away from the community of family residence
during these critical years may result in their living where Jewish
population density is different and often much lower.

With reductions in discrimination in college admissions, employment, and options for residence, Jews have had much greater
opportunity to enter institutions and workplaces where they study,
work, and socialize closely with non-Jews. Concurrently, separation from family may lead to much greater freedom in choice of
friends and dating partners, enhancing the chances for Jews and

non-Jews to interact, and, for some, to fall in love and marry. The high levels of mobility associated with higher education, open employment, and wider choice of residence as well as with greater acceptance of Jews by non-Jews as friends and marital partners has resulted in a dramatically heightened rate of intermarriage. NJPS-1990 documented that 52 percent of marriages during the five years preceding the survey consisted of persons born Jewish to persons who were not born Jewish and had not become a Jew by choice, almost a doubling in the already substantial 29 percent level measured twenty years earlier by NJPS-1970/71.

The importance of type of community in affecting intermarriage levels is illustrated by the findings of the 1991 New York Jewish population study (Horowitz, 1993; see also Horowitz, 1994). In New York the rate of intermarriage was about half that found by NJPS-1990 nationally, partly reflecting the greater density of Jewish population in the New York area and partly the general Jewish ambiance of New York which facilitates Jewish identity. Nonetheless, New York has experienced a sharp rise in mixed marriages, from the pre–1965 marriage cohort (5 percent) to the post–1985 cohort (25 percent). The strong tendency to higher rates of intermarriage characterizing American Jewry clearly also permeates even the most densely Jewish communities.

Migration can also be seen as a product of intermarriage. Couples who enter a mixed marriage (i.e., one in which the spouse was not born Jewish and has not become a Jew by choice) may regard themselves or be regarded by the larger Jewish community as marginal to it, especially if children born of such marriages are not being raised as Jews. If so, relatively more such units may engage in geographic mobility, reflecting the weaker ties they have to the core Jewish community and possibly even to the community of the non-Jewish spouse (since marginality may extend in both directions).

To assess these possible relations between intermarriage and migration, we focus on all currently married couples in the NJPS sample consisting of at least one partner who was born Jewish and identified as Jewish at the time of the survey. These couples were classified into three groups; (1) in-married, that is, both spouses were born Jewish and were Jewish at the time of the survey; (2) conversionary units, in which one spouse was born Jewish and the other either converted officially to Judaism or has chosen to regard him- or herself as Jewish, and both identified as Jewish at the survey date; (3) mixed marriages, in which the spouse who was not born Jewish chose to remain non-Jewish. Of the total core group of currently married couples, 59 percent belong to the first group, 3 percent are conversionary marriages, and 38 percent are mixed. Not surprisingly, given the sharp rise in intermarriages in recent years, most of the mixed and conversionary marriages are concentrated in the cohorts under age 45. For this reason most of the discussion will be limited to the total adults and to the youngest age group. We must stress that migration status refers to the respondent who was, in all but very few cases and by nature of the respondent selection process, a member of the Jewish core population.

The data support expectations. Whereas 15 percent of the in-married were migrants, this was true of 22 percent of those in conversionary marriages and as many as 36 percent of those in mixed marriages (table 5.6). Moreover, those in mixed marriages had the highest percentages of both intrastate and interstate movement in the previous five years. Eight percent of the in-married and 9 percent of those in conversionary marriages, compared to 18 percent of those in mixed marriages, had made an intrastate move between 1985 and 1990. The proportions were quite similar for interstate migration, with comparatively twice as many of those in mixed marriages crossing state boundaries than was true of the in-married. The levels of stability and of intra- and interstate movement of those in conversionary marriages more closely resembled the levels of the in-married than of the mixed-married. Regardless of whether we consider two born Jews marrying each other or a born Jew marrying a Jew by choice, homogamous marriage thus appears more closely associated with residential stability than is mixed-marriage.

Since migration often occurs in conjunction with marriage, we would expect the extent of migration to be greatest among intermarrieds around the beginning of the marriage. Such a pattern would be especially pronounced if intermarriage is correlated with mobility. We can control for date of marriage by comparing the five-year migration experience of the in-married and those in mixed marriages of the same marriage cohorts (table 5.7). The results support the expectation that more migration characterizes the recently married, but do not confirm that the mixed-married have higher mobility.

Table 5.6
Distribution by Five-Year Migration Status,
by Intermarriage Status and Age of Respondent:
Core Jews

	Migration Status				
Intermarriage	Non-migrant	Intra-state	Inter-state	Inter-national	Total Percent
	Total Adults				
In-married	84.7	7.0	7.5	0.7	100.0
Conversionary	77.7	8.8	10.3	3.3	100.0
Mixed married	64.1	18.4	17.0	0.5	100.0
	18–44 Years				
In-married	74.5	11.8	12.2	1.6	100.0
Conversionary	64.2	14.1	16.4	5.2	100.0
Mixed married	57.7	21.9	20.0	0.4	100.0
	45–64 Years				
In-married	92.4	3.4	4.2	—	100.0
Conversionary	—	—	—	—	—
Mixed married	77.1	11.4	10.5	1.0	100.0

Among both the mixed-married and the in-married, about half in each group of those who married during 1985–1990 migrated during that same five-year interval. This was considerably more than the proportion of migrants in the marriage cohorts of 1980–1984 or pre–1980, but the lower levels of recent migration among the earlier marriage cohorts probably reflects both their longer period of marriage and their older ages. For the 1985–1990 marriage cohort, the mixed-married and the in-married also closely resemble each other with respect to the proportions experiencing intrastate and interstate migration; and for both groups the levels of such migration were greater than for earlier cohorts, again reflecting the older age and longer marriage duration of the earlier cohorts. The close similarity in the migration experience of the recently married, whether in homogamous marriages or in mixed marriages, does not allow us to conclude that migration is more closely associated with mixed marriage than with homogamous

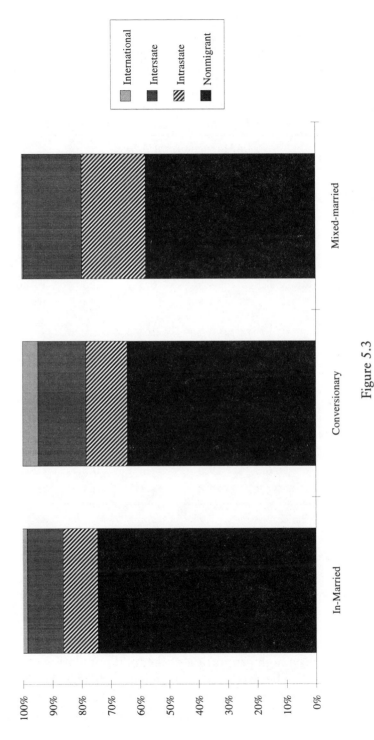

Figure 5.3
Distribution by Five-Year Migration Status, by Intermarriage Status: Core Jews, Age 18–44

Table 5.7
Distribution by Five-Year Migration Status, by Year of Marriage and
Intermarriage Status: Total Adults and Age Group 18–44

	Migration Status				
Year of Marriage	Non-migrant	Intra-state	Inter-state	Inter-national	Total Percent
In-Married, Total Adults*					
Pre-1980	91.8	4.4	3.7	0.2	100.0
1980–1984	71.7	14.3	11.4	2.6	100.0
1985–1990	48.9	23.7	23.9	3.5	100.0
Mixed Married, Total Adults					
Pre-1980	73.7	14.1	10.9	1.2	100.0
1980–1984	78.3	14.9	6.3	0.5	100.0
1985–1990	52.8	20.2	26.5	0.4	100.0
In-Married, 18–44 Years*					
Pre-1980	86.1	8.8	4.3	0.8	100.0
1980–1984	70.7	15.5	11.0	2.8	100.0
1985–1990	43.8	27.5	24.6	4.1	100.0
Mixed Married, 18–44 Years					
Pre-1980	70.5	16.8	12.1	0.6	100.0
1980–1984	76.0	19.0	4.3	0.8	100.0
1985–1990	45.7	22.6	31.1	0.5	100.0

*Includes Jews by Choice.

marriage, once date of marriage is controlled. Age may also be a factor.

We can explore the age relation by examining the experience of the 18–44-year group, controlling for date of marriage. The results closely resemble those noted in the analysis undertaken for the total adult population. This is not surprising since this age group constitutes a high proportion of the total population and is much more likely to be characterized by mixed marriage. For both the in-married and the mixed-married in this young age group, the 1985–1990 marriage cohort has the highest migration rates; more than half in both groups migrated between 1985 and 1990, but more of the mixed-married moved interstate rather than intra-state. Overall, however, the mixed-married and the in-married are quite similar. Among the other cohorts, the migration differentials between the in-married and the mixed-married groups are not consistent.

The comparisons for the 1985–1990 marriage cohort point to minimal migration differentials between the in-married and the mixed-married for the most recently married cohort. If intermarriage in the past placed the couple at the margins of the Jewish— and possibly the Christian—community and thereby created conditions conducive to migration, this situation appears to have changed. With intermarriage more common and acceptable, the impetus to migration seems equally strong among both the in-married and the mixed-married, being driven largely by factors other than those related to intermarriage status. From a policy perspective, this suggests that communities face a double challenge in integrating those at the margins who are both migrant and intermarried.

The convergence of migration patterns of the in-married and mixed married seems to parallel the reduction in differentials in fertility. In their 1963 study of Greater Providence, Goldstein and Goldscheider (1968) found the fertility of the intermarried to be lower than that of the in-married for all age segments of the population, but less so in the younger groups. They suggested that the greater social acceptance of interfaith couples by the 1960s explained the greater equality of fertility among the younger cohort. Such a conclusion is reenforced by evidence from NJPS-1990. Mott and Abma (1992) found women in the survey who were born non-Jewish to be above average in childbearing propensity.

The relation between intermarriage and migration can also be explored by comparing the mixed-married with the in-married with respect to the likelihood of future movement. For such purposes, we rely on marriage cohort, rather than age, so that the mobility expectations will be related more closely to recency of marriage.

For the adult married population as a whole, the expected relation is supported (table 5.8). Of the in-married, 70 percent thought a move in the next three years unlikely, and 13 percent thought it very likely. By contrast, only 55 percent of those in mixed marriages expected to remain settled, and 22 percent considered a move very likely.

Table 5.8
Likelihood of Moving in Next Three Years, by Intermarriage Status and
Marriage Cohort

Intermarriage Status	Likelihood of Moving			Total Percent
	Not Likely	Somewhat Likely	Very Likely	
Total Adults				
In-Married	70.4	17.1	12.5	100.0
Mixed Married	55.0	23.3	21.7	100.0
1985–1990 Marriage Cohort				
In-Married	42.6	29.8	27.6	100.0
Mixed Married	43.5	22.3	34.2	100.0
1980–1984 Marriage Cohort				
In-Married	57.0	19.1	23.9	100.0
Mixed Married	58.6	22.0	19.4	100.0

Such a pattern does not, however, hold for the most recent marriage cohort; rather, similar low levels of stability characterize both the in-married and the mixed-married. Of those who expect to move, however, the mixed-married are more concentrated among those very likely to move. For the 1980–1984 cohort, levels of expected stability are also similar for the in-married and the mixed-married; but in contrast to the 1985–1989 cohort, of those expecting to move, more of the in-married reported a change in location to be very likely. Overall, these data on anticipated mobility therefore lend weight to the earlier thesis that migration differentials between in-married and mixed-married have probably dissipated among recent marriage cohorts, reflecting the greater acceptance of mixed marriage and the stronger force of other motivating factors, such as economic considerations, in the decision-making process.

JEWISH EDUCATION

Earlier analysis has shown that level of secular education influences migration both through the movement associated with enrollment in colleges and universities and because those who have received a higher education are more likely to migrate and to move longer distances. Does Jewish education have a similar effect on migration?

To the extent that Jewish education, for most who receive it, is not intended to prepare for an occupational career, it clearly would not be expected to directly affect decisions about where to work. Moreover, since formal Jewish education for most persons ends at Bar/Bat Mitzvah at age 13 or, at best, with high school graduation, it is less likely to be associated with population movement than is general education which, for many Jews, extends into the third decade of life. Most probably, Jewish education's role in influencing mobility is quite indirect, through its impact on enhancing Jewish identity. To the extent that it fosters individuals' ties to Judaism, it may strengthen their desire to live in places where they can easily function as Jews and follow a Jewish lifestyle. If such a relation exists, we would expect those with more Jewish education to be more strongly tied to places where they have developed ties to the Jewish community and have easier access to Jewish institutions and facilities. On the other hand, those with more Jewish education who are in locations without such support may be motivated to move.

To test this complex interaction requires far more information than is available from NJPS-1990. It would also require fuller assessment than is possible here of the impact of Jewish education on community involvement. Other research (Fishman and Goldstein, 1993) has shown that the intensity of Jewish education—number of years and type of school—is closely and directly related to the level of Jewish organizational membership and giving to Jewish causes. It is also strongly related to the importance of being in a Jewish milieu and the extent of religious practices. Jewish education may therefore operate in ways similar to denomination and ritual practice in affecting the likelihood of migration. The present analysis therefore seeks to determine whether the intensity of Jewish education is related to past movement and the likelihood of future mobility.

For our purposes, the adult population has been subdivided into three Jewish education categories—low, medium, and high levels.[5] Almost half of all adults had only a low level of Jewish education; the balance were almost equally divided between those with medium and high levels. Overall, no clear pattern of differentials appear in the relation between level of Jewish education and recent migration (table 5.9). The proportion of migrants in each of the three educational categories varied only between 22 and 27 percent; the more striking differences were in the proportions who moved intrastate and interstate. A higher percentage of those with a low level of Jewish education resettled within their state of residence, whereas a majority of the medium- and high-level educated who migrated changed state of residence.

This is contrary to what one would expect based on the differentials observed among the various denominations, where Orthodox are more stable than other groups. The explanation may largely lie in the close correlation between secular and religious education. Persons with college and graduate education are also more likely to have had high levels of religious education. For example, whereas 54 percent of those with only high school education had a low level of Jewish education, this was true of only 18 percent of persons with graduate training. Conversely, only 16 percent of the high school educated had a high level of Jewish education, but 30 percent of those with graduate schooling did so.

The youngest cohort, with the generally higher migration levels, was characterized by the same lack of variation in the proportion migrating and the same pattern of distribution between intrastate and interstate migrants among those who did move. While showing far less migration overall than the youngest cohort, the middle-aged were characterized by greater migration differentials by Jewish education. Of those with low Jewish education, 10 percent were migrants, compared to 16 percent of the medium educated. Within this range, more of the latter group moved across state boundaries. Like the young, more of the low educated who migrated remained within the same state. Among the highly educated, somewhat more moved interstate rather than intrastate.

Among the low percentage of elderly who were five-year migrants, those with a low level of Jewish education were more likely to have been interstate migrants, while the medium educated moved more frequently intrastate. As for other variables examined, therefore, the pattern for the aged in the relation between Jewish education and migration differs from that of younger cohorts. This may reflect the more important role of retirement rather than career considerations in influencing the migration decisions of the aged. For all age groups, however, the level of Jewish education seems to have minimal explanatory

Table 5.9
Distribution by Five-Year Migration Status, by Jewish Education
Completed and Age: Core Jews

Jewish Education	Migration Status				Total Percent
	Non-migrants	Intra-state	Inter-state	Inter-national	
Total Adults					
Low	77.8	13.5	7.9	0.8	100.0
Medium	73.5	10.0	16.0	0.5	100.0
High	76.4	10.9	11.4	1.3	100.0
18–44 Years					
Low	67.6	20.5	11.0	0.9	100.0
Medium	62.8	13.8	22.8	0.6	100.0
High	67.5	15.2	15.2	2.1	100.0
45–64 Years					
Low	89.7	5.5	3.5	1.2	100.0
Medium	84.3	4.8	10.2	0.7	100.0
High	86.4	6.0	7.7	—	100.0
65 Years and Over					
Low	93.2	3.0	3.8	—	100.0
Medium	91.3	5.4	3.3	—	100.0
High	96.4	1.7	1.8	—	100.0

Note: Construction of the Index of Jewish Education is described in note 5 of this chapter.

value in accounting for adult Jews' migration behavior in recent years.

Considerable similarity also characterizes the potential future mobility of the three educational subgroups (table 5.10). For the total adult population, the proportion indicating that a move was not likely varied only between 52 and 54 percent. A somewhat sharper differential appeared among the three education groups in the division between those who thought a move was somewhat likely and those reporting it was very likely; 28 percent of those with low education indicated a move very likely, but only 21 percent of the highly educated did so. With age controlled, some differences exist, but the most striking finding is the absence of marked differences in expectations of future movement, supporting the conclusion that level of Jewish education in itself is not a key variable directly affecting mobility behavior among adults.

The general absence of a strong relation between Jewish education and both past and future migration reflects a series of factors. The strong correlation between Jewish and secular education

Table 5.10
Likelihood of Moving in Next Three Years, by Jewish Education
Completed and Age:
Core Jews

| Jewish Education | Likelihood of Move | | | |
	Not Likely	Somewhat Likely	Very Likely	Total Percent
	Total Adults			
Low	52.5	19.3	28.2	100.0
Medium	53.0	20.4	26.6	100.0
High	54.0	25.0	21.0	100.0
	18–44 Years			
Low	37.2	20.9	41.8	100.0
Medium	37.9	23.0	39.1	100.0
High	40.4	32.5	27.1	100.0
	45–64 Years			
Low	66.9	21.3	11.8	100.0
Medium	66.0	22.2	11.8	100.0
High	73.8	14.0	12.3	100.0
	65 Years and Over			
Low	81.2	12.6	6.2	100.0
Medium	83.4	9.0	7.6	100.0
High	83.1	9.3	7.6	100.0

Note: The Jewish education categories are described in note 5 of this chapter.

has already been noted. Other factors are also at play. Respondents received their Jewish education many years before the incidence of recent migration. For most, such education has little relevance in making decisions about where to live, especially if the decisions are career-related.

Although level of Jewish education is closely related to involvement in the Jewish community and identification as a Jew, it is not as sensitive an index of current Jewish identity or of ties to the community of residence as are organizational membership and current practices. The Jewish education being given to children by their parents, rather than the education the adults received years earlier, may be more directly related to and affected by migration.

NJPS-1990 allows some insights into the relation between mobility and the Jewish education of children. The survey asked respondents about the enrollment in programs of Jewish education of all children age 6–18 living in the household. Included were questions on whether the children had ever been enrolled, for how many years, and, for those who were currently enrolled, the type of school. Since migration refers to the five years preceding the survey, it coincides with the peak years of Jewish education of a large majority of the children. Research elsewhere (Goldstein and Fishman, 1993) has shown that very few children not being raised as Jews ever enroll in Jewish educational programs. Our analysis therefore is restricted to those children who are being raised as Jews.

Migration status is clearly related to the Jewish education of children. At each age level, a higher percentage of nonmigrant children are enrolled in programs of Jewish education than is true of those who migrated, either intrastate or interstate (table 5.11). For example, during the time of peak enrollment—ages 8–12, the pre–Bar/Bat Mitzvah years—about three-fourths of the nonmigrant children were enrolled in programs of Jewish education, but only 57 percent of the migrant children were enrolled. The differential is even greater in the early teen years, when almost three times as many of the nonmigrants were enrolled than was true of the migrants; in the later teens the difference is almost twofold. Since Jewish education beyond the elementary level is most strongly related to enhanced involvement in and identification with the Jewish community (Fishman and Goldstein, 1993), the apparent disruption caused by migration in the education of Jew-

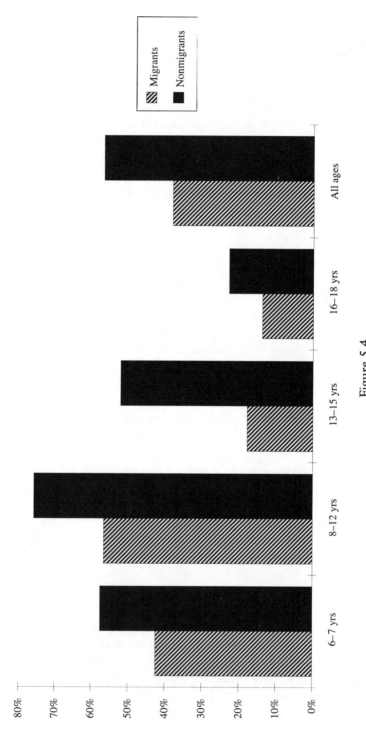

Figure 5.4
Percentage of Jewish Children Age 6–18 Currently Enrolled in Programs of Jewish Education,
by Five-Year Migration Status and Age

Table 5.11
Percentage of Jewish Children Age 6–18 Currently Enrolled in Programs
of Jewish Education, by Five-Year Migration Status and Age

	Migration Status			
Age of Child	*Nonmigrant*	*All Migrants*	*Intrastate*	*Interstate*
6–7 Years	57.5	42.5	43.3	41.8
8–12 Years	75.7	56.5	55.3	57.3
13–15 Years	52.1	17.8	19.2	*
16–18 Years	22.8	13.8	*	*
All Ages	56.6	38.1	41.0	35.5

*Fewer than 10 unweighted cases.

ish teens has particularly serious implications for their future ties to the community and also raises serious questions about the impact of migration on future Jewish identification.

VISITS TO ISRAEL

Israel has come to play a major role in the vitality of the American Jewish community, providing an important vehicle for Jewish identification in the lives of both individual Jews and the organized Jewish community. For many persons, the tie is given concrete form through visits to Israel. Whether and how many such visits are undertaken thus provides still another index of the strength of Jewish identity. Unlike some of the other indicators examined in this analysis, migration is not viewed as a direct cause or consequence of visits to Israel. Rather, to the extent that such visits reflect the strength of an individual's identity as a Jew, visits to Israel is a useful variable for evaluating whether strength of Jewish identity differs by migration status.

Just over one of every four core Jewish adults has visited Israel at least once, and almost half of these have done so more than once. The extent of such visits varied by age; almost twice as many older Jews (40 percent) visited Israel at least once as was true of those under age 45, and relatively more of the older group have done so more than once. Whether this difference represents the impact of differential opportunities to visit associated with age and income or reflects a less positive attitude toward Israel among younger Jewish Americans remains to be assessed in the future.

Migration status does not appear to be significantly related to visits to Israel (table 5.12). To the extent that any relation exists, it seems to be opposite to the hypothesis that a lower Jewish identity, as indexed by visits to Israel, characterizes migrants. For the total adult population, almost no differences characterize the proportions of interstate migrants and nonmigrants who have visited Israel. By contrast, intrastate movers had a much lower rate, and international migrants a much higher one. The latter is easily understood, given that a number of the international migrants emigrated from Israel.

When the patterns for the specific age groups are examined, they suggest that, with stage of the life cycle controlled, interstate migrants have a considerably higher than average rate of visits. For example, among those under age 45, only 15–20 percent of the nonmigants and intrastate movers had visited Israel, but just over 25 percent of the interstate migrants had done so. The same pattern characterized the middle age group. The differential was sharpest for the aged, among whom 60 percent of those who had made an interstate migration in the previous five years had visited Israel, compared to only 29 percent of the intrastate movers and 40 percent of the nonmigrants.

While these data suggest that, as indexed by visits to Israel, migrants and especially interstate migrants manifest at least as

Table 5.12
Percentage Who Have Ever Been to Israel, by Five-Year Migration
Status and Age:
Core Jews

| Migration Status | Age | | | Total Adults |
	18–44	45–64	65 and over	
Nonmigrant	19.9	27.9	39.4	26.9
Intrastate	15.8	28.7	28.8	18.0
Interstate	25.7	32.4	60.6	29.0
International	58.3	*	*	52.6
Total	20.5	28.2	39.8	26.3

*Fewer than 10 unweighted cases.

strong an identity with Judaism as the nonmigrants, an alternative explanation may be possible. Excluding the international migrants who are a special case, the interstate migrants are the most mobile of the migration status groups. Their willingness to move considerable distances may be part of a larger mindset that also involves a greater tendency to travel and willingness to be away from home. If so, it may well be that the somewhat higher than average level of visits to Israel may be more closely related to this "mobility proneness" than reflective of the strength of Jewish identity.

MOBILITY AND JEWISH IDENTITY RELATED

Of particular interest to those concerned about the vitality of the Jewish American community is the relation of mobility to various indicators of Jewish identification with and involvement in the community. Our thesis is that strong identification and traditional forms of behavior will be associated with greater stability, because strong Jewish commitments generate institutional and personal ties as well as require supportive services which may not exist in many locations. Persons who are more marginally connected to the Jewish community are expected to be more mobile and to move greater distances. Whether mobility is cause or effect of weaker identification cannot be determined from the NJPS-1990 data. Our initial exploration of the relations uses five indicators of Jewish identification: denominational affiliation, ritual practices, intermarriage, Jewish education, and visits to Israel. Our findings generally support our thesis, but the relations are not always strong or consistent.

Denominational affiliation has a clear relation to levels of stability. Those who report themselves as Orthodox, especially if they are under age 45, have been less mobile in the past and anticipate less movement in the future. By contrast, Conservative and Reform Jews resemble each other in their higher mobility rates. Elderly Orthodox are more mobile, probably because their favored destinations are retirement communities with a full complement of Jewish facilities. Those who have changed their denominational affiliation between the time of their childhood and the time of the survey also have higher levels of migration and are more likely to make interstate moves than those who have maintained a single denominational affiliation. This pattern is especially characteristic of those raised as Orthodox but currently Conservative or Reform.

Our analysis of the relation between ritual practices (as measured by an index of ritual practices) and mobility confirms the "holding power" of traditionalism. Those whose behavior conforms more closely to traditional practices are generally much more stable than the less observant. Even the youngest age group exhibits this pattern. Lower levels of ritual practice apparently remove the impediments to mobility that reside in the need for kosher facilities, appropriate schools, and other institutions enhancing traditional behavior. With a shift away from extensive ritual practice among large segments of American Jewry, mobility may well increase even further than its present level.

Previous research has suggested that intermarriage is associated with mobility because the intermarried couple feels marginal to the Jewish community and prefers to live away from strong centers of Jewish life. To some extent, our data support this finding; as a whole, the mixed-married experienced more migration and more long-distance moves than the in-married. Within the mixed-married group, however, those couples who intermarried recently show the same migration behavior as the recently in-married. Apparently, any stigma that attached to intermarriage in the past and encouraged mobility no longer exists; intermarriage is no longer a factor associated with higher mobility.

Associated with traditionalism is high levels of Jewish education. We therefore anticipated that persons with more Jewish education would be more stable than those who had little Jewish schooling. However, no clear relations between levels of Jewish education and mobility appear. In part, this is due to the high correlation between levels of Jewish and secular education. Because those with college and graduate education are among the most mobile segments of the Jewish population, the same relation obtains for individuals with considerable Jewish education. A disruptive effect is evident, however, for children. Children in nonmigrant families have higher levels of enrollment in Jewish education than do those who have moved within five years of the survey. The effect is particularly noticeable for teenagers. Since Jewish education beyond Bar/Bat Mitzvah has a particularly strong relation to enhanced levels of Jewish identification, disruption of Jewish education for mobile teens can have serious consequences for their levels of commitment in the future.

A final aspect of Jewish identity explored here is visits to Israel. Contrary to expectation, the nonmigrant population did not report the highest proportion who ever visited Israel. In fact, interstate migrants were more likely to have made visits to Israel than nonmigrants. Perhaps the propensity to move enhances propensity to travel as well.

This chapter thus documents the important relation between traditional forms of Jewish behavior and levels of mobility. Clearly, Orthodox affiliation and high levels of ritual behavior are associated with residential stability. With a gradual drift away from traditionalism, these factors may come to play a lesser role in the migration decision-making process of individuals and families. The changing impact, although opposite in direction, is already apparent in the relation between migration and intermarriage: intermarriage in the late 1980s was not associated with greater mobility than was true of the in-married couples; this may reflect the fact that mixed marriages are now much more accepted by the larger Jewish community. Our indicators suggest that community characteristics that cater specifically to Jewish needs may have little holding power in the future, and that, as a result, levels of mobility may rise even above their currently high levels. From a policy perspective, the Jewish community therefore needs to develop other mechanisms for attracting and keeping the loyalty of its population, mechanisms that are not tied to a specific location.

CHAPTER 6

Community Involvement

The comparatively high proportion of migrants among the Jewish population and their distinctive socioeconomic characteristics together present new challenges to the national Jewish community and to local communities. Geographic mobility often involves movement away from family and place of origin. For many it may also lead to movement out of centers of Jewish population concentration. Moreover, repeat movement, especially when it occurs with some frequency, may inhibit individuals and families from planting deep roots in a local Jewish community. Constraints to integration may be reinforced if community institutions have established criteria for membership (e.g., enrollment and building fees) which discourage newcomers from joining, particularly if they anticipate moving again in the near future. Geographic mobility can thereby weaken individual ties by reducing integration into a particular local Jewish community.

Steven Cohen (1983) has suggested three possible reasons why the mobile segments of the population may be less affiliated than those who are stable. First, compared to nonmovers, the migrants may have been less affiliated in their communities of origin, that is, they may have been marginal even before migration. If so, their very marginality may have contributed to their decision to migrate, or at least it may not have deterred them from doing so. Second, the act of movement itself may be disruptive of formal and informal ties to family, friends, and local institutions, while the process of reconstituting such links, if it occurs at all, may take years. Especially if movement is repeated, the time needed for reintegration in any given location may be too short.

Third, the new area of residence may have a "contextual impact" (a process demographers refer to as "adaptation"). Communities vary substantially in availability of Jewish organizations, institutions, and agencies; even individuals and families who are highly motivated to be active members of a community may be limited by the relatively weak Jewish context of a given place.

209

Indeed, such considerations may often affect decisions about whether to move and where to go. Beyond availability of facilities in the community of destination, according to Cohen, other contextual factors that affect affiliation include the socioeconomic composition of the area's population, the maturity of the area's institutions, the density of Jewish population, and the proximity to major Jewish communities and central institutions. Some, like Goldscheider (1986), have argued that weakened ties to the formal Jewish community are replaced by other sources of ethnic and identificational cohesion, such as friends and work colleagues. If so, movement into areas of low density may reflect constraints of economic factors and housing markets but not necessarily a desire to assimilate.

On a more positive note, migration may help to stimulate and/ or renew the integration of individuals and families into the larger Jewish community and to give new Jewish vitality to communities that have been too small to maintain a wide range of organizations and services. Families and individuals moving from areas with little Jewish context to ones with richer offerings may find new opportunities and new motives to affiliate and to become active; this may certainly be the case for those moving from areas of lesser to higher Jewish density. For communities that have been able to provide only limited Jewish facilities, a substantial in-migration of Jews may raise Jewish density to a point where creation of new organizations and provision of new services becomes feasible. In this way, migration may serve as "a shot in the arm" for the local Jewish community. As Lebowitz (1975) has suggested, it may also do so by bridging the traditional age and affiliation cleavages, thereby providing the "social cement" needed to hold the community together.

Concurrently, migration may contribute to the development of a national Jewish society, characterized both by greater population dispersion and by greater population exchange among various localities (Goldstein, 1987b). Both processes require more effective networking among locations to ensure continuing opportunites and stimuli for mobile individuals to maintain their Jewish identity and ties to the Jewish community, regardless of where they live or how often they move. Greater dispersion, especially to smaller communities and to more isolated ones, also requires development of means to ensure that such communities are better able through their own facilities or through links to other, larger communities to service the individual social, psychological, economic, health, and religious needs of both their migrant and nonmigrant populations.

Organizational affiliation by Jews has been regarded as "the public badge of Jewish identification" (Woocher, 1990); it has become the defining act of citizenship in the community, creating a bridge between personal Jewish identity and communal Jewish life (Cohen and Rosen, 1992:1). To the extent that concentrated areas of Jewish settlement have become diluted through the dispersion of their Jewish populations throughout the metropolitan areas as well as across metropolitan areas, with a consequent weakening of opportunities for daily informal interaction, organized affiliation can be seen as taking on increased importance, allowing Jews to interact with other Jews, express their Jewish identity publicly, and support the activities of the larger community (Phillips, 1993). How movement between communities affects such involvement therefore becomes a matter of great significance. The NJPS-1990 data do not allow full exploration of these issues; they allow only examination of the extent to which recency of migration relates to differential patterns of affiliation.

Affiliation in the Jewish community can manifest itself in varied ways, including membership in a synagogue/temple; membership and involvement in other local, regional, and national organizations; voluntary work on behalf of Jewish causes and agencies; and philanthropy. For some people, participation takes multiple forms and, as Berger (1990a) has found, is often reflected in concurrent involvement in synagogue, other organizations, and philanthropic activities. Others have suggested that different forms of affiliation are mutually exclusive (Goldscheider, 1990).

Complicating any assessment of community involvement and its relation to migration is the question of the intensity of the involvement as indicated by the extent and character of organizational and volunteer activity and by philanthropy. Judged only by membership, identification with the formal structure of the Jewish community can, according to some evidence, be rated high (Berger and Tobin, 1989), even while the intensity of such involvement is low. Berger (1990b) has concluded that "diminishing levels of participation in and commitment to Jewish institutional life" characterize the American scene. Such a conclusion may be reinforced if, concurrent with such decline, Jews increasingly participate more actively in the secular activities of the larger community.

Recognizing the importance of institutional ties as an index of Jewish identification, NJPS-1990 collected information on a variety of communal involvements, including synagogue/temple membership, other organizational affiliations, volunteer activities, philanthropy, friendship patterns, and neighborhood characteristics. The omnibus character of NJPS-1990 did not, however, allow in-depth assessment of Jewish and non-Jewish affiliations. Again, as for the Jewish identificational variables, virtually all of the information necessarily refers to the time of the survey, and much of it relates to the respondent only, rather than to all household members. We therefore cannot assess changes directly associated with the migration process.

The analysis which follows draws on the information on communal involvement to assess the degree to which migrants differ from nonmigrants in the extent and the intensity of Jewish involvement. For a number of these variables, the data also allow comparison with the extent and intensity of involvement in non-Jewish organizations and activities. Attention turns first to membership in Jewish organizations, followed by assessment of membership in non-Jewish groups.

ORGANIZATIONAL MEMBERSHIP

The key question in NJPS on Jewish organizational membership was "To how many Jewish organizations other than a synagogue or temple do you belong?" The respondent defined what constituted an "organization" and "membership." Many persons belong to national organizations, such as the American Jewish Committee, the Holocaust Museum, and various Zionist groups, largely through "paper membership" rather than active participation. To the extent that such membership is national or regional rather than local, it may not be affected by movement from one community to another. Since the names of specific organizations were not obtained in the survey, any attempt to distinguish the two levels of affiliation is precluded.

Migrants may have reported belonging to a number of organizations which were national and in which membership was therefore not affected by mobility. Indeed, migrants may especially retain such memberships as a means of maintaining a sense of integration with the larger community even as they undergo transitions in the quantity and quality of local integration. In fact, in a highly mobile society, it may be advantageous to tie local memberships to a national system to facilitate integration when individuals migrate.

In the absence of separate information on national and local organizations, a full assessment of the impact of migration on organizational membership is not possible; concurrent information would also be necessary about the existence and vitality of local affiliates of national groups. As a result, assessments of differentials by migration status will be more sensitive to the overall levels of membership rather than to the question of integration into the local organizational structure of the community of destination. Later evaluation of synagogue/temple membership will allow fuller assessment of the relation between migration and purely local affiliation.[1] Respondents were also asked about membership in organizations, agencies, groups, or clubs that were not Jewish. This question, too, did not distinguish between national and local organizations.

Of the core Jewish respondents in NJPS, only 28 percent reported belonging to one or more Jewish organizations other than a synagogue or temple (table 6.1). As expected, level of affiliation relates positively to age; only one in five of those under age 45 reported an affiliation compared to 31 percent of the middle aged, and 43 percent of the elderly. In contrast, membership in non-Jewish groups[2] is much higher (table 6.2). Just under half of all core Jewish respondents held at least one membership in a non-Jewish organization. Compared to Jewish affiliation patterns, age was not directly associated with a rise in level of non-Jewish membership. A much higher percentage of Jews under age 45 were affiliated with non-Jewish groups than with Jewish ones. For the aged, the levels were about the same.

The high levels of affiliation with non-Jewish groups among the younger cohorts suggest fuller integration into the larger community, possibly at the expense of Jewish affiliation. Whether this differential will persist as the younger generation ages bears monitoring to determine whether the basic patterns of integration are changing or whether the differential observed is a life-cycle effect. For our purposes, the key question is how do the levels of affiliation relate to migration status?

Table 6.1

Percentage Belonging to One or More Jewish Organizations and Average Number of Memberships, by Five-Year Migration Status, by Age and Sex: Core Jews

Migration Status	Percentage Belonging to One or More Jewish Organizations			Average Number of Memberships		
	Total	Men	Women	Total	Men	Women
Total Adults						
Nonmigrant	30.8	27.7	33.8	0.63	0.51	0.74
Intrastate	19.7	15.7	22.3	0.35	0.32	0.37
Interstate	18.1	15.8	20.4	0.32	0.33	0.30
International	18.2	9.0	32.9	0.27	0.09	0.57
Total	28.0	25.0	30.8	0.56	0.47	0.64
18–44 Years						
Nonmigrant	23.3	22.4	24.3	0.38	0.37	0.39
Intrastate	17.6	15.8	18.6	0.28	0.24	0.30
Interstate	16.0	13.1	18.7	0.29	0.30	0.28
International	22.4	11.1	*	0.34	0.11	*
Total	21.2	19.8	22.4	0.35	0.34	0.36

			45–64 Years			
Nonmigrant	32.5	26.8	37.8	0.71	0.54	0.86
Intrastate	27.7	12.9	37.0	0.77	0.90	0.69
Interstate	22.4	25.5	18.5	0.36	0.49	0.18
International	*	*	*	*	*	*
Total	31.4	25.7	26.5	0.68	0.55	0.81
			65 Years and Over			
Nonmigrant	43.6	39.2	48.2	1.04	0.77	1.30
Intrastate	36.3	*	*	0.64	*	*
Interstate	32.1	*	*	0.56	*	*
International	*	*	*	*	*	*
Total	42.9	37.6	48.4	1.00	0.74	1.27

*Fewer than 10 unweighted cases.

Jewish Organizations

For the total adult core Jewish population, sharp differences characterize organizational membership patterns of migrants and non-migrants (table 6.1). Whereas 31 percent of all adults who lived in the same community in 1985 and 1990 belonged to one or more Jewish organizations, just under 20 percent in each of the three migrant categories (intrastate, interstate, and international) did so.

The lower membership levels of younger persons compared to older ones characterize most age/migration categories as well (for which comparisons are possible). The relation between membership levels and migration status also obtains for men and women separately, although in every migration status group somewhat more women than men were affiliated.

Although NJPS-1990 did not allow comparisons of the before and after levels of organizational memberships, some insights are provided by research in Florida. The findings generally support the interpretations based on the national data. For example, in a study of Palm Beach County, full-year residents who had migrated to the area in the fourteen years prior to the survey were asked about their Jewish organizational involvement during the three years preceding their migration (Sheskin, 1987). This information allowed comparison of pre- and postmigration membership levels. The results suggest similar levels of membership: 42 percent in earlier community of residence and 38 percent in Palm Beach County. This did not, however, indicate a simple transfer of membership patterns. Of all those who belonged in their earlier community, only 58 percent belonged in Palm Beach County, suggesting a substantial decline in participation following migration. On the other hand, among those who did not belong to a Jewish organization before migration, 24 percent were involved after the move, compensating in part for the decline in membership among those who had been active earlier. These patterns suggest that migration can have diverse effects.

Another study in Florida, of the Sarasota-Manatee Jewish community (Sheskin, 1992), generally supports the findings for Palm Beach County. Far more (46 percent) of the respondents reported less involvement than in their former community than did those who reported more involvement (16 percent). As Sheskin (1987:160) suggests, and consistent with the interpretation offered in our analysis of the NJPS-1990 data, some of the membership decline may reflect the failure to develop commitments to the new community of residence; some may stem from a desire to forego responsibilities held earlier in favor of more leisure time or other kinds of activities. For some, the greater Jewish density may suffice in providing the types of interaction desired with other Jews. On the other hand, for those who became active after having had no involvement in their earlier place of residence, opposite factors may operate—more leisure time, reduction in family/work responsibilities, and easier access to Jewish groups, sometimes even within their condominium of residence. How typical the Florida patterns are for other areas of the country remains to be evaluated.

The differences in the proportions belonging to one or more Jewish organizations documented by NJPS-1990 extend to the average number of organizations with which adult Jews are affiliated. Since such a low proportion (only 28 percent) belong to any Jewish organization, it comes as no surprise that adult Jews averaged only 0.56 affiliations with Jewish organizations. This varies, however, from a high of 0.63 for nonmigrants to only 0.35 for intrastate movers and 0.32 for interstate migrants, about 40 percent lower than for the nonmigrants. The lowest level characterizes the international migrants, who averaged only 0.27 groups. These patterns strongly suggest that mobility either affects membership through its disruptive impact or selects persons who are differentially integrated into the community at both origin and destination.

The same basic pattern obtained for all age segments but the middle-aged group, although the sharpness of the differentials varied. For those under age 45, both intrastate and interstate migrants averaged just under 0.3 Jewish organizations, compared to 0.38 for nonmigrants. This difference of about 25 percent fewer memberships for the migrants suggests lower levels of integration into the community's Jewish organizational structure. The disparity in number of memberships of middle aged interstate migrants compared to nonmigrants was even greater, 0.36 compared to 0.71, but the intrastate movers reported about 10 percent more affiliations than the nonmigrants. The aged, like the younger cohort, conformed to the expectation that increasing distance of migration is associated with lower average memberships compared to nonmigrants.

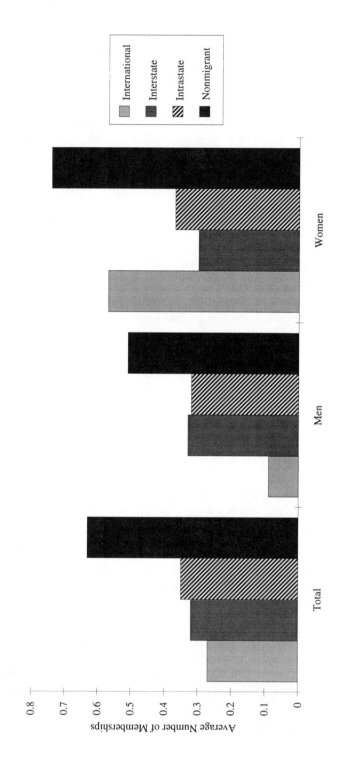

Figure 6.1

Average Number of Memberships in Jewish Organizations, by Five-Year Migration Status, by Sex: Core Jews

For women in the 18–44 and 45–64 age groups, average number of affiliations dropped from the nonmigrant to intrastate to interstate migrant categories. (Not enough cases are available for the elderly when disaggregated by migration status and sex to allow similar comparisons.) For men, the pattern is not quite as consistent, with some variations among the intrastate movers. Consistently, however, the average memberships of interstate migrants are below those of the nonmigrants, pointing to a greater impact of longer-distance movement.

Across all age and gender groups, therefore, interstate movement, either because of its greater disruptive effect or because it is selective of less affiliated individuals, is associated with lower average memberships in Jewish groups. Moreover, for most of the gender/age subcategories, the same holds true for intrastate movers.

Non-Jewish Organizations

We have seen that a much higher proportion of Jews belong to one or more non-Jewish organizations than to Jewish ones (other than a synagogue/temple). Moreover, the differentials varied inversely with age: while far fewer Jews under age 45 were affiliated with Jewish groups compared to older cohorts, the younger and the middle-aged were especially likely to be members of secular groups (table 6.2). Some of these memberships may be related to professional activities; among the elderly, professional memberships would be less important since so many are retired. Within this broad pattern, attention turns now to how the affiliation patterns of the core Jewish population in non-Jewish groups relate to migration status.

For the adult population as a whole, nonmigrants and those moving shorter distances had the highest proportions reporting at least one membership (50 percent) while the migrants from abroad understandably reported the lowest proportion. With an affiliation rate of 46 percent, the interstate migrants had only a slightly lower rate than the nonmigrants and the within-state movers. Patterns of secular affiliation thus differed in relation to migration status from membership patterns in Jewish organizations. The minimal differentials in non-Jewish memberships among the three migration groups suggests either that Jews generally integrate more easily into the secular organizational structure of a community following migration, or that more of the secular

Table 6.2
Percentage Belonging to One or More Non-Jewish Organizations and Average Number of Memberships, by Five-Year Migration Status, by Age and Sex: Core Jews

Migration Status	Percentage Belonging to One or More Non-Jewish Organizations			Average Number of Memberships		
	Total	Men	Women	Total	Men	Women
Total Adults						
Nonmigrant	50.0	50.9	49.2	1.45	1.35	1.54
Intrastate	50.0	51.8	48.9	1.44	1.25	1.56
Interstate	45.9	47.7	44.0	1.02	1.03	1.01
International	30.1	14.0	56.0	0.74	0.26	1.51
Total	49.4	50.2	48.7	1.39	1.29	1.49
18–44 Years						
Nonmigrant	52.0	49.5	54.3	1.36	1.29	1.42
Intrastate	46.2	48.4	44.9	1.32	1.11	1.45
Interstate	43.5	47.2	40.0	0.95	0.99	0.92
International	20.7	5.0	*	0.75	0.20	*
Total	49.3	48.3	50.1	1.28	1.20	1.35

			45-64 Years			
Nonmigrant	52.1	52.5	51.7	1.79	1.67	1.90
Intrastate	71.2	72.0	70.7	2.18	2.37	2.04
Interstate	68.5	65.5	72.2	1.75	1.62	1.91
International	*	*	*	*	*	*
Total	54.3	54.3	54.2	1.80	1.69	1.90
			65 Years and Over			
Nonmigrant	43.8	51.7	35.2	1.26	1.13	1.39
Intrastate	70.2	*	*	1.87	*	*
Interstate	31.8	*	*	0.46	*	*
International	*	*	*	*	*	*
Total	44.2	50.7	37.0	1.25	1.10	1.40

* Fewer than 10 unweighted cases.

memberships are not local and are therefore not disrupted by a move.

Patterns of affiliation with non-Jewish groups also differ from those for Jewish memberships when age is controlled. Non-Jewish affiliations do not show the clear inverse relation characterizing affiliation with Jewish groups. Either migration is more disruptive of organizational ties to the Jewish community than of non-Jewish memberships or it selects individuals who have fewer such ties and who are more closely tied to non-Jewish affiliations.

Adults in the core Jewish population averaged almost three times as many organizational affiliations in non-Jewish as in Jewish groups, 1.39 compared to 0.56. Considerable variation exists, however, by migration status. Nonmigrants and intrastate movers closely resembled each other, averaging about 1.45 non-Jewish affiliations per person. By contrast, interstate migrants belonged, on average, to only 1.02 organizations, and international migrants to even fewer. As for membership in Jewish groups, this pattern suggests that longer-distance movement is associated with lower levels of affiliation at destination. However, the age-specific data do not consistently support such a conclusion.

The youngest age group, which includes a disproportional number of the recent migrants, conforms closely to the pattern observed for the population as a whole. For the middle-aged, however, intrastate movers have the highest average number of affiliations, and the levels for nonmigrants and interstate migrants are similar. Among the aged, intrastate movers also have the highest averages, but interstate migrants have considerably lower levels of affiliation.

The absence of clearer patterns across the age groups parallels closely the lack of pattern already identified for the proportions belonging to any non-Jewish group. These data on average memberships therefore suggest that the same underlying factors that affect whether core Jews join *any* non-Jewish group also operate in influencing the *number* of groups they join. Migration status per se does not seem to have a consistent association with level or intensity of secular affiliation. The patterns characterize both men and women.

Evidently, migration, and especially interstate migration, affects affiliation with Jewish groups more than it does membership in non-Jewish groups. As noted earlier, this may reflect a higher level of secular memberships in national organizations,

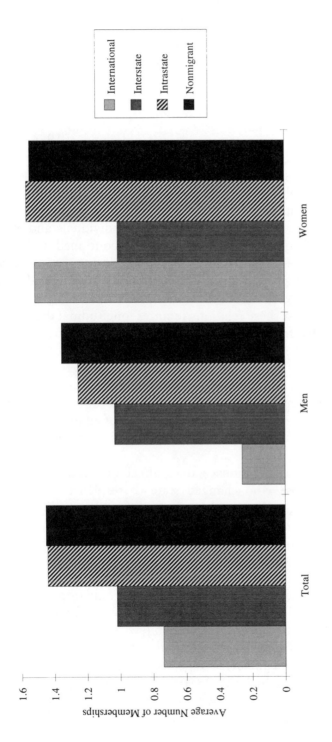

Figure 6.2

Average Number of Memberships in Non-Jewish Organizations, by Five-Year Migration Status, by Sex: Core Jews

which are not strongly affected by geographic mobility. It may also point to the greater ease, especially for intrastate migrants, of transferring memberships or in making the transition to new types of organizational involvement.

Membership in Relation to Duration

Research on various communities (Goldscheider, 1986; Cohen, 1983) has suggested that while differences between migrant and nonmigrant segments of the Jewish community are observable, much of the difference dissipates with longer duration of residence. Migrants who settle in a community for the long term take advantage of opportunities to integrate. Individuals and families who move frequently and who anticipate continued mobility are likely to be the least integrated because their comparatively short period of residence in any given community does not allow time for establishing networks and roots (Sheskin, 1992).

To fully test these relations requires longitudinal data that are not available from NJPS. Some insights can be gained, however, from use of the typology of migrants introduced in chapter 3 and used there to evaluate the extent both of recent versus long-term migration and of repeat and return migration among those who moved between 1985 and 1990. It is important to remember that this typology relies on the state as the unit of analysis, since information is not available on local areas in which respondents were born.

If duration of residence does affect integration, then early migrants (those who changed state of residence before 1985) should more closely resemble nonmigrants (those whose state of residence in 1985 and 1990 was also their state of birth) than do persons who migrated to the state between 1985 and 1990. Moreover, if repeat or return movement affects integration, then such movers should be characterized by even lower membership and participation levels than those who moved only once in the specified period. The data in table 6.3, which presents the results of such comparisons for membership in Jewish and non-Jewish organizations, lend some support to both hypotheses.

For all adults, the percentage belonging to one or more Jewish organizations is highest (29 percent) for the nonmigrants. It declines slightly for those who migrated to the state before 1985 (early migrants). However, for those who arrived during the five

Table 6.3
Percentage Belonging to One or More Jewish and Non-Jewish
Organizations, by Type of Migration and Age:
Core Jews (U.S.-Born Only)

	Age			
Migrant Type	18-44 Years	45-64 Years	65 Years and Over	Total
Percent Belonging to One or More Jewish Organizations				
Nonmigrant	23.1	37.8	35.9	29.0
Early Migrant	18.8	24.9	42.3	26.0
Primary Migrant	9.5	*	*	13.4
Repeat Migrant	17.1	22.4	37.6	19.4
Return Migrant	14.5	*	*	13.4
Percent Belonging to One or More Non-Jewish Organizations				
Nonmigrant	49.2	52.0	42.1	48.7
Early Migrant	54.5	52.1	54.2	53.8
Primary Migrant	29.7	*	*	34.3
Repeat Migrant	55.9	61.8	50.9	56.5
Return Migrant	35.9	*	*	38.9

* Fewer than 10 unweighted cases.

years preceding the 1990 survey, the level of organizational membership is only 13 percent, less than half that of the nonmigrants. Recency of move seems to operate as a deterrent to membership in Jewish organizations. While the membership levels of the repeat and the return migrants are also lower than those of the early movers and nonmigrants, consistent with expectations, they are not below the level of the primary migrants, those who made their first and only move during 1985–1990. In fact, slightly more of the repeat than of the primary migrants belonged to Jewish organizations. Since, as has been pointed out before, membership includes both local and national organizations, we cannot definitively ascertain whether, for any of the migrant groups, local memberships are curtailed as part of the migration process.

With age controlled, a similar pattern emerges for those age 18–44. For the middle-aged, too, the repeat migrants closely resemble the early migrants, but for both these groups, the level of

membership is well below that of nonmigrants. That the membership level of the repeat migrants is similar to that of the early movers remains a puzzle that can be resolved only with fuller information on the nature of the organizations to which the respective
groups of migrants belong.

The aged are unique: all three migrant status groups for whom
comparisons can be made have quite similar levels of membership
that are generally well above those of comparable younger groups
(nonmigrants are an exception). Evidently, migration does not
affect the membership behavior of older persons as much as it
does younger ones. Whether this is because more of them belong
to national groups whose membership shifts with the migrant or
because they are more likely than younger persons to join new
local groups sooner following migration remains to be tested.

Membership in non-Jewish organizations shows a somewhat
different pattern. For the total population, as well as for those age
18–44 and the elderly, early migrants and repeat migrants were
relatively more affiliated than the nonmigrants, although the difference was sharp only for the aged. Among the middle-aged, the
level for the repeat migrants was considerably higher than for
either the early migrants or the nonmigrants. By contrast, for the
adult population as a whole and for those age 18–44, primary
migrants as well as return migrants had substantially lower levels
of affiliation with non-Jewish organizations. Evidently, the mobility of repeat migrants has a markedly different relation to non-
Jewish organization memberships than for others who moved in
the same five-year period as either primary or return migrants.
Again, without more information on type of organization, the reasons for this cannot be ascertained.

A Multivariate Analysis of Organization Membership

Many factors may affect membership in Jewish and non-Jewish
organizations. Research elsewhere (Cohen, 1983) has shown, for
example, that secular education, age, and religiosity are related to
Jewish affiliations. To test here for several of these factors, a multiple classification analysis (MCA) has been undertaken for number of memberships in Jewish and non-Jewish organizations (table
6.4). Included among the covariates and variates are age, gender,
education, and Jewish identification. Our interest centers on the
differentials by five-year migration status.

Table 6.4
Relation of Five-Year Migration Status and Likelihood of Moving
on Number of Memberships in Jewish and Non-Jewish
Organizations: A Multiple Classification Analysis*: Core Jews

| | *Jewish*
Organizations | | *Non-Jewish*
Organizations | |
	Model A	*Model B*	*Model A*	*Model B*
Grand Mean	0.66	0.65	1.56	1.58
Migration Status				
Nonmigrant	0.69	0.69	1.61	1.62
Intrastate	0.59	0.54	1.70	1.74
Interstate	0.52	0.52	1.14	1.19
International	0.44	0.42	1.09	1.25
Future Move				
Very likely	—	0.54	—	1.40
Somewhat likely	—	0.55	—	1.35
Not likely	—	0.73	—	1.75

*Controlling for age, sex, education, and religious identification.

The MCA confirms the higher number of secular memberships held by persons in the core Jewish population. Beyond this differential, differences also characterize the relation between five-year migration status and number of memberships. For both Jewish and non-Jewish organizations, number of memberships drops considerably among interstate migrants, compared to those who have not moved or moved only within state (Model A). Interstate migrants belong to only 0.52 Jewish organizations and 1.14 non-Jewish ones, compared to 0.69 and 1.61, respectively, among nonmigrants. The only variation in pattern is the slightly higher number of memberships in non-Jewish organizations held by intrastate migrants.

Among the other variables entered into the model (not detailed in the table), higher education was strongly associated with more memberships in both Jewish and non-Jewish organizations. Women also average a higher number of affiliations than men. Secular Jews averaged the lowest number of Jewish affiliations among the three religious identification groups.

If anticipated future mobility is also added to the model (Model B), very little change occurs in the averages for other variables, including migration status, but future movement itself has the expected effect. Those persons who are very or somewhat likely to move within three years average fewer memberships than those who will remain more residentially stable. The impact is similar for Jewish and non-Jewish organizations. Although the differentials in membership are not large, the consistency of the patterns for both migration status and anticipated future mobility points to the importance of these factors in overall commitments to and integration into the Jewish community.

SYNAGOGUE/TEMPLE MEMBERSHIP

The survey information on affiliation with temples and synagogues can give us more direct insights into the impact of migration on local membership. Temple/synagogue affiliation is more often place-specific, reflecting the motives for membership—attendance at religious services; education of children; participation in auxiliary groups such as sisterhoods, men's clubs, and youth groups; and as a way of identifying as a Jew in the larger community. For example, Lazerwitz, Winter, and Dashefsky (1988) have noted in their study of localism that involvement with synagogues, both through membership and attendance, is related to such localistic activities as Jewish voluntarism and involvement with primary group networks of fellow Jews. Cohen (1983:100), while noting that participation in Jewish and non-Jewish organizational life and contributing to Jewish charities are not necessarily tied to the local area, posits that mobility has much more effect on synagogue membership because it is more oriented to the local community. Synagogue/temple membership therefore serves as a good indicator of the relation between migration status and integration into the local community.

To the extent that such membership directly reflects identification with Judaism and involves financial commitments in the form of membership dues and or other fees, it also serves to index an individual's or family's desire to participate in the organized religious life of the community. If migrant ties to Judaism are weaker than those of the more residentially stable, if recency of settlement in an area deters affiliation, and if anticipated out-migration argues against making large financial investments in local institutions, we can hypothesize that the levels of synagogue/temple membership among migrants, especially recent migrants, will be lower than that of natives and long-time residents.

NJPS-1990 asked respondents whether they or any members of their household were currently affiliated with a synagogue or temple and, if so, its denomination. For those households with no synagogue/temple members, earlier membership of the respondent was ascertained. For purposes of assessing the relation between migration and membership, the initial question has a possible limitation. Since it refers to the respondent or other household members, the respondent may not personally be a member. An analysis correlating the respondent's migration status with household synagogue/temple membership could therefore be confounded. This complication is minor, however, since most households covered by NJPS are nuclear and synagogue/temple membership is generally on a household rather than individual basis.

Among all core Jewish adults, only 34 percent belonged to households which were affiliated with a synagogue or temple. This overall low level of affiliation reflects several factors. Community studies have shown that in large metropolitan centers of dense Jewish settlement, membership levels tend to be low, evidently reflecting the lesser felt need for expressing Jewish identity through formal affiliation. The 1991 New York study (Horowitz, 1993; see also Horowitz, 1994), for example, found only 43 percent affiliated with synagogues or temples. In Washington, D.C., the affiliation rate in 1983 was only 39 percent, and in 1990 in Chicago (Friedman and Phillips, 1994) it was 44 percent. On the West Coast, San Francisco's rate of affiliation in 1988 was only 33 percent, and the earlier 1979 Los Angeles study found an affiliation level of only 26 percent (Sheskin, 1993). By contrast, in Rhode Island's Jewish community of approximately 15,000 core Jews, 70 percent of adult respondents were members of affiliated households in 1987 (Goldstein, Goldscheider, and Goldstein, 1988), and in Nashville the level was 78 percent in 1982 (Sheskin, 1993). In Columbus, however, with a Jewish population of 15,600 in 1990, only 46 percent of families reported synagogue/temple membership (Mott and Mott, 1994). The authors of the Columbus study suggest that this low affiliation level reflects the relative youthfulness of the Columbus Jewish population as well as the short tenure in Columbus of many of the city's Jews. It may also stem from Columbus's high intermarriage rate; about 45 percent of the Jewish respondents are married to non-Jews.

Affiliation rates also tend to be low among mixed households, and their numbers have increased. Whereas 41 percent of entirely Jewish households reported an affiliation, only 13 percent of the mixed households did so. A third factor reflects the growing proportion of Reform households, among whom membership rates are much lower (34 percent) than among the Orthodox (64 percent), who have declined as a proportion of the core Jewish population. The exceptionally low membership rates, only 6 percent, of those reporting themselves as secular Jews also lowers the overall average.

Within the low overall average, variations exist—in the predicted direction—by the migration status of respondents. Of adults who had either not changed residence between 1985 and 1990 or had only moved within the same community, 38 percent were synagogue/temple members; only one-quarter of those who had made either an intrastate or an interstate move were affiliated (table 6.5).

Table 6.5
Percentage Holding Synagogue/Temple Membership by Five-Year
Migration Status and Life-Cycle Stage:
Core Jews

		Life-Cycle Stage				
		Single Person			Parent(s) with Children	
Migration Status	Total	Under Age 45	Age 45+	Couple Only	Under Age 15	Age 15+
Nonmigrant	37.5	19.9	35.6	32.5	38.4	52.1
Intrastate	24.2	10.6	41.0	20.1	29.1	37.8
Interstate	25.4	20.4	23.2	16.0	33.4	40.7
Total*	34.4	18.2	35.1	28.9	36.1	50.8

*Includes international migrants. No separate tabulations for this migration status are presented because of the small number of cases available for this analysis.

Because synagogue/temple membership is often very closely tied to providing Jewish education for children, our attention turns next to its relation between life-cycle stage and migration status. We use life-cycle stage instead of age since the two characteristics are so closely related. Life cycle is given a five-fold classification: (1) single persons under age 45; (2) single persons age 45 and over, the large majority of whom are widowed; (3) couples with no children present in the household; (4) families (one or two parents) with children under age 15 living in the household (older children may also be present); (5) families (one or two parents) with children only age 15 and over present in the household.

The results clearly indicate the importance of life-cycle stage in levels of synagogue/temple membership (table 6.5). Young, single individuals have notably low levels of membership. The levels rise sharply for married couples, families with children, and older one-person households. Surprising are the continued, and even heightened, membership levels among households with children age 15 and over only. Since most of these children are no longer enrolled in Jewish education programs, we would have expected a concomitant drop in affiliation among their parents. The surprising differences between the two family categories (with children under age 15 and with children age 15 and over) may be due to the rather mixed age composition of the families with children under age 15: many of the children are below school age, so that the incentive does not yet exist for parents to join a synagogue/temple in conjunction with Bar/Bat Mitzvah preparation; the membership rates of this life-cycle category are therefore lower than if only families with school-age children had been considered. (More detailed division by migration status of those with children under age 15 was not possible.)

Migration status is also related to membership levels within each life-cycle stage, with nonmigrants generally having higher levels of membership than movers. For couples and households with children, nonmigrants have consistently higher levels of affiliation than either of the migrant groups. The much more mixed pattern for older and younger single-person households suggests that factors other than migration affect whether they join synagogues or temples.

Joint exploitation of information collected on current synagogue membership and on the likelihood of a future move provides further insights. We hypothesize that those who anticipate

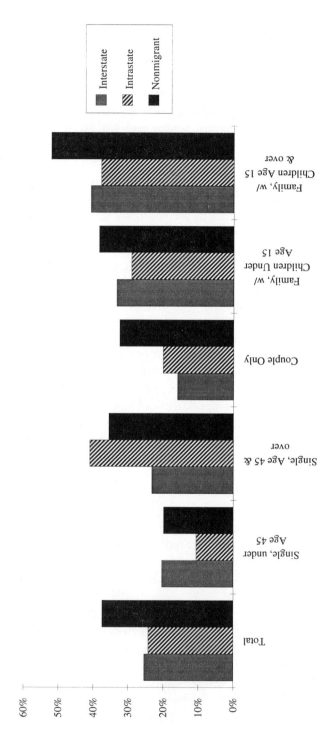

Figure 6.3

Percentage Holding Synagogue/Temple Membership, by Five-Year Migration Status and Life-Cycle Stage: Core Jews

moving in the near future would be less likely to be affiliated with a synagogue/temple since membership reflects stronger ties to community as well as financial investments. A clear differential exists in the relation between membership and prospective mobility within three years. Whereas 64 percent of the synagogue-affiliated indicated they were not likely to move in the next three years, only 48 percent of the nonmembers did so. Almost twice as many of the latter (30 percent) than of the affiliated (17 percent) thought a move to be very likely. From another perspective, whereas 41 percent of those who did not expect to move were synagogue/temple members, only 22 percent of those who thought a move very likely were affiliated (table 6.6). Clearly membership either results from residential stability or serves as a deterrent to future mobility.

The patterns by life-cycle stage support such a conclusion. Consistently, those reporting a move very likely have the lowest levels of affiliation, as low as half of those who anticipated no moves. For single-person households over age 45, couples, and households with children under age 15, even having a move somewhat likely is associated with lower levels of synagogue/temple membership. Households with children over age 15 only show the least effect of future mobility on affiliation. Again, this finding was

Table 6.6
Percentage Holding Synagogue/Temple Membership, by Likelihood of Moving in Next Three Years and Life-Cycle Stage: Core Jews

	Likelihood of Moving		
	Not Likely	*Somewhat Likely*	*Very Likely*
Single, Under 45	21.9	27.2	12.2
Single, Over 45	39.5	16.3	15.6
Couple Only	35.3	19.5	18.6
Parent(s) with Children Under 15	43.0	33.3	20.4
Parent(s) with Children 15+	52.1	50.0	44.2
Total	40.7	31.3	22.4

not expected. These households in the past may have been among the most stable and have therefore established strong roots in a community; they may also have developed a pattern of membership that is carried from one community to another when they do move. Finally, families with older children may also be among the more financially secure so that fees associated with synagogue/temple membership pose less of a burden than they do for single-person households or households with young children.

Synagogue/temple membership, because it is largely location-specific, shows a clearer relation to duration of residence than does organizational membership (table 6.7). For the adult population as a whole, 38 percent of the nonmigrants belonged to households with a synagogue/temple membership. This declined to 31 percent of the early migrants and to only 26 percent of the primary migrants, suggesting that longer duration of residence does lead to higher affiliation rates. The impact of repeat movement is evidenced in a still lower level of membership, only 20 percent. Only for return migrants is frequent movement not associated with a lower membership rate. For this group, the level was almost equal to that of the nonmigrants. Perhaps coming back to state of origin results in levels of participation similar to those of the "native" population of the location. Ties that are broken by out-migration may be

Table 6.7

Percentage Belonging to Synagogue/Temple, by Type of Migration and Life-Cycle Stage: Core Jews (U.S.-Born Only)

		Life-Cycle Stage				
		Single Person			Parent(s) with Children	
Migration Type	Total	Under Age 45	Age 45+	Couple Only	Under Age 15	Age 15+
Nonmigrant	24.8	36.9	29.7	33.8	59.3	38.0
Early Migrant	10.7	32.4	28.7	35.8	38.6	30.9
Primary Migrant	32.0	*	9.0	37.2	*	25.8
Repeat Migrant	11.1	*	11.1	26.9	43.2	20.0
Return Migrant	*	*	31.2	*	*	37.2

*Fewer than 10 unweighted cases.

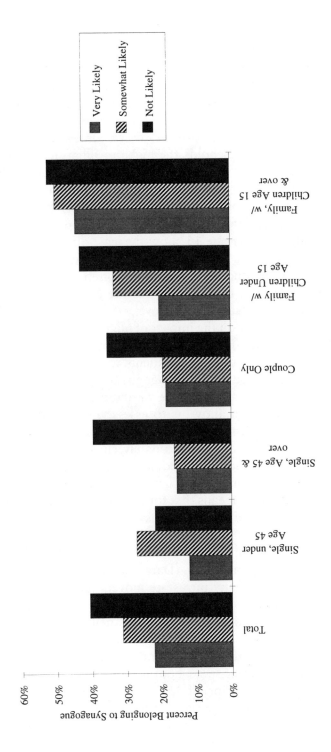

Figure 6.4

Percentage Holding Synagogue/Temple Membership, by Likelihood of Moving in Next Three Years and Life-Cycle Stage: Core Jews

restored quite easily while first-time in-migrants may find it more challenging to establish new ties; family and friends in the area very likely facilitate the reintegration process for return migrants.

These patterns are not as clear when life-cycle stage is taken into account. On the whole, repeat migrants continue to have the lowest levels of affiliation within given life-cycle groups, indicating the disruptive effect of moving several times. Surprisingly, among young single households the highest affiliation characterizes primary movers (32 percent); they may turn to such involvement as an entree into a new community. Just the opposite pattern characterizes primary migrants among couples-only households: they have the lowest affiliation rate of any group. Households including children under age 15 show the least differentiation by migration type, perhaps because they want to enroll children in programs of Jewish education, and this is often done through a synagogue/temple. Yet, even within this life-cycle group, repeat migrants have the lowest affiliation level.

Another perspective on the impact of migration on synagogue/temple affiliation is provided by information on previous membership. NJPS-1990 asked those respondents who were members of households not affiliated with a synagogue/temple in 1990 if they had ever belonged to a synagogue or temple themselves. The answers to this question allow us to assess whether, among the currently nonaffiliated, migrants differ from nonmigrants in the extent of prior membership. Unfortunately, since the exact date of prior membership was not identified, its relation to time of migration cannot be ascertained. Our use of the five-year migration interval, however, likely means that for most respondents the prior membership predates migration. We assume this to be the case.

For currently nonaffiliated respondents, minimal differences characterize nonmigrants and interstate migrants; about 30 percent reported prior membership. (Data not shown in a table.) By contrast, only half as many intrastate movers had held previous membership. All migration status groups thus have consistent patterns of high levels of nonaffiliation during their pre- and postmigration periods.

The data for all nonaffiliated respondents mask significant variations by age and life-cycle stage. For those age 18–24, more of the nonmigrants reported prior affiliation than did the interstate migrants, but with rising age the relation reverses. Among those age 25–44, about one in five of each group had been nonaffiliated;

above age 45, a much higher proportion of nonaffiliated interstate migrants than of nonmigrants had prior affiliation. For the older age segment of the population, movement across states is apparently associated with declines in affiliation. Is this a life-cycle effect?

For all ages, the nonaffiliated intrastate movers reported lower levels of prior affiliation than did either the nonmigrants or the interstate migrants. Evidently, such shorter-distance movement occurs disproportionally among persons with lower levels of affiliation.

With life cycle controlled, interstate migrants, with some exceptions, had higher levels of prior affiliation with a synagogue/temple than did nonmigrants. The major exception is couple-only households, among whom substantially fewer of the interstate and even fewer intrastate movers had been previously affiliated. For those households with children under age 15, minimal differences characterized the nonmigrants and interstate migrants, but again nonaffiliated intrastate movers had the lowest level of earlier affiliation. By contrast, among those households with children age 15 and over, as well as among single persons age 45 and over, the interstate migrants reported the highest rates of prior affiliation. These patterns suggest two points: At later stages of the life cycle, as at older ages, interstate migrants more than nonmigrants are likely to give up synagogue/temple membership. Nonetheless, regardless of age, single persons who migrate interstate experience greater reduction in affiliation than do those who remain residentially stable. Evidently, the need or incentive for rejoining after migration is not strong for the unmarried; their earlier membership may have been simply a function of parental family membership.

Both stage of the life cycle and migration experience therefore appear to interact to affect synagogue/temple affiliation rates. In general, among those unaffiliated in 1990, older persons, especially those with older children, and single persons regardless of age are more likely to have dropped their affiliations in conjunction with interstate migration. Among couples, earlier nonaffiliation is more associated with interstate migration. This may change as more of the young children in these households approach Bar/Bat Mitzvah age.

A Multivariate Analysis

Just as a number of personal characteristics affected organizational memberships, so, too, are they important variables in synagogue/temple affiliation. To test their importance, and especially that of migration status once other characteristics are controlled, an ordinary least squares (OLS) regression analysis was undertaken (table 6.8). The results indicate that education is positively related to synagogue/temple membership, as is being female compared to being male. The strongest effect characterized religious identification, with secular Jews having one-third lower levels of affiliation than Jews by religion. Life-cycle stage was also significantly related to affiliation, with single-person households and

Table 6.8
Regression Coefficients on Synagogue/Temple Membership:
Core Jews

Selected Characteristics	Model A	Model B
Sex[a]	.040	.043
Education	.016*	.015*
Life-cycle Stage[b]		
Single person, under age 45	–.261*	–.223*
Single person, age 45+	–.073*	–.094*
Couple only	–.100*	–.101*
Parent(s) + children under age 15	–.014	–.016
Religious Identification[c]		
Jews by Choice	.126*	.135*
Secular Jews	–.375*	–.361*
Five-Year Migration Status[d]		
Intrastate	–.042	–.040
Interstate	–.130*	–.101*
Future move[e]		
Very likely		–.154*
Somewhat likely		–.082*

a. Reference group is males.
b. Reference group is parent(s) with children age 15 and over.
c. Reference group is Jews by religion.
d. Reference group is nonmigrants.
e. Reference group is "not likely to move."
*Significant at the 0.05 level.

couple-only households likely to have lower affiliation rates than parent(s) with coresident children.

Turning to the focus of this monograph, the OLS also shows that levels of synagogue/temple membership do not differ significantly between nonmigrants and intrastate migrants. Interstate migrants, on the other hand, have significantly lower levels of affiliation: they are 13 percent less likely to be affiliated. Distance of move apparently plays a key role in affecting memberships, even when other variables are controlled, while relatively local changes of residence have little impact.

A second OLS model incorporated the likelihood of future moves into the analysis. The likelihood of future moves is seen as a key factor in impeding integration, since persons and families who know they will be in a given community for only a short time are much less likely to become actively involved in the institutional life of the community than those who expect to remain for long periods of time. Our analysis confirms this assumption. Persons who anticipate that they are very likely to move within three years are 15 percent less likely to belong to a synagogue/temple than are those who anticipated no move. Even among those who expect that a move is only somewhat likely, 8 percent fewer are synagogue members than the most stable group.

All other variables have about the same relation to synagogue membership as was true in Model A. For interstate migrants the coefficient drops from -.130 to -.101 when future mobility is entered into the equation. This result suggests the particular importance of anticipated movement, especially in conjunction with previous long-distance movement. Those who have been interstate migrants in the past and who also anticipate future mobility are the least likely to affiliate with a synagogue. If a significant proportion of the Jewish American population does, in fact, make repeated moves, then our findings have important implications for their integration into the community.

Such a pattern is consistent with the thesis that recent movement, and especially long-distance movement, is associated with lesser integration into the community of destination than that which characterizes natives of the community and those migrants who have lived there for longer duration. Compounding this effect is the expectation that out-migration is likely to occur in the near future. Whether individuals who do not belong to local organizations tend to move more frequently or whether frequent movement interferes with joining local groups cannot be fully tested with the available data. In either case, migration-prone individuals seem to constitute marginal members of the community when judged by membership levels; efforts to raise overall levels of community participation and to enhance the integration of the mobile population must be at least partially directed at past and prospective movers.

VOLUNTEER ACTIVITIES

A third perspective for assessing the relation between migration and community integration is participation in voluntary activities. In contrast to synagogue/temple membership, volunteering may involve little monetary investment, require no denominational choices, and be more geographically accessible. While not all volunteer activities necessarily occur in the local community, they probably do for most persons, since extensive travel would incur considerable financial costs and time. In the absence of information on the site of the activity, this analysis assumes that it occurs in the local community. Volunteer work therefore, like synagogue/temple affiliation, lends itself well to assessing the impact of migration on integration into the local social, cultural, and political milieu.

Volunteer activities were identified through a series of questions about whether individual respondents engaged in volunteer activities for Jewish and non-Jewish groups during the twelve months preceding the survey and, if so, for how many hours, on the average, per month. Definition of what constituted voluntarism was left to individual respondents. We will first examine the relation between migration and participation in Jewish activities, then in non-Jewish activities, and finally the extent to which participation in Jewish activities is affected by participation in non-Jewish volunteer work.

Jewish Voluntarism

For adults as a whole, volunteering in Jewish activities is less popular than membership in organizations and synagogues/temples. Only 18 percent reported involvement in Jewish volunteer activities, compared to 28 percent who were organization members and

34 percent who belonged to a synagogue/temple. Apparently, more persons are either "paper" members of groups or participate only in the formal activities associated with membership, such as attendance at services or meetings, rather than engaging in more active roles that involve the donation of time and services.

The extent of volunteer activity, consistent with our hypothesis, varies with the migration experience of respondents (table 6.9). One-fifth of all respondents who had been residentially stable over the previous five years reported having been engaged in volunteer work for the Jewish community in the twelve months preceding the survey, compared to only 12 percent of the five-year intrastate migrants and slightly fewer of those who had migrated interstate. Migration is thus also negatively associated with integration into the local organizational structure when defined in terms of voluntarism. Interestingly, the level of volunteer work is highest for international migrants. This is not surprising, since many immigrants are refugees who are recruited by local sponsoring agencies to help their fellow, newly arrived immigrants integrate into local community life.

With age controlled, the same basic pattern holds for the youngest and the middle-aged groups, even while level of volunteer activity is higher among those age 45–64. The absolute and relative differences by migration status were sharpest, however, for the youngest group. For both age groups, the international migrants were by far the most active of all categories. These patterns clearly show that migration status has an impact on volunteer work; the difference is not great, however, between intrastate and interstate movement, and rising age level seems to mitigate the effect. Perhaps with more experience in such activities, middle-age persons find it easier to make the transition in participation when they change communities or perhaps have the time to do so, given their later stage of the life cycle.

For the aged, the overall level of voluntarism among nonmigrants is quite similar to that of the middle-aged, about 20 percent. But it is quite different for the migrants. A much smaller proportion of the elderly intrastate movers (only 6 percent) and a higher proportion (18 percent) of the interstate migrants were engaged in volunteer work. Quite different patterns of selection and/or adaptation therefore characterize elderly intrastate movers from those moving interstate. More of the former may be moving to adjust to changing family and health conditions and may,

Table 6.9
Percentage Engaged in Jewish Volunteer Activity, by Five-Year
Migration Status, Age, and Sex:
Core Jews

Migration Status	Total	Males	Females
Total Adults			
Nonmigrant	19.5	17.3	21.7
Intrastate	12.0	8.2	14.4
Interstate	11.1	9.0	13.3
International	35.5	27.0	49.2
Total	17.8	15.6	20.0
18–44 Years			
Nonmigrant	18.6	17.8	19.5
Intrastate	11.8	8.4	13.9
Interstate	9.5	7.4	11.5
International	34.9	33.4	*
Total	16.2	15.1	17.3
45–64 Years			
Nonmigrant	20.7	18.8	22.4
Intrastate	16.2	12.9	18.4
Interstate	16.9	15.6	18.5
International	*	*	*
Total	20.3	18.1	22.4
65 Years and Over			
Nonmigrant	19.9	15.0	25.0
Intrastate	6.5	*	*
Interstate	18.1	*	*
International	*	*	*
Total	19.3	14.3	24.7

because of these changed conditions, find it more difficult to actively volunteer in community life. Among the elderly interstate migrants, the same factors that lead middle-aged movers to maintain a high level of voluntarism may operate. That a considerable proportion of aged interstate migrants move to areas of comparatively high Jewish residential density may also help account for their high level of involvement in voluntary Jewish activities, much of which may be within relatively short distances of their homes. The absence of many aged international migrants precludes attention to their patterns.

As was true of organizational membership, women are more active in volunteer activities than men: for all respondents, 20 percent of women and 16 percent of men reported some volunteer work for Jewish groups. The gender difference characterized all three age subdivisions, but was most pronounced for the elderly.

For all age groups combined, migration status, whether intra- or interstate, is strongly associated with a drop in volunteer activity for both men and women. Only about half as many of the men who were migrants engaged in such activity as did men who were nonmigrants (17 percent). Among women, the levels of voluntarism were generally higher, but whereas 22 percent of the nonmigrants were volunteers for the Jewish community, this was true of only 13–14 percent of the migrants. Again, international migrants were much more involved, especially the women, among whom almost half reported some Jewish volunteer activites. The general patterns by age identified for the total population characterize the two gender groups as well, even while the levels of voluntarism are consistently higher for women than for men in each age/migration category where comparisons are possible.

Recent past migration helps to explain variation in participation in voluntary Jewish activities; is the effect compounded by anticipated future mobility? Anticipated moves may make individuals reluctant to become involved in the community as active volunteers. The effect becomes exacerbated with repeated movement. Conversely, those who are actively involved may be reluctant to break their ties to the community. For purposes of assessing these relations, men and women are treated jointly.

Among adult core Jews who do not engage in Jewish volunteer activities, 52 percent reported that they had no plans to move, compared to 61 percent of the volunteers (table 6.10). As many as 27 percent of the nonvolunteers thought it very likely that they would move in the next three years, but only 18 percent of the volunteer workers did. Voluntarism is thus correlated with greater integration into the community and seems to serve as a deterrent to future movement. This overall pattern especially characterizes those under age 45. With rising age, the differentials disappear or are reversed.

The relation between likelihood of moving and voluntarism can also be examined in terms of the percent who volunteer, by likelihood category (table 6.10, bottom panel). Again, for the youngest age group, level of voluntarism is clearly and directly

Table 6.10
Likelihood of Moving in Next Three Years, by Current Engagement in Jewish Volunteer Activity, by Age:
Core Jews

Volunteer Activity	Likelihood of Move			Total Percent
	Not Likely	Somewhat Likely	Very Likely	
Total Adults				
Volunteer	60.9	21.0	18.1	100.0
Nonvolunteer	51.8	21.2	26.9	100.0
18–44 Years				
Volunteer	46.7	28.5	24.8	100.0
Nonvolunteer	36.0	24.6	39.3	100.0
45–64 Years				
Volunteer	73.9	14.5	11.6	100.0
Nonvolunteer	67.5	21.0	11.4	100.0
65 Years and Over				
Volunteer	82.0	8.9	9.0	100.0
Nonvolunteer	82.7	10.9	6.4	100.0

Age	Percentage Engaged in Jewish Volunteer Activity		
18–44	20.4	18.6	11.1
45–64	21.4	14.7	20.1
65 and over	19.2	16.4	25.2
Total	20.4	17.7	12.7

associated with expected stability. The middle-aged show less difference in level of volunteer work by mobility expectation, and the
relation is irregular. For the aged, more of those who think a move
very likely are involved in Jewish volunteer work than is the case
for those not as sure about moving. The same reasons posited for
the reversal in pattern among the aged with respect to synagogue/
temple membership may hold for Jewish volunteer activity. If the
expectation is to move to other areas which are also characterized
by high Jewish density, there may be less concern that such a move
will interfere with volunteer activity. Still another possibility is
that the aged discontinue such activity because of physical constraints or as part of retirement, and not directly because of actual
or anticipated mobility.

Non-Jewish Volunteer Activities

A much higher proportion of all age segments of the core Jewish
population were engaged in non-Jewish than in Jewish volunteer
work, and differences by gender were much less pronounced
(table 6.11). For the adults as a whole, 41 percent reported being
active in non-Jewish volunteer work, compared to only 18 percent
in Jewish activities. The differentials were sharpest for the younger
segments of the population. Among those age 18–44, almost three
times as many reported non-Jewish (46 percent) than Jewish (16
percent) volunteer work. For those age 45–64, the ratio was just
over two to one. Even the aged were more engaged in non-Jewish
than Jewish volunteer activities, although the differential was less
sharp. As with organizational memberships, these findings raise
the question whether the much greater difference characterizing
the youngest segments reflects a life-cycle effect or is indicative of
a shift toward lesser involvement by Jews in the Jewish community and greater integration into the general community. Only follow-up studies of the younger cohorts as they age can indicate
firmly which explanation is the more valid.

Current migration status seems to have less effect on the levels
of non-Jewish (secular) than on Jewish voluntarism. For the core
population as a whole, for example, only half as high a percentage
of interstate migrants were volunteers in Jewish activities as were
nonmigrants. By contrast, the differentials by migration status for
voluntarism in secular activities were minimal. The absence of
sharper differences between the nonmigrants and internal

Table 6.11
Percentage Engaged in Non-Jewish Volunteer Activity, by Five-Year
Migration Status, Age, and Sex:
Core Jews

Migration Status	Total	Males	Females
Total Adults			
Nonmigrant	40.4	41.7	39.2
Intrastate	45.4	38.7	49.7
Interstate	43.7	43.4	43.9
International	29.1	25.1	35.4
Total	41.3	41.4	41.2
18–44 Years			
Nonmigrant	46.2	46.2	46.3
Intrastate	46.8	38.9	51.6
Interstate	44.1	48.1	40.3
International	28.3	18.8	*
Total	45.8	45.1	46.4
45–64 Years			
Nonmigrant	42.0	43.7	40.5
Intrastate	50.9	55.0	48.2
Interstate	54.3	38.9	73.9
International	*	*	*
Total	43.2	43.9	42.5
65 Years and Over			
Nonmigrant	27.3	31.0	23.5
Intrastate	16.5	*	*
Interstate	22.5	*	*
International	*	*	*
Total	26.7	29.5	23.9

*Fewer than 10 unweighted cases.

migrants suggests that such involvement is less affected by movement, possibly because more of the activities are in association with local branches of national groups, such as service organizations, environmental groups, and health-related organizations. Local secular groups may also be more effective than the Jewish community in recruiting newcomers into their programs. Migrants may also feel less attached to the Jewish community and find it easier to become involved in the non-Jewish voluntary sector.

In the secular sphere, then, migration status is less marked for volunteer work than for organization membership, suggesting that migration may interfere less with informal activity than with formal membership in organized groups. That this differential does not characterize Jewish organizational affiliations and volunteer activity may reflect the closer links between these two forms of identification in the Jewish community so that migration affects both in similar ways.

The relation observed for the total population characterizes the two age and gender groups as well for which comparisons are possible, although the differences are somewhat more marked for men than women and not consistent in direction in relation to migration status. Nonetheless, among the middle-aged, women are least affected by migration, even when it involves a change in state of residence. They are either selected from among those who are already highly involved in secular voluntarism or are stimulated to engage in such activity soon after making a move.

For the total adult population, involvement in non-Jewish volunteer activity also seems to have a somewhat less inhibiting effect on future mobility than being active in Jewish volunteer work (table 6.12). The differential suggests that greater integration into the Jewish community, as indexed by involvement in Jewish volunteer activities, is correlated with a set of factors that lead such active persons to be somewhat more residentially stable than those whose links are through more secular activities. While only 18 percent of those in Jewish volunteer activity (table 6.10) thought it very likely they would move, up to 24 percent of those engaged in secular voluntarism did so. By contrast, about equal proportions of those not active in Jewish volunteer programs and those not involved in secular volunteer activities reported a move to be very likely. However, compared to active volunteers, the likelihood of a move was far greater among those not involved in Jewish volunteer groups than among those not engaged in secular activities. Thus, nonactive persons were most likely to anticipate a move, and more of those active in Jewish volunteerism expected to be stable. This finding suggests that ties to the Jewish community through volunteer activities are associated with lower expectations of future moves, especially for the youngest age cohort.

For this group, which is characterized by the highest level of both recent and potential mobility, considerably more of the persons active in secular than in Jewish activities considered it very likely that they would move in the next three years: 39 percent, compared to 25 percent of the nonvolunteers. Yet, whether they

Table 6.12
Likelihood of Moving in Next Three Years, by Current Engagement in Non-Jewish Volunteer Activity, by Age: Core Jews

Volunteer Activity	Likelihood of Move			Total Percent
	Not Likely	Somewhat Likely	Very Likely	
Total Adults				
Volunteer	53.5	22.7	23.8	100.0
Nonvolunteer	53.0	19.1	27.9	100.0
18–44 Years				
Volunteer	40.3	21.0	38.7	100.0
Nonvolunteer	35.3	29.1	35.6	100.0
45–64 Years				
Volunteer	71.9	19.4	8.7	100.0
Nonvolunteer	66.0	19.7	14.3	100.0
65 Years and Over				
Volunteer	80.3	9.5	10.2	100.0
Nonvolunteer	53.5	10.8	5.7	100.0

Age	Percentage Engaged in Non-Jewish Volunteer Activity		
18–44	49.0	39.7	47.7
45–64	46.4	43.9	32.5
65 and over	25.9	24.1	39.5
Total	41.5	37.6	45.6

were involved in secular activities made little difference in anticipated movement; just over one-third of both volunteers and nonvolunteers in secular activities thought a move very likely. This suggests that, for the younger group, factors related to engagement in Jewish activities are also associated with greater residential stability than either those correlated with involvement in the secular realm or those associated with noninvolvement in the Jewish sphere.

For the middle-aged and elderly groups, the differences in migration intentions between those engaged in Jewish and in secular voluntarism were less striking and even mixed in direction. Overall, nonvolunteers in both Jewish and secular activities showed a lower likelihood of stability. Within this general pattern, more of the active elderly in both spheres thought a move very likely. This again suggests that the motives underlying mobility of the elderly, the nature of their destinations, and their intention to continue established patterns may together account for the deviation in patterns from those characterizing younger groups.

Voluntarism in Relation to Duration

Attention focusses next on whether duration of residence affects levels of participation in volunteer activities, using the five-fold migration typology (see chapter 3 for definition). For the total adult population, virtually identical levels of participation in Jewish volunteer work were reported by both the nonmigrants and the early movers (those who changed state of residence before 1985) (table 6.13). This similarity suggests that duration of residence exceeding five years leads to full integration into the Jewish voluntary sector at destination. Such a conclusion is reinforced by the much lower level of volunteer activity on the part of primary migrants; only one-third as many were so engaged.

Contrary to expectations, but similar to the pattern observed for organizational membership, repeat migrants had higher levels of voluntarism than did recent migrants, although lower than those of the early movers and the nonmigrants. While this points to some impact of migration on involvement, it also suggests that either repeat migrants engage in a different kind of volunteer activity, possibly more national in orientation, or that the experience of moving more frequently than the primary migrants gives repeat migrants an experiential advantage in gaining entree to the

Table 6.13
Percentage Engaged in Jewish and Non-Jewish Volunteer Activity,
by Type of Migration and Age:
Core Jews (U.S.-Born Only)

| | Age | | | |
Migrant Type	18–44 Years	45–64 Years	65 Years and Over	Total
Percentage Engaged in Jewish Volunteer Activity				
Nonmigrant	15.4	22.2	15.7	17.2
Early Migrant	15.5	17.6	20.8	17.4
Primary Migrant	2.7	*	*	6.8
Repeat Migrant	13.3	12.3	10.9	13.0
Return Migrant	0.0	*	*	0.0
Percentage Engaged in Non-Jewish Volunteer Activity				
Nonmigrant	44.9	38.0	23.1	42.2
Early Migrant	51.7	48.5	29.1	45.3
Primary Migrant	34.1	*	*	35.3
Repeat Migrant	51.3	62.8	30.2	51.7
Return Migrant	57.8	*	*	53.7

*Fewer than 10 unweighted cases.

formal and informal social structure of their new communities. Among the comparatively small number of return migrants, none reported engagement in Jewish volunteer activities.

With age controlled, the same general pattern characterizes the different migration status groups. Compared to nonmigrants and early migrants, however, among the middle-aged and elderly, repeat migration seems to be more disruptive of voluntarism than it is for the youngest group.

The levels of participation in non-Jewish volunteer activities are consistently much higher than they are for Jewish voluntarism for every migration status group used in this typology. Moreover, the underlying pattern in relation to duration and frequency of movement also differs somewhat. Early migrants and nonmigrants do have quite similar levels of participation, and the level for the primary migrants is lower, pointing to a negative impact of recency of migration on integration. However, the difference is not nearly as sharp as for Jewish volunteer activity, suggesting either greater ease in becoming a volunteer for local non-Jewish groups or more involvement in regional and national programs that are transferable and therefore not affected as much by migration.

Most different from the patterns characterizing Jewish volunteer activity are the very high participation levels of both repeat and return migrants, higher than even the nonmigrants. For the repeat migrants, this parallels a pattern noted for non-Jewish organizational membership, suggesting that one or more common unidentified factors underly the relation. The specific age groups all conform to the pattern noted for the population as a whole for those migration status groups for which comparisons with non-Jewish volunteer activity can be made.

Multivariate Analysis

As was done for synagogue/temple membership, an ordinary least squares (OLS) regression analysis was undertaken to incorporate the effects of several variables simultaneously into the equation. In addition to attention to the migration variables (five-year migration status and likelihood of future move), several sociodemographic variables were also included: age, gender, education, and religious identification (Jew by religion, convert, or secular Jew). Two models were developed: The first included the sociodemographic characteristics and migration status; the second added likelihood of future move.

In general, the OLS regressions[3] corroborate the findings of the bivariate analyses (table 6.14). With all other variables controlled, voluntarism in Jewish activities is 7 percent less among intrastate migrants than among nonmigrants, and 11 percent less among interstate migrants. Anticipation of a move in the near future does not significantly affect voluntarism, although the effect is in the expected direction—it reduces participation. Non-Jewish voluntarism is less affected by migration; the coefficients are negative but very small and not significant. Nor does expected future movement have a significant impact. Nonetheless, for both non-Jewish and Jewish voluntarism, the coefficient for interstate migrants increases when likelihood of future movement is added to the model; persons who were interstate migrants in the past and who anticipate another move are least likely to participate in volunteer activities. As was apparent for organizational membership

Table 6.14
Regression Coefficients on Volunteer Activities:
Core Jews

Selected Characteristics	Jewish Activities	Non-Jewish Activities
Age	0.005	–0.002*
Sex[a]	0.060*	0.008
Education	0.012*	0.025*
Religious Identification[b]		
Jews by Choice	0.038	0.134*
Secular	–0.172*	0.160*
Five-Year Migration Status[c]		
Intrastate	–0.073*	–0.005
Interstate	–0.109*	–0.018
Likelihood of future moves[d]		
Very likely	–0.031	–0.006
Somewhat likely	–0.024	–0.042

a. Reference group is males.
b. Reference group is Jews by religion.
c. Reference group is nonmigrants.
d. Reference group is "not likely to move."
*. Significant at least at the 0.05 level.

and synagogue/temple membership, the more mobile segments of the population are likely to be the least integrated into the community, Jewish and general.

INTERRRELATIONS AMONG FORMS OF INVOLVEMENT

The foregoing assessment of the relation between migration and participation in the organized life of the Jewish community has focussed on each category of membership or activity independent of the others. In actuality, individuals and families vary the extent of their participation, depending on stage of the life cycle and particular needs for Jewish identity and expression. Some are not active or affiliated at all; others may belong to a synagogue/temple and to Jewish organizations as well as engage in Jewish volunteer work; still others may rely on different combinations of these three aspects of involvement in the community. Furthermore, the balance between involvement in Jewish and non-Jewish affiliations and volunteer activities may also vary by migration status.

Interrelations in Jewish Involvement

It is important therefore to examine whether migrants resemble or differ from nonmigrants in their "aggregate" patterns of involvement. Do migrants engage in more or fewer types of Jewish activities than do nonmigrants? Does the combination of such activities differ for the two groups and for different types of migrants? Are individuals who expect to move characterized by different levels and combinations of overall involvement? The underlying expectation, as in the previous analyses, is that migrants are less involved, that this difference declines with longer duration of residence, and that those who expect to migrate in the near future are less involved than those who anticipate remaining in their community. The data lend considerable support to these propositions.

Although data for all migration status groups are presented in table 6.15, the initial comparison will be restricted to the nonmigrants and those who migrated across state lines in the previous five years, since these migrants are most likely to have moved beyond commuting distance to institutions in their previous community of residence. The table does not show the specific categories of affiliation or activity in which respondents were involved, but limited reference to selected combinations will be made in the discussion.

A sharp difference in level of involvement characterizes nonmigrants and interstate migrants. Just under half of all nonmigrants were not involved in any type of Jewish organization, synagogue/temple, or volunteer work, in itself a high proportion. However, this was true of 63 percent of the interstate migrants, strongly suggesting that such movement is associated either as cause or effect with particularly low levels of overall involvement by movers in the Jewish community. This conclusion is reinforced by the finding that only half as many, only 12 percent, of the migrants as of the nonmigrants (26 percent) are involved in at least two kinds of involvement.

Table 6.15
Aggregate Involvement in Jewish Organizations, Synagogue/Temple,
and Jewish Volunteer Activity, by Five-Year Migration Status and Age:
Core Jews

Migration Status	Level of Involvement				
	None	One Only	Two	All Three	Total Percent
Total Adults					
Nonmigrant	49.0	24.6	15.9	10.5	100.0
Intrastate	65.7	17.7	11.6	5.0	100.0
Interstate	63.4	25.0	5.0	6.5	100.0
International	45.6	36.3	18.0	—	100.0
Total	52.5	24.0	14.2	9.3	100.0
18–44 Years					
Nonmigrant	54.3	23.7	13.5	8.4	100.0
Intrastate	70.4	13.5	11.4	4.5	100.0
Interstate	62.8	28.6	3.5	5.1	100.0
International	41.8	44.9	13.4	—	100.0
Total	58.3	23.0	11.6	7.1	100.0
45–64 Years					
Nonmigrant	47.5	24.7	14.1	13.7	100.0
Intrastate	43.5	38.7	10.0	7.8	100.0
Interstate	68.0	12.0	4.3	15.7	100.0
International	*	*	*	*	*
Total	48.7	24.3	13.5	13.4	100.0
65 Years and Over					
Nonmigrant	40.1	27.2	21.8	10.8	100.0
Intrastate	39.5	38.8	15.2	6.5	100.0
Interstate	61.5	11.5	20.6	6.4	100.0
International	*	*	*	*	*
Total	41.0	27.0	21.5	10.5	100.0

*Fewer than 10 unweighted cases.

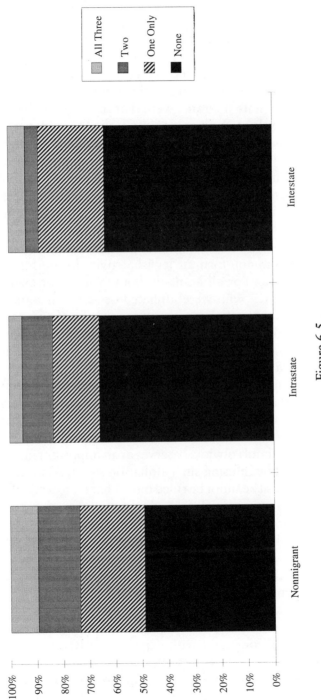

Figure 6.5

Aggregate Involvement in Jewish Organizations, Synagogue/Temple, and Jewish Volunteer Activity, by Five-Year Migration Status: Core Jews

Although the difference between nonmigrants and interstate migrants in level of involvement is slightly less for the 18–44 age group, the migrants continue to be characterized by a considerably higher level of noninvolvement: 63 percent compared to 54 percent. The difference is sharper when two or more types of activity are considered: 22 percent of the nonmigrants but only 9 percent of the interstate migrants were that broadly involved.

The overall levels of noninvolvement decline for older groups, with just under half of those age 45–64 not involved in any way and even fewer (41 percent) of those 65 years and over reporting no involvement in any of the three dimensions being examined here. But for these two age groups, wide differences characterize the nonmigrants and interstate migrants, even more so than for those age 18–44.

Of those who are involved, synagogue/temple membership is by far the most common form of Jewish activity for both nonmigrants and migrants. For all adults in both groups, for example, just over seven of ten who were affiliated or active in some way belonged to a synagogue/temple, including six out of every ten of those who had only one form of involvement. By contrast, for both nonmigrants and migrants, only about 3 percent were exclusively involved in voluntarism, suggesting that monetary costs are not the sole barriers to involvement. Clearly, synagogue/temple membership represents the single most important gateway to involvement with the organized Jewish community for those who choose to be involved. Attendance at religious services and/or enrollment of children in religious schools obviously serves as an important incentive for affiliation, although using such affiliation simply as an expression of Jewish identity cannot be ruled out. What is most significant is that so many more, especially among the migrants, chose not to affiliate at all nor to engage in volunteer activity.

The relation between duration of residence and frequency of migration on the one hand and level of involvement on the other can be explored through attention to the differentials characterizing the various migrant types. They generally point to the impact of both duration and frequency of move (table 6.16). The highest level of involvement characterized the nonmigrants, followed by the early migrants, consistent with expectation. Return migrants closely resembled early migrants. Primary migrants and repeat migrants had the lowest levels of participation, almost one-third less than the nonmigrants. In turn, the nonmigrants and early migrants also included the highest proportion of individuals involved in two or three types of affiliations and/or activities.

The pattern is not as clear for those age 18–44. All categories of migrants, except return migrants (who closely resembled non-migrants), had lower rates of involvement than nonmigrants. The exception characterizing the younger return migrants suggests that having previously lived in the general area facilitates involvement. By contrast, nonmigrants and early migrants were quite similar in the proportion involved in two or three different types of affiliations/activities; primary and repeat migrants, as hypothesized, had lower levels of involvement. Overall, for this age group, primary and repeat migrants had lower levels of involvement, as expected. Consistent with our previous findings, a disproportional number of those affiliated or otherwise active are members of synagogues or temples. For example, of the 30 percent of primary migrants with only one type of involvement, two-thirds were members of synagogues/temples, compared to the 7 percent who belonged to other organizations only, and the little more than 1 percent who participated in Jewish volunteer work.

For both those age 45–64 and 65 years and over, the comparisons must be restricted to nonmigrants, early migrants, and repeat migrants. For both age groups, the nonmigrants have the highest levels of involvement and repeat migrants far lower ones, differences that are similar in direction to those of the youngest group but greater in magnitude. For the middle-aged group, as for the youngest, the early migrants clearly fall intermediary, but for the aged they closely resemble the nonmigrants, suggesting fuller integration among the aged. Thus, while varying in degree, the patterns for all age groups point to a fairly clear association between duration of residence and frequency of movement on the one hand and involvement in the community on the other.

The differences noted for past migration extend to expected future movement (table 6.17). For the total adults and for those age 18–44, the likelihood of a move in the next three years varies inversely with the level of involvement in the community. The pattern is illustrated by the data for the total population. Almost one-third of those who were not at all involved in the community anticipated that a move was very likely. This declines to only 11 percent of those involved in three types of affiliations/activities. While the exact extent of difference varied, the same basic pattern characterized those age 18–44: 43 percent of those not at all

Table 6.16
Aggregate Involvement in Jewish Organizations, Synagogue/Temple, and Jewish Volunteer Activity, by Type of Migration and Age: Core Jews (U.S.-Born Only)

Migration Status	Level of Involvement				
	None	*One Only*	*Two*	*All Three*	*Total Percent*
		Total Adults			
Nonmigrant	50.1	25.4	14.3	10.1	100.0
Early Migrant	56.1	22.5	13.1	8.2	100.0
Primary Migrant	64.9	27.1	4.8	3.1	100.0
Repeat Migrant	66.4	21.9	4.8	7.0	100.0
Return Migrant	57.7	32.8	9.6	—	100.0
		18–44 Years			
Nonmigrant	56.7	22.7	12.8	7.8	100.0
Early Migrant	62.4	20.8	10.1	6.7	100.0
Primary Migrant	66.8	29.9	2.7	0.6	100.0
Repeat Migrant	66.5	24.3	2.8	6.5	100.0
Return Migrant	54.3	35.4	10.3	—	100.0
		45–64 Years			
Nonmigrant	40.3	28.2	15.5	15.9	100.0
Early Migrant	55.2	22.8	11.0	10.9	100.0
Primary Migrant	*	*	*	*	*
Repeat Migrant	67.7	15.3	4.7	12.3	100.0
Return Migrant	*	*	*	*	*
		65 Years and Over			
Nonmigrant	41.4	31.5	18.0	9.0	100.0
Early Migrant	43.6	26.0	21.8	8.6	100.0
Primary Migrant	*	*	*	*	*
Repeat Migrant	62.4	11.5	26.0	—	100.0
Return Migrant	*	*	*	*	*

*Fewer than 10 unweighted cases.

Table 6.17
Likelihood of Move in Next Three Years by Aggregate Involvement in
Jewish Organizations, Synagogue/Temple, and Jewish Volunteer
Activity, by Age: Core Jews

Level of Involvement	Likelihood of Move			Total Percent
	Not Likely	Somewhat Likely	Very Likely	
Total Adults				
None	46.5	22.2	31.3	100.0
One Only	57.0	20.7	22.3	100.0
Two	61.1	20.5	18.4	100.0
All Three	69.7	18.9	11.4	100.0
18–44 Years				
None	33.2	23.9	42.8	100.0
One Only	37.7	27.7	34.6	100.0
Two	46.9	27.0	26.1	100.0
All Three	58.8	25.8	15.3	100.0
45–64 Years				
None	61.9	24.7	13.5	100.0
One Only	75.5	14.9	9.6	100.0
Two	73.1	15.0	11.9	100.0
All Three	77.3	14.8	7.9	100.0
65 Years and Over				
None	82.4	10.8	6.8	100.0
One Only	87.5	8.5	4.0	100.0
Two	75.3	14.2	10.5	100.0
All Three	82.1	9.0	8.9	100.0

involved compared to only 15 percent of those most involved
reported a move in the next three years to be very likely. For the
middle-aged, more of those not at all involved also expressed a
greater expectation to move compared to more active groups, but
the differentials among the more active community participants
covered a narrow range and were mixed in direction.

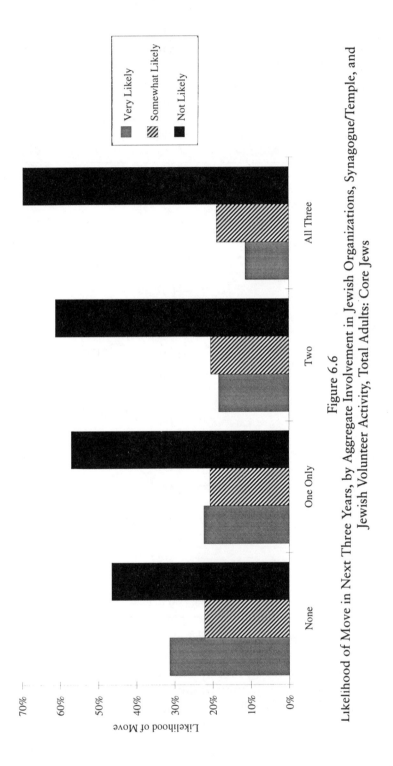

Figure 6.6

Likelihood of Move in Next Three Years, by Aggregate Involvement in Jewish Organizations, Synagogue/Temple, and Jewish Volunteer Activity, Total Adults: Core Jews

For the elderly, the pattern was even more mixed, and the highest expectation for future mobility characterized those engaged in two types of affiliations/activities. Here, as for some of the earlier assessed relations, migration associated with retirement appears to bear a different relation to affiliation and volunteer activity. Elderly persons expecting to move in conjunction with retirement may also plan to transfer memberships and to be active in volunteer groups in their community of destination, so involvement at origin does not act as a deterrent to mobility.

With the exceptions noted, the differences between intensity of involvement in the Jewish community and expected mobility reinforce the differentials noted for the recent migration experience. Together, these patterns point to considerably lower levels of involvement in the community of the more mobile segment, especially those under age 45. They suggest that migration, either as a selective process or through disrupting the usual linkages of individuals and families to the community's organized structure, is associated with lesser integration of migrants into the Jewish community. To the extent that involvement in Jewish organizations, synagogues/temples, and volunteer activities provides channels for reinforcing Jewish identity and oportunities for developing new networks of Jewish ties, the complete absence or low levels of such involvement associated with migration may well contribute to the weakening of other forms of Jewish identity among younger segments of the mobile population.

Jewish/Non-Jewish Involvement Compared

In considerations of membership and voluntarism patterns, research has shown that those who are involved in Jewish organizations and activities are also most likely to be involved in non-Jewish ones (A.Goldstein, 1990). Conversely, inactivity cuts across Jewish/secular lines. Apparently, active secular involvement is not used as a substitute for Jewish activites; the two seem to complement each other. Whether such a pattern holds for migrants as well as natives, and whether the lower levels of involvement documented by the preceding analyses obtain when membership and voluntarism in Jewish and non-Jewish activities are considered jointly, is the focus of the ensuing discussion.

The data from NJPS-1990 for total adults (table 6.18) suggest that the level of no memberships at all is directly related to migra-

Table 6.18

Memberships in Jewish and Non-Jewish Organizations, by Five-Year Migration Status and Age:
Core Jews

Migration Status	Neither Jewish nor Non-Jewish Organizations	Jewish Organizations Only	Non-Jewish Organizations Only	Both Jewish and Non-Jewish Organizations	Total Percent
Total Adults					
Nonmigrant	36.5	12.4	32.7	18.4	100.0
Intrastate	41.2	8.3	39.1	11.4	100.0
Interstate	47.5	6.2	34.4	11.8	100.0
International	64.3	5.5	17.5	12.6	100.0
18–44 Years					
Nonmigrant	38.9	8.7	37.8	14.7	100.0
Intrastate	46.4	7.5	36.1	10.1	100.0
Interstate	49.1	7.4	34.9	8.6	100.0
International	72.5	6.8	5.1	15.6	100.0

45–64 Years

Nonmigrant	34.3	11.8	33.4	20.5	100.0
Intrastate	12.9	14.2	59.5	13.5	100.0
Interstate	31.5	—	46.1	22.4	100.0
International	*	*	*	*	*

65 Years and Over

Nonmigrant	34.0	20.7	22.1	23.2	100.0
Intrastate	18.4	10.1	45.3	26.3	100.0
Interstate	56.9	5.1	11.0	27.0	100.0
International	*	*	*	*	*

*Fewer than 10 unweighted cases.

tion status, rising from 36 percent for nonmigrants to 48 percent for interstate migrants and 64 percent for international migrants. Conversely, belonging to both Jewish and non-Jewish organizations is highest for nonmigrants, but shows little variation by type of migration. More important from the point of view of the Jewish community, membership in non-Jewish organizations seems little affected by migration status, whereas membership in Jewish organizations is clearly affected: Nonmigrants have almost twice the level of affiliation in Jewish organizations as do interstate migrants, but these two migrant status groups differ minimally in non-Jewish memberships.

In general, these patterns are replicated among the 18–44 age group. For the two older groups, the patterns are not as clear and often reversed. For example, total nonmembership is exceptionally low for the intrastate migrants in these two age groups, when compared either to the younger cohort or to other migration status groups in the same age cohorts. Yet membership in both Jewish and secular organizations is highest among the interstate migrants in these age groups. The data thus suggest that many factors other than migration status impinge on the particular combination of memberships in Jewish and non-Jewish organizations, including career development, family life cycle stage, and geographic availability of organizations.

When patterns for voluntarism in Jewish and non-Jewish activities are considered jointly (table 6.19), similar conclusions can be drawn. For all adults, as well as for those age 18–44, nonvoluntarism is more characteristic of migrants than nonmigrants. Being active in only Jewish volunteer activities is particularly sensitive to migration status, declining from 11 percent of the nonmigrants to only 3 percent of the interstate migrants for all adults, with similar differences for those age 18–44. Being active in only non-Jewish activities or volunteering in both sectors does not appear to be directly related to migration status. These mixed patterns appear in every age group.

International migrants are an exception. Not surprisingly, in view of previous findings, they have much higher levels of participation in Jewish volunteer activities than any other migration status group and are less likely to be involved in non-Jewish activites. The many special organizations focussing on and dealing with new Americans in which the newcomers themselves become active participants makes this pattern quite understandable.

Table 6.19
Volunteer Work in Jewish and Non-Jewish Activity, by Five-Year
Migration Status and Age:
Core Jews

Migration Status	Volunteer Activity				
	Not Active in Jewish or Non-Jewish	Active in Jewish Only	Active in Non-Jewish Only	Active in Both Jewish and Non-Jewish	Total Percent
Total Adults					
Nonmigrant	48.9	10.8	31.6	8.7	100.0
Intrastate	49.2	5.4	38.9	6.5	100.0
Interstate	53.5	2.9	35.4	8.2	100.0
International	42.4	28.6	22.1	6.9	100.0
18–44 Years					
Nonmigrant	45.1	9.1	36.2	9.6	100.0
Intrastate	48.0	5.2	40.2	6.6	100.0
Interstate	53.1	2.8	37.4	6.7	100.0
International	45.3	26.3	19.8	8.6	100.0
45–64 Years					
Nonmigrant	45.7	12.0	33.6	8.6	100.0
Intrastate	41.6	7.5	42.1	8.7	100.0
Interstate	44.5	1.2	38.6	15.7	100.0
International	*	*	*	*	*
65 Years and Over					
Nonmigrant	59.9	12.7	20.2	7.2	100.0
Intrastate	78.9	4.7	14.7	1.8	100.0
Interstate	71.1	6.4	10.8	11.7	100.0
International	*	*	*	*	*

*Fewer than 10 unweighted cases.

Overall, when nonmigrants and interstate migrants are compared, several differentials emerge. For both membership in organizations and participation in volunteer activities, nonmigrants are generally more involved than interstate migrants. Of those involved, the nonmigrants have a higher level of being active in Jewish groups; by contrast, involvement in non-Jewish groups varies minimally and is less consistent across age groups. Longer-distance movement therefore appears to be associated with a lower level of involvement in the Jewish community, but it makes little difference for involvement in the non-Jewish community.

PHILANTHROPY

Philanthropic giving serves as another index of commitment to the larger community and to identity as a Jew (Rimor and Tobin, 1991; Kosmin and Ritterband, 1991). To the extent that migrants are less integrated into the community, we can expect their level of giving to charitable causes to be lower than that of nonmigrants. Full testing of such a hypothesis requires a clear distinction between donations to local and to national or regional causes. Unfortunately, NJPS-1990 did not seek such distinctions in its questions, except for separate measurement of contributions to Federation/United Jewish Appeal (UJA). To the extent that donations to this specific fundraising effort are locally oriented, it may serve as a better indicator of the links between migration and philanthropic giving than contributions to Jewish causes generally.

The survey did collect separate information on donations to Jewish and non-Jewish (secular) causes. More frequent giving to secular than to Jewish causes may indicate weaker commitments to the Jewish community. The question on donations in the past year to philanthropies, charities, causes, and organizations was asked of all respondents but referred to contributions made by them or other members of their household. It excluded membership dues or fees.

Recent Migration and Giving

Just half of all respondents reported not making any contribution to a Jewish cause during 1989 (table 6.20). This varied by migration status. More of the nonmigrants were givers (54 percent) than of those who moved into the community after 1985. Only 33 percent of those moving within the state gave to a Jewish cause, as did 38 percent of the interstate migrants. About 41 percent of the international migrants reported making Jewish contributions.

Philanthropic giving tends to vary directly with age. Only 39 percent of the respondents under age 45 made contributions to

Table 6.20
Percentage Making Charitable Contributions, by Five-Year
Migration Status, by Age:
Core Jews

	Age Group			
Migration Status	18–44 Years	45–64 Years	65 Years and Over	Total
Percentage Contributing to Any Jewish Cause				
Nonmigrant	42.8	57.1	73.6	54.0
Intrastate	29.9	57.7	31.2	32.6
Interstate	35.4	33.8	77.6	38.4
International	26.7	*	*	40.6
Total	39.1	56.1	72.2	49.5
Percentage Contributing to Federation/UJA				
Nonmigrant	26.2	46.4	62.6	40.6
Intrastate	15.1	37.9	51.7	19.5
Interstate	21.0	26.2	66.4	24.8
International	8.6	*	*	19.9
Total	23.2	44.8	62.4	36.1
Percentage Contributing to Any Secular Cause				
Nonmigrant	62.4	72.9	66.7	66.3
Intrastate	61.4	75.8	57.3	62.6
Interstate	60.4	68.6	47.2	60.3
International	45.2	*	*	43.8
Total	61.7	72.6	65.6	65.0

*Fewer than 10 unweighted cases.

Jewish causes, compared to 56 percent of those between ages 45 and 64, and almost three quarters of the aged. However, within each age group, migration status was associated with substantial differentials, although these were not always consistent in magnitude or direction.

In the youngest group, the percentage of donors is lower for each migrant category than for nonmigrants, but the lowest differential is between the nonmigrants and the interstate migrants. For those age 45–64, nonmigrants and intrastate migrants are quite similar; about 57 percent of both groups gave to Jewish causes. By contrast, only 34 percent of the interstate migrants were donors.

Among the aged, the interstate migrants have the highest level of giving, almost matched by the nonmigrants; the intrastate migrants have the lowest proportion of donors. Perhaps those older persons who move interstate for retirement are wealthier and continue to donate to causes regardless of location, in contrast to middle-aged migrants who move for other reasons. Such an assumption is supported by the high proportion of elderly interstate migrants who donate $500 and over (data not in table). The data by age therefore only partially corroborate the thesis that migrants are characterized by lower proportions of philanthropic givers because they are not as integrated into their new community. It is true of those under age 65, but not of the aged. In part, the mixed pattern may reflect the inability, as for organization memberships, to isolate local from national/regional donations.

The availability of separate information on contributions to Federation/UJA allows limited attention to the extent of local philanthropy, if we assume that for most givers such donations are made through the local federation rather than to the national office. The pattern of such contributions closely parallels those noted for donations to Jewish causes as a whole. For the total adult population, as well as for those in each age group, the proportion of donors is lower for intrastate migrants than for nonmigrants. Interstate migrants also have a smaller proportion of donors than the nonmigrants, except among the aged. For the youngest group, more interstate migrants than intrastate movers are donors. Among both groups under age 65, fewer movers than nonmigrants contributed to Federation/UJA, suggesting that migration is associated with lower levels of community integration. For the aged, interstate transfer of residence evidently does

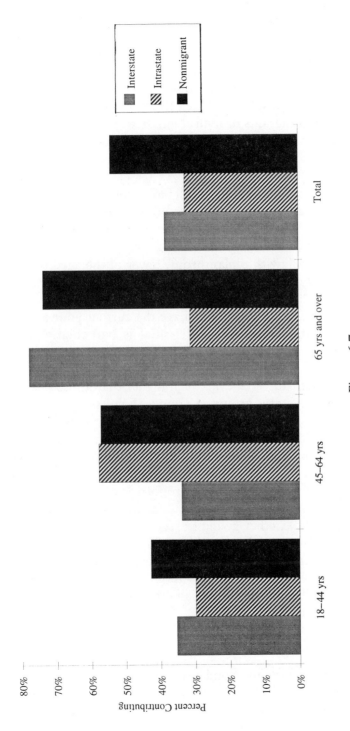

Figure 6.7

Percentage Contributing to Any Jewish Cause, by Five-Year Migration Status, by Age: Core Jews

not disrupt the high levels of giving characterizing this segment of the population.

While the differences for giving to secular charities are less sharp, the patterns are generally more consistent. The percentages making donations are also higher than for Jewish causes. For the adult population as a whole, as well as for each of the three age subdivisions, nonmigrants have the highest level of charitable giving and interstate migrants the lowest among internal migrants. The differences are not, however, especially large, except for the elderly.

For all adults, for example, while 66 percent of nonmigrants gave to secular causes, this declines to 60 percent of the interstate migrants. As was true of donations to Jewish causes, the youngest age group reported the lowest levels of giving.

In contrast to Jewish philanthropy, fewer of the aged than of the middle aged are givers to secular causes. This difference suggests that in earlier years this cohort may not have integrated as fully into the larger community as have the current younger segments of the population. The differential is particularly sharp among the migrant subcategories of the aged population. For example, over half of the elderly interstate migrants did not donate to secular causes, a level much higher than those of comparable migration status groups in younger cohorts.

Overall, these data point to quite different patterns of giving to Jewish and secular charities among the different age segments of the population. Nonetheless, a pattern of lesser participation in charitable giving by migrant households emerges, with interstate migrants tending to have the lowest proportion of givers. This pattern is more often the case for secular contributions than for Jewish philanthropy. Whether giving to secular causes is more likely to be disrupted by migration or whether loyalties to Jewish causes are sufficiently strong to withstand the negative effects of changes in residence cannot be ascertained without more detailed information on the specific contributions and on how they compare with the before-migration situation.

Duration of Residence and Philanthropy

In his assessment of the relation between geographic mobility and philanthropic giving, Cohen (1983:104–107) found that contributions were less frequent among the residentially mobile than among their more mobile counterparts. However, control for an array of background variables suggested that the disruption effect persisted only for up to five years; thereafter, patterns of giving showed little differentiation by duration of residence. Only one-third of those who had lived in the Boston area less than five years gave at least $50 to Jewish philanthropic causes other than to synagogues compared to 40 percent or more of those living in the area five years or more.

The NJPS-1990 data allow assessment of the impact of duration of residence on philanthropic giving, as they did for other indicators of Jewish identity, through use of the migrant typology introduced earlier. Again, migration is measured by change in state of residence. The results (table 6.21) point to a migration effect, but one that is attenuated by longer residence and other factors.

Among all adult interstate migrants, 55 percent of the nonmigrants and half of the early movers gave to Jewish causes, compared to only 38 percent of the primary migrants, suggesting that with longer residence migrant patterns of philanthropic giving are similar to those of the nonmigrants. Although lower percentages of repeat and return migrants than nonmigrants and early movers made donations to Jewish causes, the higher percentage of givers among repeat migrants suggests that disruptions associated with frequency of move do not necessarily lead to reduced participation in philanthropy. Contrary to expectations, such an effect was only evident for the return migrants, whose level of giving was far below all other groups. Whether these general patterns hold for the different age cohorts needs to be examined, since levels of giving vary considerably by age.

The data for the youngest age group suggest that the age composition of the various migrant types may account for some of the differentials noted for the total adult population. As among total adults, among those age 18–44, fewer of both the primary and the early migrants than of the nonmigrants reported charitable giving to Jewish causes, but the differentials had narrowed, possibly because the younger early migrants, on average, had shorter duration of residence because of their age. In contrast to the adults as a whole, the younger repeat migrants had the highest level of giving. As for the total adults, the lowest level of giving characterized the return movers. Perhaps the return migrants were disproportionally persons who had been less successful in their previous

Table 6.21
Percentage Making Charitable Contributions, by Type of
Migration and Age:
Core Jews

	Age Group			
Migration Type	18–44 Years	45–64 Years	65 Years and Over	Total
Percentage Contributing to Any Jewish Cause				
Nonmigrant	42.8	67.4	76.6	54.5
Early Migrant	38.6	52.1	71.6	50.0
Primary Migrant	35.6	*	*	37.5
Repeat Migrant	45.5	34.0	56.0	44.6
Return Migrant	17.9	*	*	20.0
Percentage Contributing to Federation/UJA				
Nonmigrant	25.1	50.3	49.4	35.5
Early Migrant	19.6	40.7	68.9	36.8
Primary Migrant	19.7	*	*	21.0
Repeat Migrant	25.4	25.7	55.5	27.6
Return Migrant	14.5	*	*	16.9
Percentage Contributing to Any Secular Cause				
Nonmigrant	65.3	76.2	72.9	69.3
Early Migrant	65.3	77.0	68.9	69.1
Primary Migrant	57.2	*	*	59.4
Repeat Migrant	72.0	84.1	26.7	70.9
Return Migrant	50.6	*	*	52.0

*Fewer than 10 unweighted cases.

locations, and were therefore less likely to be able to make charitable contributions.

The pattern changes for the middle-aged. The proportion of givers among the early migrants was sharply lower than among the nonmigrants, and that of the repeat migrants is only half as high as of the nonmigrants. For the aged, however, early migrants more closely resemble the nonmigrants even while the repeat migrants have a substantially lower level of givers. The mixed pattern for the aged group and the limited number of cases in some categories precludes any clear conclusion about the impact of duration of residence and frequency of movement on philanthropic behavior. More often than not, fewer migrants are givers, and repeat and especially return migrants include the fewest contributors. The exceptions suggest, however, that other factors not encompassed by the analysis also affect philanthropic behavior. The fact that the information on giving refers to the household as a whole and not just to the respondent, coupled with the problems stemming from the lack of information on strictly local donations, precludes a finer assessment. Contributions to Federation/UJA, as noted earlier, is an exception that may be more sensitive to local integration.

Levels of Federation/UJA giving in relation to type of migration basically replicate the patterns noted for contributions to all Jewish causes. This is true of the adult population as a whole and of the 18–44 and 45–64 age groups. The only noticeable difference is the much higher proportion of elderly early migrants who contributed to Federation/UJA compared to nonmigrants, and the fact that the elderly repeat migrants also had a higher percentage of donors than nonmigrants. As suggested earlier, older interstate migrants, many of whom move in conjunction with retirement, may belong to higher-than-average income status groups who are more likely to make contributions than are either elderly nonmigrants or younger migrants. For the younger groups, migration, except for repeat movement among those age 18–44, is associated with lower proportions of charitable givers. Whether this reflects the effect of disruption or selection cannot be ascertained in the absence of fuller information.

Do the same patterns hold for giving to secular causes? The evidence is even more mixed. Between 52 percent and 71 percent of all adults who migrated donated to secular causes, but for both early migrants and repeat migrants the proportion differed minimally from that of the nonmigrants. Fewer of the primary migrants and still fewer of the return migrants were donors, a pattern similar to but less sharp than that characterizing contributors to Jewish causes.

As for contributions to Jewish causes, among those in the youngest age group, repeat migrants had the highest proportion of donors to secular causes, and the return migrants had the lowest proportion. Early migrants and nonmigrants had almost equal percentages, suggesting that, unlike the patterns for Jewish causes, with longer duration of residence, migration has less impact on contributions among the younger segment of the population. For the middle-aged and the elderly, there are minimal differences between the early migrants and the nonmigrants for contributions to secular causes. Like the youngest group, middle-aged repeat migrants included a comparatively high percentage of donors to secular causes, well above the proportions giving to Jewish causes. Most exceptional is the very low percentage of elderly repeat migrants who gave to secular charities.

Overall, then, while giving to both Jewish and secular causes is affected by duration of residence and frequency of move with longer residence mitigating the impact of migration, the relation appears clearer for Jewish giving. The same seems true for the impact of frequency of migration. As for other indicators of integration in which participation in Jewish and non-Jewish activities can be compared, these data suggest that migrant Jews are more fully integrated into the non-Jewish spheres of activities than into the Jewish ones. Whether this reflects the characteristics of the migrants or of the institutional structure of the Jewish and the larger community warrants further exploration.

The Impact of Expected Mobility

Analyses of the relation between migration on the one hand and organizational memberships, synagogues/temple affiliation, and volunteer activities have all shown the important impact of expected future mobility on levels of involvement. Given the high percentage of the Jewish population who anticipate such movement, the relation takes on great relevance for local communities and pertains to philanthropic giving as well. Again, the impact of mobility can be expected to be greatest if most donations are to local groups. This may be particularly true if newcomers are not fully integrated into the local community and, as a result, have a lower probability of being contacted in fundraising campaigns. On the other hand, the ties of mobile persons and households to the general Jewish community may also be weaker than those of more stable households, so that even contributions directed at national/international causes may be affected.

For the adult population as a whole and for both the young and the middle-aged segments, anticipated mobility is clearly related to the level of philanthropic giving to Jewish causes (table 6.22). Whereas 57 percent of all those adults envisaging no likelihood of moving within three years reported giving to Jewish charities, only 42 percent of those who thought a move somewhat likely, and even fewer (38 percent) of those who thought a move very likely, reported such contributions. Evidently, anticipation of a move is associated with a complex of factors, including possibly a history of prior mobility, which results in lowered commitment to making donations to the community.

A similar pattern characterizes the younger segment of the community, compounding the overall lower level of giving characterizing this age group. Compared to the nearly half (46 percent) of the not-likely-to-move who gave to Jewish charities, only 39 percent of the somewhat likely movers and 34 percent of the highly likely ones did so. In fact, the latter group had the lowest

Table 6.22
Percentage Making Charitable Contributions, by
Likelihood of Future Move, by Age:
Core Jews

| | Age Group | | | |
| | *18–44* | *45–64* | *65 Years* | |
Likelihood of Move	*Years*	*Years*	*and Over*	*Total*
Percentage Contributing to Any Jewish Cause				
Very Likely	34.5	49.2	76.6	38.2
Somewhat Likely	38.6	46.2	63.2	42.5
Not Likely	45.7	59.4	71.1	57.1
Percentage Contributing to Federation/UJA				
Very Likely	15.0	36.0	69.4	20.2
Somewhat Likely	25.1	35.2	60.3	30.5
Not Likely	29.7	47.6	60.2	44.0
Percentage Contributing to Any Secular Cause				
Very Likely	57.0	57.2	63.4	57.3
Somewhat Likely	60.5	72.8	74.1	64.6
Not Likely	68.3	74.5	66.5	69.6

level of giving of all subcategories of the population controlled by age and anticipated mobility status. Among the middle-aged, too, possible mobility was associated with lower levels of giving, although the difference between the somewhat likely and the very likely movers was reversed in direction.

Regardless of prospective mobility, the aged consistently gave more often to Jewish causes (63–77 percent) than either of the younger groups, and the level of giving did not vary directly with mobility expectations. Evidently, older persons have developed overall high levels of giving so that prospective mobility does not detract from their continuation. It may also reflect the particular nature of the charities to which funds are given. If the commitment is more heavily to national and international causes, the particular location of residence may be less relevant than the cause itself. Also, to the extent that in the immediate past the elderly had been more stable than younger persons, the aged may have developed stronger ties both to the community and to specific charitable causes. The different pattern characterizing the aged lends weight to the important way in which mobility may affect the attitudes and behavior of younger persons with respect to Jewish philanthropy.

We can also try to isolate the impact of likelihood of future movement on contributions to local Jewish causes by focussing on donations to Federation/UJA. Consistent with the earlier evidence on total contributions to Jewish causes, far more of those who do not expect to migrate reported donations to Federation/UJA than did those who considered a move in the next three years very likely. Again, this pattern is true of both those age 18–44 and those age 45–64, but especially of the younger group. For the aged, those who thought a move very likely were characterized by the higher donor rate. As suggested before, this reversal among the aged may reflect the association between retirement migration and economic status. For the others, weaker links to the community, judged by expected geographic mobility, are clearly linked to lower levels of participation in local philanthropic activities, indicated by Federation/UJA contributions.

The way prospective mobility affects charitable giving is evidently not unique to Jewish causes. When assessed in relation to donations to secular causes, those who anticipate a move in the next three years are less likely to make charitable contributions. Whereas 70 percent of all adults who did not expect to move made such contributions, only 65 percent of the somewhat likely movers and 57 percent of the very likely ones did so. Virtually the same patterns characterized the young and the middle-aged. Only among the aged was the pattern irregular and the difference between the not-likely and the very-likely groups minimal. The absence of a clear and sharp pattern in giving to secular causes among the aged parallels the absence of a pattern for Jewish giving. The reasons may be somewhat similar, although the cross-cohort levels of overall giving suggest that the aged are not unique in having high levels of giving to secular causes.

RELATIONS BETWEEN COMMUNITY INVOLVEMENT AND MOBILITY

It has been our thesis that migrants, especially those with shorter duration of residence in a given community, are less likely to be involved in its formal organizational structure than nonmigrants. This thesis rests on the assumption that migration is selective of persons who are least involved at place of origin and replicate this pattern in their new location, or that migration is disruptive of community ties. Both effects are, of course, possible and may work in conjunction with each other. The NJPS-1990 data do not allow full testing of these relations due to the absence of information on organizational involvement before migration. We have, however, explored the relations between migration and involvement by examining organizational memberships, synagogue/temple affiliations, voluntarism, and philanthropic giving at the time of the 1990 survey. Our findings suggest that migration is associated with lower levels of involvement, but that the effect varies by age and is not always strong.

Jewish organizational membership was generally at a low level for all segments of the core Jewish population; only about one-third indicated that they belonged to any Jewish organization. Low levels were particularly characteristic of the younger segments of the population, while greater proportions of the elderly reported memberships. Among all groups, although the differences were often quite small, migration was associated with lower membership levels in Jewish organizations. This was especially true when duration of residence and possible future mobility were taken into account. The relation was least pronounced, however, among the elderly. In part, the lack of a stronger relation between membership and mobility may be due to the substantial number of Jewish organizations that are national rather than only local, so that membership can easily be maintained despite moves to a different community.

These patterns are different from those characterizing membership in non-Jewish organizations. Non-Jewish memberships are generally higher—about half of all core Jews report such memberships—and less affected by mobility. Apparently, quite different forces operate to stimulate memberships in Jewish and non-Jewish organizations. These may be related to the national character of some organizations, so that membership is not location-specific; to the larger number of non-Jewish organizations; or to the greater ability of non-Jewish organizations to locate newcomers to a community and draw them into a network of belonging. Since organization membership is often stimulated by friendship networks, if Jews move disproportionally to non-Jewish neighborhoods, they may more easily learn about non-Jewish organizations than about Jewish ones. Learning about the latter may require a concerted effort on the part of new arrivals and a strong desire to be involved in Jewish organizations, even without prior personal contacts. Thus, while migration deters individuals from joining Jewish organizations, it does not affect non-Jewish organizational connections as much.

Much more clearly location-specific is membership in synagogues/temples. Again, affiliation levels are generally quite low, with about one-third of the core Jewish population reporting that their households held such memberships. But because of the local nature of synagogue/temple affiliation, it is much more closely linked to migration than organizational membership. Longer duration of residence clearly is associated with higher levels of affiliation and, conversely, repeated mobility lowers affiliation rates. The likelihood of future moves is particularly associated with lower affiliation levels.

The strong relation between synagogue/temple membership and migration suggests that migration may be especially disruptive of such involvement. When membership involves dues and other, sometimes substantial, financial assessments (like building pledges), households may be slow in making such a commitment. They may not make it at all if they anticipate moving again in a relatively short time. On the other hand, movers may be selective of persons who are least likely to belong to a synagogue/temple; the nonmigrants would then disproportionally include persons with strong proclivities to belong and with deep roots in particular locations and institutions.

One form of community involvement that involves little financial outlay but that is quite location-specific is voluntarism. As was true of organizational membership, levels of voluntarism in Jewish activities are lower (only one in five volunteer) than in non-Jewish ones (two in five). And again, compared to volunteering in non-Jewish activities, voluntarism in Jewish activities is more sensitive to migration, with migrants having lower levels of involvement than nonmigrants. The relation is most pronounced among the youngest age group, especially if they also anticipate moving in the near future.

The final aspect of involvement assessed in this chapter was philanthropic giving. On the whole, nonmigrants had the highest rates of giving, both to any Jewish causes and to UJA/Federation specifically. Type of move had no regular relation to giving, but those who anticipated future mobility were less likely to give than those who expected to remain stable. Again, younger core Jews had lower rates of contributing than the middle-aged or elderly, and proportions giving to non-Jewish charities was higher among the two younger groups.

When all three forms of community involvement—organizational membership, synagogue/temple affiliation, and voluntarism—are considered jointly for the core Jewish population as a whole, lack of involvement is clearly associated with greater mobility, and involvment in several types of activity is more likely for nonmigrants. The exception is international migrants, who have a relatively high level of participation, but are most likely to be involved in just one type of Jewish activity—most usually organization membership or volunteer activity. This is not surprising, since immigrants often participate in activities designed either to assist them in adjusting to their new situation or to help newer arrivals.

When the core population is divided by age, different patterns emerge. Not only does the youngest group have the lowest levels of involvement, their involvment is also most sensitive to migration, especially anticipated mobility. Their low levels of involvement with the organized Jewish community may thus be compounded by this group's migration patterns. Being at a stage in their life cycle when career opportunities and family formation often involve geographic mobility increases the tendency not to belong or be active in organized Jewish communal life.

A quite different pattern characterizes the elderly. In general, they report higher levels of memberships and voluntarism than younger groups. Moreover, they tend to be less affected by mobility, especially moves that are interstate, even though migration continues to be related to somewhat lower levels of involvement. Several factors may be operating. The aged may be continuing patterns of involvement from earlier periods in their life cycle, and they may have stronger attachments to the Jewish community. Since many are retired, they may have more time to devote to community involvement and greater affluence with which to do so. For those who move, mobility may be to areas of high Jewish density, like Florida, where involvement is relatively easy to continue because of the large number and proximity of Jewish organizations and institutions.

Given the high levels of mobility among Jewish Americans, we can anticipate that migration will continue to be associated with lower involvement with and integration into the formal Jewish community as explored in this chapter. Whether this relationship, which is clearest for the younger segments of the population, will become attenuated as they age and come to resemble the less-pronounced differentials of the elderly needs to be monitored. The overall patterns of lower levels of involvement and continuing high levels of mobility present a major challenge to the community's leadership to draw younger Jews into the orbit of the formal organizational structure of the community and to maintain that contact as they move between communities.

CHAPTER 7

Informal Networks

Jewish identity is manifested and reinforced not only by participation in the formal, organized life of the community and through observance of a variety of ritual practices. Having Jewish friends and living in Jewish neighborhoods also indicate the strength of individual identification with the larger Jewish community and provide a mechanism for maintaining that identity. Indeed, some scholars would maintain that as the more traditional indices of identity and cohesion diminish in importance, the informal ones represented by choice of friends and neighborhood assume complementary or substitute roles as mechanisms for insuring continuity in individual identity and maintaining ties to the larger Jewish community (Goldscheider, 1986:165–169).

Our analysis turns now to use of the data collected by the 1990 National Jewish Population Survey (NJPS-1990) on a variety of indicators of the Jewish milieu in which the respondents operate. The analysis addresses the basic thesis that, assuming such informal connections with other Jews positively reinforce Jewish identity, the migrants' connections will be fewer/weaker. This relation is hypothesized because (1) the very act of moving disrupts local ties and (2) those with weaker/fewer ties will feel less bound to a given location and therefore more prone to migrate when appropriate opportunities arise elsewhere. Without longitudinal information on friends and neighborhood before and after the move, the data from NJPS-1990 do not allow testing which of these specific alternatives offers the best explanation or whether both may hold.

FRIENDSHIP PATTERNS

Attention turns first to friendship patterns. NJPS-1990 asked: "Among the people you consider your closest friends, would you say that: none, few, some, most, all or almost all are Jewish?" No distinction was made in terms of the specific locations of friends who might be living in the new or in earlier places of residence. Moreover, to measure exactly the extent of friendship with other Jews, we would need to know the Jewish density levels of the areas within which such friendships have been developed. Within these limitations, the data point to a clear association between migration and friendship patterns with other Jews.

For most adult Jews, friendship networks include other Jews. For as many as one-third, most or all of their close friends were Jewish and for an additional 54 percent, few or some were. Only 8 percent reported having no Jewish friends. Migration status, however, has a negative association with the extent of Jewish friendship networks.

Whereas four in ten of all nonmigrants reported that all or most of their friends were Jewish, only one in five of the intrastate movers and one-quarter of the interstate migrants did so (table 7.1). That only a small minority (less than 10 percent) of any migrant status group had no Jewish friends at all points to the important role that such interaction with other Jews has for most Jews. For those who have moved internationally, friendship with other Jews occurs even more often than among nonmigrants, probably reflecting the much narrower social circles in which recent immigrants operate—disproportionally with fellow immigrants. An extensive Jewish friendship network may also reflect the conditions from which the immigrants came: many had been involved in heavily encapsulated Jewish networks in their countries of origin (e.g., the Soviet Union, Iran, Israel) and tended to replicate these once they settled in the United States.

As for many variables, age is also clearly related to Jewish friendship levels. The percentage of Jewish friends rises consistently and sharply with rising age: just over one-quarter of the respondents under age 45 reported most or all of their friends to be Jewish, compared to 45 percent of the middle-aged, and 60 percent of the oldest group. Whether the younger group will increase their proportion of Jewish friends as they move into later stages of the life cycle is a major question that requires monitoring in the years ahead. Yet even within the youngest age group, the strong level of Jewish friendships of the internal migrants is substantially below that of the nonmigrants and the international movers. Again, a small minority of each group reported no Jewish friends, but for this age group more of the nonmigrants did so.

Table 7.1
Number of Jewish Friends, by Five-Year Migration Status, by Age: Core Jews

| Migration Status | Number of Jewish Friends | | | Total Percent |
	None	Few or Some	Most or All	
Total Adults				
Nonmigrant	7.6	49.7	42.7	100.0
Intrastate	9.7	68.9	21.4	100.0
Interstate	9.4	66.4	24.2	100.0
International	*	42.3	57.7	100.0
Total	8.0	53.8	38.2	100.0
18–44 Years				
Nonmigrant	11.2	57.9	30.9	100.0
Intrastate	9.8	71.4	18.8	100.0
Interstate	7.1	72.5	20.4	100.0
International	*	45.3	54.7	100.0
Total	10.2	62.3	27.4	100.0
45–64 Years				
Nonmigrant	5.0	47.9	47.1	100.0
Intrastate	3.7	56.3	40.0	100.0
Interstate	25.6	53.8	20.6	100.0
International	*	*	*	*
Total	6.1	48.5	45.3	100.0
65 Years and Over				
Nonmigrant	3.2	35.3	61.5	100.0
Intrastate	19.3	56.3	24.5	100.0
Interstate	7.2	25.7	67.1	100.0
International	*	*	*	*
Total	3.9	35.6	60.5	100.0

*Fewer than 10 unweighted cases.

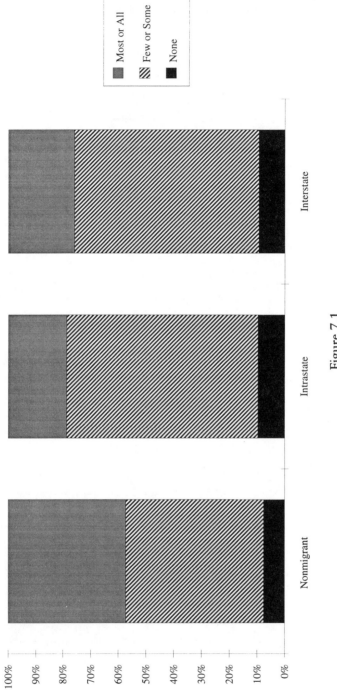

Figure 7.1
Number of Jewish Friends, by Five-Year Migration Status: Core Jews

Middle-aged nonmigrants also had more Jewish friends than did migrants, but the difference was especially pronounced for those moving interstate. Only one in five of the interstate migrants reported all or most friends as Jewish compared to almost half of the nonmigrants; a much higher proportion of the interstate migrants also reported no Jewish friends.

The aged deviate from the patterns characterizing the two younger age groups. The level of friendship with other Jews is highest for the interstate migrants and not too different from that of the nonmigrants; by contrast, intrastate migrants reported the lowest level, and considerably more reported no Jewish friends. Since the elderly, as a total group, have more intensive Jewish friendship patterns and many move primarily in connection with retirement or changed housing arrangements, more are likely to choose to move to areas of high Jewish population concentration, locations that sometimes even include friends from the same origin, as in movement from New York to retirement communities in Florida. In the postretirement period, they can therefore easily continue to have and choose friends who are Jewish. This is especially possible when, in their new places of residence, such as Florida, they live in condominiums where a high proportion of residents are Jewish (cf. Sheskin, 1992).

For short-distance movers, the situation is evidently different and results in fewer Jewish friends. More may move to be nearer their children who themselves, judging by the data for younger cohorts, have fewer Jewish friends and perhaps live in less densely Jewish areas. Others may be moving into assisted-care facilities that encompass few other Jews.

Overall, therefore, these data for adults as a whole and for the two youngest age cohorts indicate that some forms of migration are associated with lower levels of friendship with other Jews. Interstate migration, in particular, is strongly related to a lower level of Jewish friends for those under age 65. Whether migration operates as cause or effect cannot be ascertained here. The exception provided by the aged is, as noted, understandable in the context of their generally high levels of friendship with other Jews and the choice of destination of those who move interstate. Thus, to the extent that high levels of friendship and interaction with other Jews constitute a mechanism for reinforcing or encouraging Jewish identity and closer ties to the larger community, these data suggest that migration may contribute to weakening of such ties and, in turn, of Jewish identity generally.

We can expect that friendship patterns may change with length of residence in a given place. Nonmigrants may well have formed friendships as children, and these are likely to have been with other Jewish children who shared educational and informal activites under Jewish auspices. Among in-migrants, by contrast, initial friendships may be formed with coworkers and colleagues, while longer duration may lead to the development of ties to people met through organizational affiliations and informal activities. We can generate an approximation of the effect of duration of residence on friendship patterns by again turning to the migrant typology.

The findings (table 7.2) generally corroborate those based simply on the five-year migration status data. Those who have spent substantial periods of time in the community—as either nonmigrants, return migrants, or early migrants (resident more than five years)—have a much higher percentage of friends who are mostly Jewish than do the primary migrants and repeat movers. For example, among nonmigrants, four of ten indicated that most of their friends were Jewish; this was true of only two of ten of the primary migrants and the repeat movers.

Generally similar patterns characterize the various age groups. Particularly noteworthy is the high percentage (28 percent) among repeat migrants age 45–64 who report no Jewish friends. While friendships are often formed through informal associations, the reverse is also true—those whose friends have connections to the Jewish organized community are also most likely to make the same kind of connections themselves (cf. A. Goldstein, 1990). Special outreach to newcomers to a community may therefore be especially effective in helping them to establish ties to the Jewish community.

Having Jewish friends in a given location may not only be influenced by past migration and the recency of arrival in the new community; it may also be related to whether an individual anticipates leaving a given location, since strong social ties may hinder out-migration. To test such a thesis fully requires information on both the extent and intensity of friendship patterns with Jews and non-Jews in the specific location. Moreover, insofar as decisions to move are usually family decisions, we should have information for all members of the family rather than just the respondent. Unfor-

Table 7.2
Number of Jewish Friends, by Type of Migration and Age: Core Jews

Migration Type	None	Few or Some	Most or All	Total Percent
		Number of Jewish Friends		
	Total Adults			
Nonmigrant	7.7	51.6	40.7	100.0
Early Migrant	9.5	56.5	34.0	100.0
Primary Migrant	13.0	68.3	18.7	100.0
Repeat Migrant	9.7	70.1	20.2	100.0
Return Migrant	5.6	61.5	32.8	100.0
	18–44 Years			
Nonmigrant	10.1	61.1	28.8	100.0
Early Migrant	13.4	64.8	21.7	100.0
Primary Migrant	9.3	74.3	16.5	100.0
Repeat Migrant	6.8	74.5	18.7	100.0
Return Migrant	6.1	60.8	33.1	100.0
	45–64 Years			
Nonmigrant	4.1	41.6	54.4	100.0
Early Migrant	6.3	55.9	37.7	100.0
Primary Migrant	*	*	*	*
Repeat Migrant	28.3	53.3	18.3	100.0
Return Migrant	*	*	*	*
	65 Years and Over			
Nonmigrant	4.4	33.5	62.0	100.0
Early Migrant	4.5	40.0	55.5	100.0
Primary Migrant	*	*	*	*
Repeat Migrant	—	58.2	41.8	100.0
Return Migrant	*	*	*	*

*Fewer than 10 unweighted cases.

tunately, the omnibus nature of NJPS-1990 precluded collection of such detailed information. Within these limits, the evidence points to a considerable association between the level of Jewish friendships and the likelihood of a future move.

Having a high proportion of Jews among one's friends seems to serve as a deterrent to mobility or at least is associated with factors that impede migration (table 7.3). Whereas only 44 percent of those who reported no Jews among their circle of friends indicated that it was unlikely that they would move in the next three years, this rose to almost half of those reporting a few or some friends and to 61 percent of those reporting that most or all of

Table 7.3
Likelihood of Moving in Next Three Years,
by Number of Jewish Friends and Age:
Core Jews

	Likelihood of Move			
Number of Jewish Friends	Not Likely	Somewhat Likely	Very Likely	Total Percent
Total Adults				
None	43.5	29.1	27.4	100.0
Few or Some	49.3	21.1	29.6	100.0
Most or All	60.8	19.8	19.4	100.0
18–44 Years				
None	37.9	27.6	34.5	100.0
Few or Some	36.5	25.0	38.5	100.0
Most or All	40.2	24.8	35.0	100.0
45–64 Years				
None	59.2	33.8	7.0	100.0
Few or Some	71.4	16.3	12.3	100.0
Most or All	66.4	21.6	12.1	100.0
65 Years and Over				
None	58.6	32.2	9.2	100.0
Few or Some	81.6	8.0	10.4	100.0
Most or All	84.7	10.9	4.4	100.0

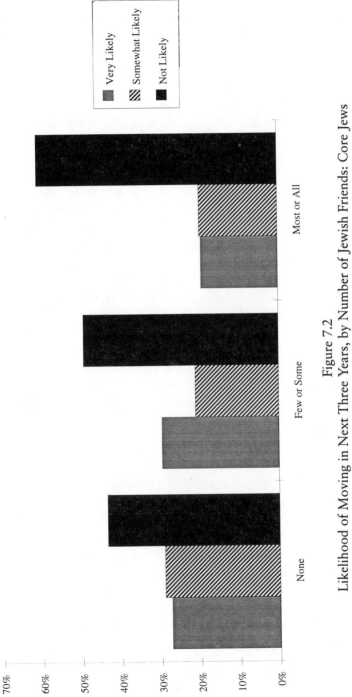

Figure 7.2

Likelihood of Moving in Next Three Years, by Number of Jewish Friends: Core Jews

their friends were Jewish. The opposite is also true. That is, only 19 percent of those who indicated that most of their friends were Jewish thought a move was very likely, but this was true of 27–30 percent of those with lower levels of Jewish friendship.

The patterns are less sharp for the younger age group than for the middle-aged and the elderly. Forty percent of those under 45 years who had mostly Jewish friends did not intend to move in the next three years, as did only slightly fewer of those with some or no Jewish friends. This finding suggests that for this younger age cohort, the extent of Jewish friendship networks does not significantly influence decisions on whether to move. By contrast, among those age 45–64 and among the aged, the proportions expecting no move were considerably higher among those reporting most or some of their friends were Jewish than among those who said none of their friends were Jews. That the differential was less sharp among younger people may mean that Jewish friendship networks have less significance in their daily living and therefore play less crucial roles in influencing mobility decisions. That far fewer younger core Jews also reported most of their friends as being Jewish fits such an interpretation. Whether their friendship patterns will change as they age or whether this lower level of interaction with other Jews and corresponding lesser influence of Jewish ties on mobility decisions will persist as they move on in the life cycle remains to be determined in future research.

NEIGHBORHOOD COMPOSITION

For a good part of their history in the United States, Jews have adjusted to life in America through residential clustering. Doing so made it easier for them to maintain their Jewish identity through close, daily interaction with other Jews and easy access to facilities essential for a Jewish life style, observance of religious rituals, and the religious/cultural education of their children. Residential clustering reflected not only preference for a Jewish neighborhood, but also reactions to anti-Semitism and restrictive property covenants which made it impossible for Jews to live in certain neighborhoods.

As earlier chapters have documented, since the 1950s Jews have become redistributed across the regions of the United States, and within and between metropolitan and nonmetropolitan areas.

Jewish residential clustering in a limited number of urban neighborhoods has declined as Jews have participated in the general suburbanization movement. Jewish neighborhoods in central city areas and in older suburbs have declined in importance as newer outer suburbs have grown. The population within given metropolitan areas has thereby become more dispersed just as the national population has been dispersing. Concurrently, in many metropolitan areas Jewish institutions have relocated at widely separated points; in areas of low Jewish density, they may either not exist or be quite distant.

Although residential clustering will undoubtedly continue in metropolitan areas, especially those with large Jewish populations (cf. Horowitz, 1993:4–16, 1994), the continuing dispersal and integration of the Jewish population into the larger American community that seem likely to continue may weaken the ties that deeper residential roots have facilitated in the past and could encourage in the future. New York, with its preeminent concentration of Jewish Americans, is a case in point.

Between 1981 and 1991, the Jewish population of the New York area declined by 13.5 percent (Horowitz, 1993, 1994). The city itself decreased almost 8 percent, but suburban Nassau, Suffolk, and Westchester counties declined by 25.5 percent. Whereas in 1981 Jews constituted 16 percent of the city's total population and 15 percent of the suburban population, by 1991 their percentage of the city and suburban populations had declined to 14 and 11 percent, respectively. These differential rates of change resulted in an increase in the percentage of Jews living in New York City proper from 67 percent to 72 percent of the eight-county area covered by the survey and a decline in the suburban segment from 33 percent to 28 percent. This suburban decline, while partly accounted for by an increase in Manhattan's Jewish population, probably stems in larger measure from movement to outer suburbs (not covered in the New York survey) in Connecticut, New Jersey, and elsewhere in New York State. But part of the exodus is undoubtedly also explained by the overall Jewish population shifts noted in this monograph, from the Northeast to the West and South.

NJPS-1990 shows that the indicators of Jewish identity in the newer regions of growth tend to be weaker than in the more established areas. We have previously suggested that this differential may be caused by selective migration: persons moving from the older, more established areas of Jewish settlement to newer ones may be selective of those who are more marginal to the Jewish community and less strongly identified as Jews; in so doing, they leave behind the more committed and affiliated. While not giving attention to the characteristics of out-migrants between 1981 and 1991, the findings from the New York survey lend support to this thesis.

Between 1981 and 1991, the New York area showed a sharp decline in number of Jews, but had generally low rates of change in levels of observance and organizational affiliation, and it had intermarriage levels below the national average. These patterns suggest the exodus of relatively more of the less observant and less affiliated, leaving behind those who have higher levels of identity. They thereby serve to maintain the greater religiosity and Jewish density of the New York milieu. At the same time, those who have moved out of the area seem likely to lose the reinforcing influences on their Jewishness that living in the Jewishly dense New York area provides, unless they move to other areas of similar density.

Such speculation is reinforced by the NJPS-1990 data showing that far more secular Jews (82 percent) reported living in neighborhoods that were not at all Jewish than did Jews by religion (57 percent). By contrast, only 3 percent of the secular Jews, but 11 percent of the Jews by religion reported living in very Jewish neighborhoods. Similarly, 56 percent of the secular Jews, but only 23 percent of the Jews by religion reported that residence in a Jewish neighborhood was not of any importance to them; a majority of the Jews by religion (53 percent), but only one in five of the secular Jews, considered Jewish density very important.

A different assessment of the relation between Jewish density of neighborhood and Jewish identity has been made by Goldscheider (1986) using data from the 1965 and 1975 Boston surveys. He concluded that those living in areas of low Jewish density were not alienated from other Jews, nor did they seem to be living on the edge of ethnic survival. Based on this finding, he suggests that we need to look beyond neighborhoods to identify the social ties and networks which link Jews to each other and to their community (Goldscheider, 1986:40). If Goldscheider is correct, then the thesis that greater dispersion will contribute to a weakening of Jewish identity may prove wrong.

Population movement is a major factor in the changing Jewish composition of neighborhoods. The history of cities is replete with evidence of changing patterns of residential distribution, concentration, and segregation of different racial and ethnic groups as the members of the different groups integrate more fully into the larger society. (See, for example, Lieberson and Waters, 1988; White, 1987.) Our ability is very limited, however, to assess the changing ecological patterns of Jews on a community level, because of the virtually complete absence of studies that encompass more than a short time period or contain adequate data on small areas within the community.

A unique data source for addressing this issue are the Boston surveys of 1965, 1975, and 1985. They clearly document that over the course of twenty years, the overall population trend has been one of continued movement outward and westward (Israel, 1987:78–84). In 1965, almost 60 percent of the Boston area's Jews lived in Boston proper, Newton, and Brookline. By 1985, only 45 percent lived in these three communities, and Boston itself was no longer among the three communities with the highest percentage of Jews; areas to the west had become more popular.

Studies of the Jewish population of Rhode Island allow similar assessment of change over time. In Greater Providence, 88 percent of the 1951 population was located in the central cities of Providence/Pawtucket, but by 1987, this had declined to only 46 percent (Goldscheider and Goldstein, 1988). The decline would have been even sharper if data had been available in 1951 for towns in Rhode Island outside the Greater Providence area. Just between 1970 and 1987, on a statewide basis, the proportion of Jewish households in the central cities declined from 57 percent to 42 percent, and the dispersal of the population encompassed a much wider range of census tracts, pointing to much lower levels of Jewish density than in earlier decades.

The modest growth of the Columbus Jewish community between its 1969 and 1990 surveys has also been accompanied by population dispersion (Mott and Mott, 1994). As Mott and Mott note, the "spreading," while not yet fully defined, undoubtedly has important implications for the future of the community, especially regarding the location of and ability to provide religious, social, and communal services. For many communities, the effect of residential clustering on Jewish identity therefore constitutes a key concern. In this monograph, our interest lies in how such density relates to migration.

In NJPS-1990, two questions were asked to allow some evaluation of the impact of residential clustering on Jewish identity: Respondents were asked to describe the Jewish character of their neighborhood on a scale ranging from very Jewish to not Jewish at all; and they were asked the importance they attached to their neighborhood having a Jewish character. Both questions are obviously subjective, tapping the perceptions of the respondents and not necessarily objective conditions. Data from Boston, however, provide some confidence for use of these questions. For the Boston area, Goldscheider (1986:32) was able to compare perceptions of Jewish neighborhood density with measures of census-tract Jewish residential concentration. The high correlation (+.69) between the two suggests that perceptions serve as a reasonably good proxy for actual density.

The NJPS-1990 data therefore lend themselves to assessment of whether geographically mobile individuals live in more or less densely Jewish neighborhoods than do nonmobile persons. To the extent that the mobile persons moved within the previous five years, the data may provide some insights into whether they are more or less likely to choose Jewish neighborhoods than would be expected on the basis of the residential patterns of the nonmobile. Unfortunately, the absence of information on the Jewish density of previous residential neighborhoods precludes a more direct evaluation of whether movers settle in areas of more or less Jewish character.

Jewish Character of Neighborhood

Although the NJPS-1990 survey asked respondents to indicate whether their neighborhood was very, somewhat, little, or not at all Jewish, for this evaluation we have combined the last two categories. Because change in residences within the same community may also affect the character of the neighborhood of residence, this analysis treats movers within the same community as a separate category, whereas in most other analyses they are combined with the nonmigrants.

In contrast to data for metropolitan centers with large Jewish populations (cf. Goldscheider, 1986:33), NJPS-1990 found that a large percentage of core Jews lived in areas of comparatively low Jewish density. Sixty-two percent reported their neighborhood was not at all or only a little Jewish. This high proportion reflects the continuing dispersion of the Jewish population and especially the fact that NJPS-1990 encompassed the full range of communities in the United States—those with large and small Jewish populations, and those in regions of high and low Jewish concentration. Only 9 percent considered their neighborhood to be very Jewish. That core Jews tend to live in more Jewish neighborhoods is suggested by the fact that 84 percent of those in the NJPS-1990 sample who were not currently Jewish but were Jews by background lived in neighborhoods with little or no Jewish character, and only 1 percent in neighborhoods which were very Jewish.

Within the core population, the data for all adult Jews point to a strong relation between the Jewish character of the neighborhood and mobility status (table 7.4). About six in ten of those Jews who were living in the same house in 1990 as in 1985, or who had moved only within their community, resided in a neighborhood with little or no Jewish character. By contrast, just over three-quarters of those migrating to their new community of residence from elsewhere in the same state or from another state settled in neighborhoods that they regarded as having little Jewish character. Evidently, either by choice or because places of destination had few Jews living in them, migration was associated with settlement in largely non-Jewish neighborhoods.

These patterns are complemented by the percentage living in neighborhoods classified as very Jewish. Whereas 11 percent of the nonmobile Jews and 9 percent of those moving only within their community lived in such areas, only 3 percent of the interstate migrants did so. Clearly, for adults as a whole, movement into a new community is associated more frequently than for non-movers or local movers with residence in neighborhoods that have little Jewish character. To the extent that neighborhood plays any role in integrating individuals into the larger Jewish community, such a pattern suggests that integration may be impeded for migrants. Of course, if migrants are not concerned about integration into the local Jewish community, the very choice of destination and neighborhood may facilitate integration into the larger non-Jewish community. Some insight into preferences will be possible through later assessment of the importance of the Jewish character of the neighborhood to the respondent.

The general pattern of mobility differentials with respect to the Jewish character of the neighborhood is also generally characteristic of the young and middle-aged segments of the population.

More of those who had migrated to the communities from elsewhere lived in neighborhoods which were either not or little Jewish in character. Interstate migrants had the lowest proportion living in very Jewish neighborhoods.

Table 7.4
Jewish Composition of Neighborhood, by Five-Year Migration
Status, by Age:
Core Jews

| Migration Status | Jewish Composition of Neighborhood | | | |
	Not or Little Jewish	Somewhat Jewish	Very Jewish	Total Percent
Total Adults				
Nonmobile	56.9	32.2	10.9	100.0
Local Mover	60.7	30.0	9.4	100.0
Intrastate	78.0	14.8	7.2	100.0
Interstate	76.2	20.0	3.8	100.0
International	82.5	17.5	*	100.0
Total	62.4	28.3	9.3	100.0
18–44 Years				
Nonmobile	66.4	24.3	9.3	100.0
Local Mover	63.1	29.1	7.8	100.0
Intrastate	78.4	14.9	6.7	100.0
Interstate	76.7	20.6	2.6	100.0
International	86.1	13.9	*	100.0
Total	69.3	23.4	7.3	100.0
45–64 Years				
Nonmobile	54.6	36.3	9.0	100.0
Local Mover	65.9	28.0	6.1	100.0
Intrastate	71.5	15.7	12.9	100.0
Interstate	88.6	10.0	1.4	100.0
International	*	*	*	*
Total	58.9	32.8	8.3	100.0

Table 7.4 (continued)

Migration Status	Jewish Composition of Neighborhood			
	Not or Little Jewish	Somewhat Jewish	Very Jewish	Total Percent
65 Years and Over				
Nonmobile	47.8	37.8	14.4	100.0
Local Mover	30.5	41.0	28.6	100.0
Intrastate	82.8	12.1	5.1	100.0
Interstate	50.8	28.3	20.8	100.0
International	*	*	*	*
Total	47.5	36.9	15.6	100.0

The aged again provide an exception to the general pattern. Overall, as expected, many more reside in somewhat or very Jewish neighborhoods. However, migration status does not seem to have a clear relation to type of neighborhood. The high of 83 percent of elderly intrastate migrants living in areas described as having little or no Jewish character contrasts sharply with the approximately half of both the nonmobile and the interstate migrants who did so. The intrastate movers may have shifted to homes with or near children in the same state or to facilities for the aged, both of which may involve moves to less Jewish areas. In contrast, those moving locally and interstate may both be choosing areas with greater Jewish character to be near Jewish friends and facilities. This is consistent with the relation between migration and proportion of Jewish friends identified earlier.

Our assessment of residence patterns suggested that migrants tend to locate more often than nonmigrants in neighborhoods that have little if any Jewish character, and that this is especially true of persons who had moved interstate during the previous five years. In turn, this suggests that, either by choice or as a result of mobility, such longer-distance migrants are residentially more marginal to the Jewish community. In response to economic and other incentives or a disinterest in living in a Jewish neighborhood, they may intentionally live in neighborhoods that have lower Jewish density, or they may move to areas which have few Jews in them.

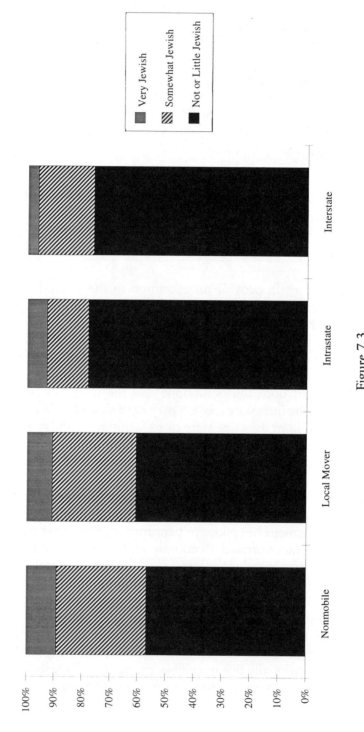

Figure 7.3

Jewish Composition of Neighborhood, by Five-Year Migration Status: Core Jews

Flowing out of the observed inverse relation between movement and perceived density of Jewish neighborhood is whether this relation changes with longer duration of residence in a given location. To explore this relation, we again turn to use of the migration typology (table 7.5). As noted earlier, the majority of Jews live in neighborhoods that have little or no Jewish character, regardless of migration type. Nonetheless, nonmigrants and those who arrived at their place of residence more than five years before the survey are more likely than other migrants to live in neighborhoods that are very Jewish. By contrast, less than 2 percent of either return or repeat migrants do so. The primary and repeat migrants have the highest proportion living in neighborhoods with little or no Jewish character.

This pattern is generally replicated by the 18–44 age group, although not as strongly; the primary migrants, who arrived within five years of the survey, include the highest percentage (85 percent) living in neighborhoods with little or no Jewish character. Again, the pattern for the aged is distinctive. Repeat migrants, like the elderly nonmigrants, tend to live in areas with more Jewish character than younger Jews, and an especially high percentage (18 percent) of the elderly repeat migrants report living in neighborhoods that are very Jewish. As has been pointed out before, this clustering may well be related to retirement migration to areas of high Jewish density, like parts of Florida, or to other housing arrangements for the elderly.

As we have done with other indicators of Jewish identity, we can assess whether the type of neighborhood in which mobile persons settle is meaningfully associated with the likelihood of future mobility. If strong Jewish identity leads individuals to want to live in neighborhoods which are more Jewish in character, we would expect that once in such areas, they would be reluctant to leave. The data support such an expectation (table 7.6). Half of those living in neighborhoods with little or no Jewish character thought a move in the next three years was not at all likely, and 28 percent considered a move to be very likely. This pattern changes as the neighborhood becomes more Jewish in character. Among those living in very Jewish areas, 63 percent reported a move was not likely, and only 16 percent deemed a move very likely. Clearly, for the adult population as a whole, the less Jewish the neighborhood, the more frequently do its residents report that they are very likely to leave it.

Table 7.5
Jewish Composition of Neighborhood, by Type of Migration and Age: Core Jews

Migrant Type	Jewish Composition of Neighborhood			
	Not or Little Jewish	Somewhat Jewish	Very Jewish	Total Percent
Total Adults				
Nonmigrant	57.1	32.8	10.1	100.0
Early Migrant	66.3	25.0	8.7	100.0
Primary Migrant	83.9	10.1	6.0	100.0
Repeat Migrant	75.7	22.9	1.4	100.0
Return Migrant	62.8	35.3	1.9	100.0
18–44 Years				
Nonmigrant	65.3	26.1	8.6	100.0
Early Migrant	72.2	21.2	6.6	100.0
Primary Migrant	84.7	9.3	6.0	100.0
Repeat Migrant	75.5	24.5	—	100.0
Return Migrant	61.5	38.5	—	100.0
45–64 Years				
Nonmigrant	46.2	41.7	12.1	100.0
Early Migrant	68.1	26.9	5.0	100.0
Primary Migrant	*	*	*	*
Repeat Migrant	95.2	4.8	—	100.0
Return Migrant	*	*	*	*
65 Years and Over				
Nonmigrant	44.8	43.4	11.8	100.0
Early Migrant	52.1	31.1	16.8	100.0
Primary Migrant	*	*	*	*
Repeat Migrant	45.2	36.7	18.1	100.0
Return Migrant	*	*	*	*

*Fewer than 10 unweighted cases.

Table 7.6
Likelihood of Moving in Next Three Years,
by Jewish Composition of Neighborhood, by Age:
Core Jews

Jewish Composition of Neighborhood	Not Likely	Somewhat Likely	Very Likely	Total Percent
		Likelihood of Move		
	Total Adults			
Not or Little Jewish	50.4	21.4	28.2	100.0
Somewhat Jewish	56.8	20.5	22.7	100.0
Very Jewish	62.7	21.5	15.8	100.0
	18–44 Years			
Not or Little Jewish	38.0	23.9	38.1	100.0
Somewhat Jewish	37.5	26.8	35.7	100.0
Very Jewish	41.0	31.9	27.1	100.0
	45–64 Years			
Not or Little Jewish	68.4	19.3	12.3	100.0
Somewhat Jewish	68.4	18.8	12.8	100.0
Very Jewish	66.9	25.3	7.9	100.0
	65 Years and Over			
Not or Little Jewish	80.2	13.0	6.8	100.0
Somewhat Jewish	81.4	10.5	8.1	100.0
Very Jewish	91.5	3.6	4.9	100.0

The patterns differ some by age. For the young and middle-aged, the proportions expecting no move varies minimally in relation to Jewish density of neighborhood. For the aged, however, a group characterized overall by the highest level of stability, living in very Jewish neighborhoods heightens stability. Evidently, living in a Jewish area and wanting to stay there is especially strong among the elderly. Many elderly lived in heavily Jewish neighborhoods when growing up and moved into mixed neighborhoods at later stages of the life cycle; more of them may therefore prefer to spend their later years in a more Jewish environment. By contrast, in all three age groups, but especially among the young and the middle-aged, those living in very Jewish neighborhoods are least likely to report an anticipated move as very likely. Whether the weaker relation between the Jewishness of neighborhood and the likelihood of future mobility of the two younger cohorts means that they attach less significance to living among Jews remains to be tested. It may change as these persons age. The similarity in pattern to the relation between Jewish friendship patterns and migration suggests that the same underlying processes related to Jewish networks are operating to affect future mobility.

Importance of Jewish Neighborhood

Additional insights into these relations can be gained from examination of information collected on the attitudes of respondents toward the importance they place on the Jewish character of their neighborhood. For the core Jewish sample as a whole, just under half considered the Jewish character of the neighborhood to be very important; yet as many as 30 percent held the view that it was not important (table 7.7). In general, the range of differentials among the various mobility status groups was quite narrow, although international migrants attached greater importance to the matter, probably because they prefer to live close to fellow eth-

Table 7.7
Importance of Jewish Character of Neighborhood,
by Five-Year Migration Status, by Age:
Core Jews

	Jewish Character of Neighborhood			
Migration Status	Not Important	Somewhat Important	Very Important	Total Percent
	Total Adults			
Nonmobile	28.0	23.4	48.6	100.0
Local Move	31.8	20.0	48.2	100.0
Intrastate	34.9	27.6	37.5	100.0
Interstate	27.6	30.3	42.0	100.0
International	23.7	10.4	65.9	100.0
Total	29.6	23.8	46.6	100.0

Table 7.7 *(continued)*

Migration Status	Jewish Character of Neighborhood			
	Not Important	Somewhat Important	Very Important	Total Percent
18–44 Years				
Nonmobile	28.8	26.1	45.1	100.0
Local Move	32.2	22.5	45.3	100.0
Intrastate	32.9	28.3	38.8	100.0
Interstate	25.2	32.1	42.6	100.0
International	27.6	12.1	60.3	100.0
Total	29.9	26.2	43.9	100.0
45–64 Years				
Nonmobile	24.9	26.9	48.1	100.0
Local Move	36.1	14.0	49.9	100.0
Intrastate	39.2	26.8	34.0	100.0
Interstate	40.7	26.5	32.9	100.0
International	*	*	*	*
Total	28.2	24.9	47.0	100.0
65 Years and Over				
Nonmobile	30.4	16.3	53.2	100.0
Local Move	17.8	7.9	74.3	100.0
Intrastate	56.8	19.1	24.2	100.0
Interstate	31.7	18.2	50.1	100.0
International	*	*	*	*
Total	30.3	15.8	53.9	100.0

*Fewer than 10 unweighted cases

nics who are also immigrants. Nonetheless, somewhat fewer of the intrastate movers and, to a lesser extent, the interstate migrants, compared to nonmigrants and local movers, thought the Jewish character of their neighborhood was very important. These small differences are consistent with the thesis that migrants are more marginal to the Jewish community.

The discrepancy between the importance attached to the Jewish character of neighborhood of residence and the actual Jewish composition of neighborhoods in which respondents lived warrants comment. Although almost half of all respondents thought the Jewish character of the neighborhood was very important (varying from 38 percent of intrastate migrants to as many as two-thirds of international movers), a substantial majority (table 7.4) reported their neighborhood as being little Jewish or not Jewish. This suggests that residential integration and assimilation is much more prevalent than the declared preferences of the respondents; the discrepancies between preferences and actual residence are greatest for the intrastate and interstate migrants. These patterns in turn suggest that, while some migrants may integrate because of preference, many may do so because other forces operate in connection with their move, including generally lower Jewish residential density at destination, operation of housing market factors, and lack of familiarity with the new area.

As expected, the importance of the Jewish character of one's neighborhood varies inversely with age. While a similar proportion in each age cohort, about 30 percent, did not attach any importance to the issue, the percentage who considered it very important rose from 44 percent of those under age 45, to 54 percent of the aged. Among the youngest and especially the middle-aged groups, fewer of the intrastate and interstate migrants attached great importance to the matter compared to nonmovers and local movers. For the aged the pattern is very mixed. Half or more of each group, except the intrastate movers, attach great importance to the Jewish character of their neighborhood. As suggested earlier, the deviation among intrastate movers may relate to their changing housing needs because of health concerns or changed family status. If they are moving to areas closer to children or to special housing for the aged, these considerations more than the Jewish character of the neighborhood may take precedence. For those who have migrated interstate, by contrast, the stronger preference for areas with concentration of Jewish populations may also color views about neighborhood composition.

Is the importance attached to the character of the neighborhood meaningfully related to the likelihood of a change in residence in the next three years? Overall, there seems to be little relationship (table 7.8). Among the adult core Jewish population as a whole, quite similar percentages of those who considered the Jewish char-

Table 7.8
Likelihood of Moving in Next Three Years, by Importance of
Jewish Character of Neighborhood, by Age:
Core Jews

Importance of Jewish Neighborhood	Likelihood of Move			
	Not Likely	Somewhat Likely	Very Likely	Total Percent
Total Adults				
Not Important	54.2	18.8	27.0	100.0
Somewhat Important	50.1	24.1	25.8	100.0
Very Important	53.6	21.9	24.5	100.0
18–44 Years				
Not Important	38.8	20.8	40.4	100.0
Somewhat Important	36.4	27.2	36.4	100.0
Very Important	37.6	27.4	35.0	100.0
45–64 Years				
Not Important	70.0	20.0	10.0	100.0
Somewhat Important	74.7	18.3	6.9	100.0
Very Important	63.9	20.6	15.5	100.0
65 Years and Over				
Not Important	83.6	11.4	5.0	100.0
Somewhat Important	73.3	19.2	7.5	100.0
Very Important	83.9	8.6	7.5	100.0

acter of their neighborhood to be very important (24 percent) than
of those who attached no importance to it (27 percent) thought that
a move in the near future was very likely. Moreover, this pattern
stems entirely from the variation characterizing the youngest age
cohort. Among the middle-aged and the aged, the pattern was irregular, with more of those attaching great importance expecting to
move compared to those who were not concerned. Some of this difference may result from compositional changes in current neighborhoods of residence, which would more likely affect older residents who have lived in their areas longer.

OVERVIEW OF JEWISH MILIEU

To assess the joint importance of Jewish friends and Jewish neigh-borhood (both of current residence and importance) a Jewish Milieu Index has been constructed combining all three indicators.[1] Each indicator of the index was given a score of 0 to 2, and the index was constructed to equal the sum of the scores; it has a range of 0 to 6.

Using the Jewish Milieu Index, a multiple classification analysis (MCA) was performed to assess the relation between it and both migration status and likelihood of future mobility. For this analy-sis, nonmigrants and those who moved only within the community were combined into the nonmigrant category. The results generally support the findings of the earlier analyses (table 7.9). With a grand mean score of 3.06 (Model A), nonmigrants score slightly higher and both intra- and interstate migrants score lower; international migrants score the highest of all. The overall significance of migra-tion status on the Jewish Milieu Index is not high. In fact, of all the variables included in the model, only religious identification (not shown in the table) has a strong relation to the index, with those identified as Jews by religion having by far the highest score (3.27) and secular Jews scoring much lower (1.90). When antici-pated future mobility is added in Model B, the averages for the migration status categories remain virtually unchanged, but antic-ipated mobility lowers the average slightly. The relation is not sig-nificant.

These results suggest that having Jewish friends and living in Jewish neighborhoods are more likely to occur if individuals have had time to integrate into the local Jewish community. Longer-dis-tance (interstate) migration especially tends to disrupt these pat-terns. That international migration has the opposite relation is not surprising, since immigrants are much more likely to find their first circle of socialization and adjustment within either their own immigrant community or within the community (in this case prob-ably Jewish) that has sponsored their settlement in the United States.

The multiple classification analysis serves to highlight the complex interplay of factors determining the nature of informal networks. Nonetheless, when considered in conjunction with the findings of the bivariate analyses undertaken earlier, the results again point to the potentially negative association between migra-

Table 7.9
Relation of Five-Year Migration Status and Likelihood of Moving
on Jewish Milieu: A Multiple Classification Analysis:*
Core Jews

	Model A	Model B
Grand Mean	3.06	3.04
Migration Status		
Nonmigrant	3.14	3.14
Intrastate	2.83	2.84
Interstate	2.69	2.67
International	3.48	3.44
Future Move		
Very Likely	—	3.01
Somewhat Likely	—	3.10
Not Likely	—	3.04

*Controlling for age, sex, education, and religious identification.
Note: Jewish Milieu incorporates scores for Number of Jewish Friends; Jewish Character of Neighborhood; and Importance of Jewishness of Neighborhood.

tion and strength of Jewish identity. Whether those who move prefer a less intense Jewish milieu or whether their integration into the informal (as well as formal) Jewish community simply takes a number of years of residence in a given place cannot be determined directly from the NJPS-1990 data. For a combination of reasons, some identified in the MCA analysis, migrants, especially younger ones and those who move interstate, are less likely to report many close Jewish friends and less likely to live in neighborhoods of some Jewish density than is true of those who had not moved in the five years preceding the survey.

Our analyses have thus identified a cluster of variables associated with Jewish identification and involvement in the Jewish community, the strength of which vary by a number of demographic characteristics, including migration status. Younger Jews, especially if they are living alone, have lower levels of involvement, both with the formal community structure and with informal networks. This group is most likely to be geographically mobile and among the most likely to move to areas of low Jewish density. Since migration has been shown to be associated with lower identification levels, the challenge of integrating young Jewish adults into the Jewish community's structure becomes particularly acute. By contrast, the elderly not only have generally higher levels of memberships and more extensive Jewish networks, but for them migration makes little difference. Many move to areas where such intensity of involvement can be continued relatively easily. Nonetheless, for all groups, stability of residence, in terms of previous moves and likely future mobility, is related to higher levels of formal and informal Jewish association.

CHAPTER 8

Jews on the Move:
Implications for American Jewry

Dramatic changes have occurred in the demographics of the Jewish American community over the past half century. Among the most important of these has been the redistribution of the population across the nation. Because of the low Jewish birthrate and virtual zero population growth, migration is now the major dynamic responsible for the growth or decline of many individual communities. Population dispersion and the emergence of a continental Jewish community have serious implications for the national organization of the community, for regional and local institutions, and for individual Jews and their families. The preceding chapters have described some of these changes and explored their relations to Jewish identity and commitment. In this summary chapter, we highlight the major findings, suggest their relevance for the future of American Jewry, and point to possible coping mechanisms.

TOWARD A NATIONAL JEWISH COMMUNITY

From a community heavily concentrated in the Northeast at the beginning of the twentieth century, ensuing decades witnessed the heavy movement of Jews into the Midwest, the South, and the West. In this respect, they closely resembled the general American population. In 1930, after massive immigration from Eastern Europe had stopped, an overwhelming 68 percent of America's Jews were living in the Northeast. This settlement pattern was quite different from that of earlier German Jews, who tended to scatter widely, following other German immigrants. Their settlement in the South and West thus formed the foundations of Jewish communities that became the core of later larger centers of Jewish life (Ritterband, 1986).

The pattern of distribution began to change in the 1950s as Jews emulated their non-Jewish counterparts. Economic considerations, new transportation networks, housing markets, and leisure-time tastes all stimulated movement out of older centers of settlement. The result in 1990 was a Jewish American population more nearly resembling the general population in its distribution pattern across the states. In the process, the South and the West gained large numbers of Jews while the Northeast and the Midwest lost. The patterns of change are continuing, but during 1985–1990, movement out of the Northeast slowed a bit, and the South and the West, with their larger population base, saw an increase in out-migration, even though they continued to have a net gain of population.

The numbers tell the story most dramatically and indicate how many persons were involved in the shifts. Of the 5.5 million core Jews identified by the 1990 National Jewish Population Survey (NJPS-1990), almost 1.4 million had changed their region of residence since birth. The streams of movement out of and into regions were quite unequal. For example, some 839,000 Jews moved out of the Northeast, offset by only 162,000 in-migrants. The result was a loss of almost 677,000 Jews for the Northeast. By contrast, the South gained some 485,000, due to the in-movement of 618,000 Jews and the out-migration of only 133,000. The West also grew substantially, with a net in-flow of 411,000 Jews.

Even if we restrict our attention to the five years preceding the survey, the numbers continue to be striking. Fully 186,000 Jews changed region of residence within this limited time. Again, the flows were uneven and large numbers of movers in one direction were offset by those migrants going in another direction. For example, 49,000 Jews moved to the West, while 31,000 left the region; the net gain in the West of 18,000 gives little indication of how many persons were actually involved.

The impact of so much mobility is felt not only by the communities of origin and destination, but even more so by the many individuals involved. Community ties, as expressed through memberships in organizations and synagogues/temples and ties to family, friends, and neighborhoods, are broken or, at best, disrupted. Old networks are abandoned, and new ones may take many years to establish. Lack of familiarity with new surroundings and a lingering sense of loyalty to old ties may retard new involvements; commitments to new places of residence may be weaker, especially if further mobiity is anticipated. As a result, newcomers are often lost to the formal structure of the Jewish community to which they have moved and may, in fact, turn more to the general community for a sense of belonging. The end result may be weakened ties to the Jewish community, for themselves and perhaps even more for their children.

Even within regions and states, shifting of populations occurred. Central cities, where immigrants had formed cohesive, dense Jewish neighborhoods, became areas of Jewish out-movement, while suburbs became attractive alternative places of residence. Even within suburbs, movement was progressively outward, toward newly built-up areas sometimes called "edge cities" (Elazar, 1993). Some Jews forsook large metropolitan areas altogether and settled in small cities and towns, even while countercurrents saw the demise of Jewish life in numerous small locations throughout the nation.

A recent news account of the situation in Sioux City, Iowa, illustrates the situation. In a pessimistic assessment, Tim Klass (1994) documents the "last stand" of 560 Jews, the remnants of a community that numbered about 3,000 between the two world wars. He indicates that around Iowa a number of once thriving Jewish communities are down to single or double digits. Many have out-migrated, seeking greater opportunities and perhaps more thriving Jewish life elsewhere. Servicing the remnant becomes a major challenge to the larger community, especially given the aging composition of the population left behind.

The challenge that wide dispersion poses has both positive and negative features. On the positive side, Jews living in communities with few co-religionists are often drawn into active involvement because in these places every Jew counts in the survival of the organized Jewish community. Furthermore, even limited migration to areas of previously low Jewish density has provided "transfusions" of Jewishness that have been critical to the maintenance and strengthening of basic institutions and services.

On the negative side, wide dispersion creates great difficulties for the provision of institutions and services necessary for a vital and vibrant Jewish community. The difficulties extend from the broad coverage of federations, to the more narrow range of Jewish community centers and Jewish educational institutions, to the even more local provision of kosher meats and other ritual needs. With the extension of Jewish settlement to the fringes of metropolitan areas, federations designed to encompass given areas are finding it necessary to expand their geographic coverage ever further, into a regional organization (Elazar, 1993).

The Jewish Federation of Los Angeles, for example, dealt with the large geographic area over which its Jewish population was dispersed by establishing area councils to coordinate and administer the campaign in local areas, provide education and leadership development, and plan for new local programs (*RI Herald*, 8 May 1980). While more of the population is thereby covered, the cohesiveness of a geographically more circumscribed federation is lost. Active participation is often limited to those living close to headquarters—the same core who were active before expansion. Jews living on the community's margins are generally marginally involved and marginally served.

Distance is also an important factor in the catchment area of Jewish community centers and, to some extent, of Jewish schools, particularly at the secondary level and above. Few are willing to commute more than a limited distance to take advantage of such facilities. The integrating function that community centers serve therefore remains restricted to a central area. Similarly, few families will volunteer to provide transportation to youngsters to attend Jewish schools more than a circumscribed distance from their homes. Long commutes are especially difficult if teens are involved in extracurricular activities in their general schools. Other services, like kosher butchers, depend on a certain volume of business in order to remain viable. If a population is too spread out, most may forego buying kosher meat or do so only sporadically, not often enough to support a business.

Jews moving to small communities outside metropolitan areas face an even greater sense of isolation from the organized Jewish community. For them, travel to the nearest synagogue/temple or Jewish community center may involve not extra minutes, but extra hours. The Jewish education of children poses a special problem where Jewish density is not great enough to support even a small school. Several attempts have been made to provide networks for Jews scattered over broad geographic areas (e.g., "Serving Isolated Congregations," 1991; *New York Times*, 22 May 1988), but they cannot substitute for the intensity of Jewish life available in more densely populated areas.

Synagogues may be somewhat less affected by dispersion because they may be able to relocate to meet the new geographic configurations (Elazar, 1993). Such a change in venue takes place at considerable cost, however, and in the process members may be lost. Again, the losses are likely to affect particularly those most tenuously affiliated at the previous location.

The very migration process that has helped produce the national community has, through its selective character, helped to ensure the maintenance of often sharp differences among localities. To the extent that migration is a response to various kinds of opportunities, people who move are concentrated disproportionally in certain ages; educational, occupational, and income groups; and marital status categories; they are also likely to be in groups with certain religious-identificational tendencies. The exodus of migrants with selected characteristics from some communities and their settlement in others contributes to the distinctive socioeconomic profiles that communities develop. Thus, the genesis of a "national society" occurs simultaneously with the perpetuation and, in some cases, exacerbation of the unique features of local communities. As a result, both movers and stayers develop familial, social, and economic networks that span the nation. The process is dynamic, with both the national and local communities in continual states of change. From a demographic perspective, we must recognize both the existence of a national community concurrent with distinctive local communities and the fluidity of their composition; the complexity of the situation must be taken into account in planning.

WHO IS MOBILE?

In view of the large numbers of persons involved in the regional redistribution of the Jewish American population, a key question is "Which Jews are moving?" Previous research on individual Jewish communities as well as on other populations found that migration is very often selective. Most likely to move are young persons entering careers and establishing families; older persons may also relocate in connection with retirement. The higher educated and those with high-status occupations are also more likely to move than lower educated, low occupation persons. These findings are particularly relevant for the situation among America's Jews.

A distinctive feature of American Jewry is its very high level of education and its clustering in upper white-collar occupations.

Taken together, these characteristics are particularly conducive to high levels of mobility. Indeed, our analysis (chapter 4) found that, other things being equal, persons with a postgraduate education were three times as likely to move long distances as those with only a college degree. Their mobility may be related to a search for the best possible career opportunities or to their positions with large corporations that require occasional relocation; since many others are self-employed, in professions that allow considerable autonomy in deciding on location (doctors, lawyers, educators), their mobility may be relatively easy and particularly sensitive to local economic conditions. What is perhaps surprising is that, despite the high proportion of Jewish Americans with high levels of education and high-status occupations—characteristics strongly associated with high mobility levels—Jewish mobility rates are very similar to those of the general American population. Apparently, other factors, including considerations having to do with Jewishness, also play an important role in migration decision-making, and these may be conducive to stability.

Closely related to career development is age. Not surprisingly, younger people are more likely to migrate, especially longer distances, than are the middle-aged or elderly. Since such large proportions of young Jewish Americans leave home to attend colleges and universities, further movement in connection with employment is often a logical next step: propensity to move is strongly conditioned by previous mobility. Migration by young adults is also exacerbated by the decline of the family-owned business, which in earlier decades drew children back to their home communities. The result of high mobility among the best and brightest may be to create in some Jewish communities—those with poor economic conditions—a brain drain that can have serious consequences for future leadership and development. In the long run, the exodus of a community's most talented members may also affect fundraising. For other communities—those receiving the in-migrants—mobility may provide new energies and new perspectives to revitalize existing institutions, if newcomers are easily integrated.

The national Jewish community has become very conscious of the migration of elderly Jews to southern Florida and other destinations in sunbelt areas. Yet mobility among the elderly is at a much lower level than among the young, and the relation between migration and indicators of Jewish identification and involvment among the elderly is quite different than for younger segments of the Jewish population. Those elderly who do move are often motivated by place-specific amenities like weather, cultural and recreational facilities, and presence of kin. Others move because of their health.

For the elderly, then, the distance of movement may be closely related to reasons for move: those who move for health-related reasons may tend to relocate not far from their previous home; those involved in retirement migration may move much greater distances. The result may be a reconcentration of elderly in certain locales—certain areas of Florida are, of course, the primary example. The burden this may impose on the local Jewish community may be especially onerous if the in-migrants retain loyalties to previous community of residence and continue their charitable contributions there, or if, as they age, their health deteriorates and they require special services. The problems created by elderly mobility were voiced as early as 1980 by the president of a Florida Jewish community: "The major problem is the identification of new members in the Jewish community; we have requested the assistance of the Northern Federations to help us with this process. We must begin to think in national terms" (*RI Herald*, 8 May 1980).

Also intensifying the relation between age and mobility is marital status. Marriage and the establishment of a household is often associated with migration, especially interstate, for at least one of the partners to the marriage. In a parallel relation, marital dissolution may also lead to mobility, although generally not over long distances. Divorce is also more likely to lead to migration than is widowhood. With rising divorce levels among Jews and higher incidence of widowhood as the population ages, we can expect a continuation of mobility at least at present levels. The single-person households that often result from marital dissolution and subsequent migration may create special challenges and opportunities for the Jewish community if it wishes to retain these individuals as active members.

Another dimension of individual characteristics of particular importance to the Jewish community is religious identification. Through a series of screening questions, NJPS-1990 was able to classify respondents as (1) Jews by religion; (2) secular, or ethnic, Jews; (3) Jews by choice, and (4) a peripheral population that includes persons born/raised Jewish who switched to another religion, adults of Jewish background who were never themselves Jewish, and non-Jews living in households containing one or more persons either currently Jewish or Jewish by background. On the assumption that Jews by religion are more strongly identified as Jews and committed to the Jewish community, their migration pattern vis-à-vis other categories has great relevance for issues of Jewish cohesion and vitality.

The Northeast has in the past and continues in the present to encompass a disproportionate number of Jews by religion, while the Midwest and the West, especially the latter, contain relatively more secular Jews. Migration over the past few decades has mitigated these discrepancies to some extent. Large numbers of Jews by religion left the Northeast to settle in the South and West, so that Jews by religion are now much more dispersed across the nation. Nonetheless, taken as a whole, Jews by religion have been the most residentially stable of all groups, and more likely to move short distances (intrastate) rather than across state boundaries or interregionally.

The infusion of Jews by religion in those areas that are heavily secular can revitalize Jewish life and play an important role in the maintenance of the community. Organized Jewish communities in the South and West have gained strength because of the in-migration of strongly identified Jews. On the other hand, few communities—other than such large cities as New York, Philadelphia, Boston, and Baltimore—have the density of Jewish population to be able to withstand substantial out-migration, especially of their most committed members. For them, the out-migration in particular of Jews by religion may reduce the density necessary for a viable community.

The advanced education, high-status occupations, and changes in marital status of Jews in conjunction enhance the likelihood of migration. Mobility is even more likely among young adults. Since it is these persons who hold the key to the future viability of the Jewish community, both locally and nationally, their high mobility levels may have serious implications. If migration is disruptive of community involvement, and integration into a new community of residence extends over several years, highly mobile Jewish Americans may well be at the margins of the community. Whether such lack of integration is documented by the NJPS-1990 data is the focus of our ensuing discussion.

MIGRATION AND JEWISH IDENTITY/INVOLVEMENT

Theoretical Issues

Integration into a community may be seen as the development of personal social networks that tie an individual to a particular place or group. In this way, an individual can structure a private, meaningful life somewhat apart from the larger, more impersonal, cosmopolitan world. When such a network is disrupted, as migration is likely to do, it takes time to rebuild it in another location, and for some, the network may never be rebuilt at all. Such a perspective on the impact of migration on community involvement presupposes an existing network at place of origin. Persons who move repeatedly may never develop such ties, and for them migration may be a much simplified process.

A different explanation for the marginality of migrants is also possible, however. Those who move may be persons who even at place of origin had only minimal connections with the Jewish community. Migration may be selective of the least involved. In that case, they may not be inclined to become actively integrated into their new Jewish community, and community efforts may have only minor results.

In either case, because the majority of Jewish Americans are strongly desirous of participating in the secular social and cultural life of the wider society, migration may accelerate assimilation. The process is also made easier by the wide acceptance of Jews by the larger society—educationally, occupationally, residentially, and even in marriage. Few areas have a high enough Jewish density to ensure that a newcomer's first contacts will be with other Jews without a concerted effort on the part of the migrant. The greater dispersion of American Jewry across the nation and, in particular, movement to cities and towns or to regions of the country with very few Jews may be especially conducive to assimilation. Thus, even Jews who may have had high levels of religious observance and community participation in their places of origin may adapt to the less intense Jewish life at their destinations.

These perspectives clearly assume that migrants will be less integrated into their communities of destination, that they will have lower levels of Jewish identification, and that their marginality contributes to weakening the continuity of Judaism in the United States. On this basis, we expect that migrants will score lower on a range of indicators of Jewish community involvement, that they will have lower levels of personal religious practices and behavior, and that they will be more likely to be intermarried. We also assume that distance of migration, which we measure in terms of intrastate and interstate movement, will be differentially related to these indicators; to the extent that it contributes to more disruption of family and community ties, long-distance migration is expected to have a stronger association with lowered levels of involvement than short-distance mobility. Finally, because of the potentially disruptive effects of migration, we also assume that persons who have strong ties to their community, in the form of extensive kinship and friendship networks and intensive involvement in the organized life of the community, and who require institutional support for their observance of Judaism (e.g., *mikveh*, kosher meat) will be less mobile than other Jews.

Methodological Issues

The relations between migration and Jewish identity/involvement are obviously very complex, incorporating community factors, personal characteristics, and specifically Jewish background. Moreover, many aspects of Jewish identity and behavior change over time, in tandem with changes in life-cycle status and other changes in the larger society. While NJPS-1990 collected data on many of the relevant variables, most refer only to the time of the survey. We have no way of knowing, therefore, the level of a person's integration into the Jewish community at any time in the past, and specifically not in the period immediately preceding a move. We cannot tell whether those who move were selective of the marginally identified or whether behavior changed because of the move. As a result, we cannot directly determine cause-effect relations; that would require more in-depth, longitudinal data such as are impossible to collect in an omnibus survey like NJPS-1990. Nonetheless, patterns of association can point to the problems that migration may cause for individuals and communities and indicate directions for policy development and for further research.

In our analyses, we defined migration in a variety of ways to measure both distance moved—in terms of intrastate, interstate, and interregional—and duration of residence, by using a migration typology based on residence at three points in time. We also examined the effect of anticipated mobility in the three years after the survey, since the likelihood of future moves may have an important relation to current behavior.

Mobility and Jewish Identity

We turned first to direct indicators of Jewish identity—denominational affiliation, ritual practices, intermarriage, Jewish education, and visits to Israel (chapter 5). We anticipated that the more traditional would be the least mobile because of their greater need for appropriate supportive institutions. This was generally true for some indicators but not for others. The Orthodox were less mobile than the Conservative and Reform; and respondents who adhered to more traditional ritual practices, like *kashrut*, were among the most stable. Presumably, their levels of observance and the concommitant need for a religious community and certain facilities limit their choice of residential locations and make movement somewhat problematic. The elderly are an exception. For them, traditional observance did not hinder migration, probably because so many move to retirement communities in areas of high Jewish density where the necessary facilities are generally and easily available. With the drift away from more traditional to less traditional behavior and away from Orthodox toward Conservative and Reform affiliation, we can expect mobility levels to remain at least at current levels and quite likely to rise.

We also anticipated that, because of its relation to levels of observance, more intensive levels of Jewish education would be associated with greater stability. In fact, because level of Jewish education is highly correlated with level of secular education, this relation was not supported. As we have seen, the more highly educated are the most mobile, and this is often also true for those with the most Jewish education. Any relation between Jewish education and mobility for adults is captured in the differences by denominational affiliation and ritual practice.

For children, especially teens, however, migration is associated with less Jewish education; those in nonmigrant households have higher levels of enrollment than do those who moved. In part, lower enrollment may result from moves to communities where Jewish educational programs are limited and Jewish high school studies of any kind are unavailable. Because of the strong connection between Jewish education beyond Bar/Bat Mitzvah and Jewish identification, the disruption associated with migration is especially serious.

In past decades, intermarriage often occasioned movement away from home community to areas where greater anonymity was possible. Such behavior reflected the opprobrium with which intermarriage was viewed. And our data show that couples who intermarried before 1980 were indeed more mobile than others. These couples present a particular challenge for the community, which must attempt to integrate those at the margins both because of their intermarriage and their migration status. The greater acceptance of intermarriage and its greater prevalence in the 1980s has changed this relation; intermarriage itself no longer seems to stimulate migration at levels higher than for the in-married.

A final indicator of Jewish identification explored with the NJPS-1990 data was visits to Israel. To our surprise, within the generally small overall proportion who had ever visited Israel, long-distance migrants were somewhat more likely to have done so. Perhaps the greater cosmopolitanism associated with moving internally accounts for the inclination to travel internationally as well.

Community Involvement

If our assumptions about the disruptive effect of migration are correct, and integration into a community is achieved only after some period of residence, then Jews who are recent in-migrants will be less involved in their new community's formal structure than those who have lived in the community five years or more. To explore this relation, we examined organizational membership, voluntarism, synagogue/temple affiliation, and philanthropic giving.

Membership in Jewish organizations was generally low, especially among the young, so that differences by whether respondents had moved were quite small. Nonetheless, migrants did show a lower level of membership, less so for the elderly than for the young. Anticipated future moves increased the differences. That the relation was not stronger may be because many of the Jewish organizations are national and membership can be easily transferred from one place to the next. The relation between migration and membership was quite different for non-Jewish organizations. At a generally higher level than Jewish organizational membership, non-Jewish affiliations are not as affected by mobility, although long-distance moves continue to be associated with lower levels of membership.

An interesting exception to these patterns characterizes international migrants. Immigrants are generally more likely to be members of Jewish organizations and less likely to belong to non-Jewish ones. Since many of the Jewish organizations specifically cater to immigrants and are ethnically homogeneous, they serve as an important bridge between country of origin and the American community of destination and can therefore be particularly attractive to immigrants. From the Jewish community's point of view, such organizations can become important catalysts for the integration of persons who have often had only tangential contact with Judaism.

More specifically locally oriented than organizational memberships are volunteer activities. Voluntarism is thus more sensitive to time spent in the community, since it often depends on the establishment of informational and friendship networks. Migrants are less involved in Jewish voluntarism. The relation is especially pronounced among the youngest age group and those who anticipate a move in the next three years. Again, like organizational membership, non-Jewish voluntarism is at higher levels and less affected by migration. The networks leading to involvement in non-Jewish activities apparently become established more easily than the ones related to Jewish voluntarism. Community efforts to promote networks that can easily incorporate newcomers to the community may be instrumental in increasing levels of Jewish voluntarism.

Dependent to some extent on networks and often seen as a prime vehicle for entree into the Jewish community, but also related to religious needs, is synagogue/temple affiliation. At the same time, high membership fees and other assessments may discourage affiliation, especially if the migrants anticipate making another move soon. Since such membership is almost universally local, it becomes a good indicator of involvement in the local Jewish community.

Synagogue/temple affiliation is clearly linked to mobility. Persons with longer duration of residence in the community generally have higher levels of affiliation, and repeat migrants have much lower levels. Yet, because of the association between affiliation and Jewish education for children (especially leading up to Bar/Bat Mitzvah), life-cycle stage is a key variable in determining membership levels. Families with children have consistently higher affiliation rates than single persons or couple-only households. Moreover, once membership has been established—often in connection with the Bar/Bat Mitzvah education of children (cf. Liebman and Cohen, 1990)—it seems to remain at the higher level even after children are in their teen years. Yet even among families with children, migration is associated with somewhat lower levels of affiliation. Anticipated future mobility lowers them much more, at every life-cycle stage.

These findings on synagogue/temple affiliation point to the strong family orientation of these institutions, or at least the perceived view that they are most relevant for families with children, but also to the effect of duration of residence on membership levels. A community's best opportunity to have an impact on both the children and their families may therefore be at the time the children enter school. If the impact is positive, it may help individuals and families to "carry" the Jewish cultural environment with them in subsequent years, even if mobility and/or disaffiliation follow. The high percentage of young Jews who leave home to go to college means that another opportunity for such an impact may arise on campuses through organizations like Hillel and through student peers where Jewish density is high. To what extent these opportunities for maintaining, recreating, or establishing a Jewish environment are used to advantage requires in-depth asssessment.

One final perspective for measuring community involvement is philanthropic giving. Nonmigrants generally were more likely to make contributions to Jewish causes than those who had moved in the past and those who anticipated a move in the future. The proportions giving were lowest among the youngest age groups, who were also likely to have a higher percentage making contributions to non-Jewish causes. A strong contrast is provided by the elderly, among whom the percent of interstate migrants making contributions to Jewish causes is at levels as high or higher than among the nonmigrants, but at much lower levels for giving to non-Jewish causes.

When all forms of involvement in the Jewish community are considered jointly, lack of involvement is clearly associated with greater mobility, and membership/voluntarism is more prevalent among the nonmigrants. At the same time, age is also a critical differentiating characteristic. Young adults have lower levels of involvement than the middle-aged and elderly, and for the young, mobility is related more strongly to even lower levels of involvement. Since younger Jews are the most mobile, and are in the process of career development and family formation, their low participation rates are compounded by a host of factors. They may also be the ones most attuned to the larger society (as indicated, for example, by their relatively high levels of non-Jewish organizational membership and voluntarism) and therefore less likely to affiliate with the Jewish organizational structure. Whether their orientation to the general community and away from the Jewish one at the early stage of their adulthood will carry over into later life remains to be seen. In the meantime, programs designed to draw them into Jewish activities may help to enhance their later identification and to enrich the pool of potential leaders for the Jewish community.

The elderly form a striking contrast. The growing proportion of aged in the Jewish population, and their continued movement, often as bilocal residents but also as permanent in-migrants to sunbelt communities, argues sharply for in-depth attention to their movement patterns and the problems such movement presents for the aged, their families, and the communities of in- and out-migration (Rosenwaike, 1989). Not only are their levels of involvement generally higher, but mobility also is less clearly related to decreases in membership, philanthropy, and voluntarism. They may thus be continuing patterns developed at younger ages and perpetuating ties and networks developed over several decades. Because most are retired, they may also have more time for leisure activities, including voluntarism, and greater affluence with which to do so. Mobility for many may simply be a relocation from one area of relatively intense Jewish activity to another, often even in conjunction with the movement of friends and relatives. How much of these patterns is attributable to aging and changes in the life cycle and how much to underlying differences from the young in attachments and commitments to the Jewish community cannot be determined with our data. The answer can have serious implications for community planners and policy makers.

Informal Networks

We have assumed that networks can have a crucial effect on involvement in Jewish activities. Assessment of the relation between migration on the one hand and number of Jewish friends and the Jewishness of neighborhood on the other can provide some indication of their interaction and how they may relate to other aspects of integration into the Jewish community. Migration is clearly related to lower levels of informal Jewish associations although this effect is mitigated with longer duration of residence. The relation between migration and lower informal associations is also sharper for the young than for the elderly. As we have seen before, the migration of the elderly is not as disruptive of community ties as it is for younger persons. That many elderly move to relatively dense areas of Jewish settlement may reflect their desire to recapture some of the sense of community that characterized their youth. Many who grew up in Jewish neighborhoods found themselves in less densely Jewish areas in middle-age; some are apparently reconcentrating upon retirement, when locational features rather than economic opportunities determine destination.

The disruptive impact is not necessarily desired by the migrants: many more indicate that Jewishness of neighborhood is important to them than indicate that they live in an area that is very Jewish. This finding suggests that, in fact, many Jews would prefer to associate with other Jews but that a variety of forces prevent their doing so. Included among these may be the location of career opportunities, availability of affordable housing, and preference for general amenities. That these often take priority over Jewish-oriented preferences is clear from the small percentage of respondents who actually live in what they consider Jewish neighborhoods. The challenge for the Jewish community, then, is to find ways to either channel migrants to the more Jewish areas of a given place or to provide Jewish networks for them from within a wider area of settlement.

THE CHALLENGE OF MOBILITY

A complex set of factors that include socioeconomic characteristics of individual Jews, the context of the greater American society, and the historical legacy all have conjoined to bring about major changes for Jewish Americans and the Jewish communities in which they live. Broad dispersion across the fifty states has come to be associated with weakening identification with and involvement in the organized Jewish community and a changing configuration of family and friendship networks.

NJPS-1990 has documented the high levels of mobility of Jewish Americans; the concentration of migrants in certain age, occupation, and education categories; and the association of mobiity with decreased involvement in the Jewish community. As yet, we understand these relations only imperfectly. An omnibus survey can provide only limited insights into the causal direction between migration and strength of Jewish identification. Nor do we know the constellation of motivating factors that determine whether to move, where to relocate, and how to relate to the new community of residence. More particularly, we lack adequate information to assess the role of specifically Jewish factors in influencing these various aspects of the migration process. In-depth data that allow us to identify characteristics and behavior before and after the move will help disentangle the cause-effect relations; qualitative data, such as are obtained from unstructured interviews or focus groups, can provide more information on motivational factors and on the values of Jewish ties to the individuals and families.

The next national Jewish population survey, planned for 2000, should include additional questions on premigration conditions related to Jewish identity and to basic socioeconomic characteristics, such as labor-force status, occupation, and education. This will permit fuller assessment of the relations between migration and identity. It will help us to understand whether migration selects persons who are Jewishly less identified or whether movement contributes to lowering identity levels because it is disruptive. Information on premigration conditions would also allow fuller assessment of whether migration involves movement from areas of higher to lower Jewish density or vice versa, and how migrants adjust to the changing environmental conditions.

Even with the imperfect information obtained from NJPS-1990, however, we can recognize the important role that migration plays in the changing dynamics of American Jewry. What can national and local Jewish communities do to meet the challenges migration poses?

At the local level, planning must be sensitive to shifting residential patterns, the overall physical configuration of the community, and the types of access to given locations. Gary Tobin (1989) has stressed that, as the Jewish population has shifted South and West and developed new spatial patterns within older cities in the Northeast and Midwest and across metropolitan areas, Jewish community centers, and by implication other organizations as well, must confront the needs of a highly mobile population and make decisions about spatial locations in response to or in anticipation of population movement.

In many communities, migrants from other places settle outside the traditional areas of Jewish clustering, where their first informal contacts are likely to be with non-Jews. If they are to be incorporated into the existing Jewish community, overall planning must take cognizance of their location. An assessment of the impact of greater population dispersion in the Rhode Island community recognized: "With all this shifting and moving, there is a tremendous sense of loss that people may not realize until they're in their new environment: a loss of friends, associates, and the familiar network of daily life. . . . There is an urgency to compensate for one's losses as quickly as possible" (Goldberg, 1988). Information about the location of synagogues/temples, Jewish community centers, day schools, and other Jewish institutions should be made readily available to newcomers, preferably even before they move. Since most can be expected to become only slowly involved with their new Jewish community of residence, efforts by the organized community to draw the newcomers into existing networks will help to speed the process (see Eisen, 1993).

Special outreach efforts may be particularly important to identify children newly arrived in the community and to facilitate their enrollment in programs of Jewish education. In those communities with limited educational programs, substitutes may have to be found in informal activities to provide Jewish experiences for their youth.

One step in the direction of helping Jews to relocate in a new Jewish community has been the Shalom Newcomers Network, developed by the Jewish Community Center Association, which provides community fact sheets and guides for the movers, and alerts the sending and receiving communities about the move. Some local federations have similarly implemented programs to facilitate access to the Jewish community. Jewish information and referral services have already been established in over twenty cities across the United States to help people locate information and connect with resources primarily within the Jewish community. Funded by local federations, and often staffed by volunteers, they provide information about organizations, service agencies, synagogues, and a host of other programs and volunteer oppportunities that both locals and newcomers may need in their efforts to develop stronger links to the community and to make fuller use of its services.

A number of privately organized real estate networks also cater to Jewish clients and help them to relocate in neighborhoods where access to Jewish facilities and services will be facilitated. The very existence of such private relocation agencies points to the need for their services. For example, Shalom Home, a national real estate relocation service, is designed to help individuals and families locate homes appropriate to their needs and to preserve their connections with the Jewish community by putting them in contact with Jewish organizations, programs, and facilities in their new community.

Individual community organizations can also develop outreach programs to identify newcomers and enhance their sense of belonging. Often, just facilitating connections between members and migrants can serve to establish informal friendship networks that over time lead to involvement in more formal structures. To accelerate this process, special membership fee structures may be needed to attract new members. This may be especially necessary for organizations like synagogues and temples that have additional fees (such as building pledges) associated with membership. Since migrants are heavily concentrated among the young who are just beginning careers and families, high initiation fees may be strong deterrents to membership. They may especially serve as barriers if newcomers anticipate another move to still another community in the foreseeable future.

The importance of all such efforts to improve the integration of newcomers and the unaffiliated is reflected in steps being undertaken by the Council of Jewish Federations' Research Department to assess how CJF member communities maintain, enrich, and update their population lists (Council of Jewish Federations, 1994). Preliminary findings, based on 127 communities, indicate that only about half of the federations claim to update their lists on a continuing basis, but the exact practices followed provide no basis for estimating how complete the lists are or how many extinct households continue to be listed.

List sharing occurs with some frequency, undoubtedly contributing to greater coverage. List sharing occurs most commonly with synagogues and Jewish community centers; other Jewish organizations such as schools, country clubs, and hospitals, do so more rarely. About two-thirds of the communities indicated they cooperated with other locations in exchanging information about migrating households, but the survey did not ascertain the degree to which this was actually done or how the exchange was handled.

Few federations had a formal system for encouraging individuals to report the names of newcomers or of unafffiliated households in the community, but a large proportion use local news media, including local newspapers and synagogue and organization bulletins, for such purposes. Many report success in using Jewish and non-Jewish realtors, but only one in ten said they turned to commercial research companies for new listees. Networking within the federations does, however, prove valuable in identifying individuals, especially through professional and occupational groups associated with the federation.

Many local federations have clearly become aware of the need to identify newcomers and unaffiliated residents if the federation is to achieve its mission fully. A variety of methods are used to meet this challenge, but how effective they are remains to be ascertained; more widespread use of the most effective approaches also should be encouraged.

At the national level, the continuing dispersion of Jewish Americans out of large centers of Jewish settlement, and often into smaller and more isolated communities containing few Jews, requires that some recognition be given to incorporating such localities into the national community structure. Many fall outside even those federations that encompass large geographic areas. They therefore have little contact with mainstream developments in the Jewish community and little access to the very institutions and programs that are designed to promote cohesiveness among Jewish Americans. National or regional federations should develop programs to take responsibility for this scattered population. A model may be found in the cooperative arrangements established by the Council of Jewish Federations to allow sharing the cost of resettling immigrants from Eastern Europe among the more than two hundred federations in the country. Under this arrangement, communities not absorbing their appropriate share of new Americans contribute to a fund that is used to help those communities that absorb more than their designated share. A parallel program for Jewish Americans moving among communities may be worth exploring.

Other solutions might take the form of circuit rabbis and teachers; traveling lending libraries of Judaic books and tapes; and wider use of television and videos. Development of educational videos and electronic classrooms may also help to reach Jews in communities without the density to support a Jewish educational program. Several such outreach programs have been initiated, including the Reform movement's (UAHC) Small Congregations Department, which provides guidance as well as intellectual and spiritual support to Reform Jews living in small and isolated communities and helps to train lay leaders (UAHC, 1994); a long-term program instituted by the North Carolina Association of Jewish Men, which sponsored a "synagogue on wheels," complete with a circuit-riding rabbi and educational materials (Gerber, 1974; see also, Edelman, 1974); and the Jewish Theological Seminary's Cantorial Outreach program, "rabbi sharing" initiatives, and "Brit Kodesh" designed to train *mohelim* (ritual circumcizers) in areas where no such service is available ("Serving Isolated Congregations," 1991). Sometimes, the small communities have initiated cooperative efforts of their own. An example is the Conference on Rural Jewry in New England, which serves as a network for Jews living in the small communities of northern New England. The organization has stated the following as its aim: "that we not allow far-flung Jews to fall off the edges of the Jewish world" (*Kfari*, January 1990).

At the national level, too, community leaders must reorient their thinking to recognize the evolution of a national Jewish society. Sending communities must become more willing to share information on mobile persons with the community of destination. Such cooperative efforts can be quite easy using the electronic "infohighway" available through computers. The technology exists, all that is lacking is the will to use it for such purposes. A national mindset is necessary, which recognizes that one community's loss will be another's gain and also a gain for the American Jewish community as a whole.

As the 1993–1994 deliberations of the North American Commission on Jewish Identity and Continuity recognized, some of the underlying dynamics that have weakened Jewish identity in North America, including high levels of Jewish mobility, are continental phenomena which can be dealt with only through collaboration across local boundaries. Initiatives emerging locally to strengthen identity and institutions are unlikely to realize their objectives fully without parallel supportive changes and activity at the continental level. These range from facilitating the flow of information, to creating a positive climate for new partnerships, to massing the resources of many systems and organizations to tackle some of the most challenging problems faced in seeking to expand Jewish identification and involvement (North American Commission, 1994:30).

The Commission's deliberations stressed that special attention in recruitment, training, and placement of professional personnel should be given to the needs and problems of smaller, isolated communities. Models for sharing and rotating personnel (especially Jewish educators) among communities needed to be developed (North American Commission, 1994:32).

A national initiative should also take the lead in developing a system of "tracking" Jews as they move from communitiy to community or life stage to life stage (e.g., college student leaving the campus). This information should be made available to the full range of organizations in the communities into which individuals or families are moving (North American Commission, 1994:34)

One area where such sharing and cooperation has begun to develop is in connection with the migration of elderly to the Sunbelt regions. Their moves often separate them from their children just at a time when children's support is most necessary for the parents' well-being. Both community and private linkages have been developed to allow for long-distance problem solving and regular communication between the separated family members.

A national perspective should also inform institutional structures. If membership involves considerable financial investment, it can, as we have suggested, deter persons from joining if they anticipate moving from the community. This may not be a major problem for some national organizations, for which membership is easily transferrable between communities; Hadassah life membership is an example. But it may even be possible for more locally situated institutions through development of a "Jewish Community Express Card" that has a national cachet and carries with it credit in whole or part for contributions made elsewhere.

In the twenty-first century, the number of Jews in the United States will probably either remain stable or more likely decline; Jews will certainly be a smaller percentage of the total American population. Migration will continue to be a central feature responsible for the changing profile of American Jewry, as Jews become more dispersed across metropolitan areas and across the nation, as some major centers of Jewish population decline and new centers and smaller communities with quite different characteristics develop. Such movement and redistribution will create both problems and opportunities.

National and local institutional structures must recognize the challenges and learn to facilitate the linkages among communities and individuals. Mechanisms must be adopted that provide for "portable locability," facilitating integration into new communities of residence by allowing individuals who move to change local community loyalties while maintaining loyalty to the larger community. This requires that planning be broad in scope and based on solid research. The future vitality of the Jewish American community may well rest both on such realistic assessments and on innovative planning based on them.

APPENDIX A

The Methodology of the National Jewish Population Survey

by Joseph Waksberg

Large-scale sample surveys are frequently carried out in a number of discrete steps and the National Jewish Population Survey (NJPS) followed such a pattern. The steps consisted of: determination of the subjects to be included in the survey; development of specific question wording; testing questions and procedures; decisions on survey procedures; preparation for data collection, including recruitment and training of staff; sample selection; data collection; weighting and other aspects of data processing; internal analysis of potential sources of errors; tabulations; analyses and preparation of reports. This methodological report concentrates on the technical aspects relating to sampling, survey procedures and data collection, weighting, and issues relating to accuracy of the data. There is a brief description of the questionnaire development. Data analysis and preparation of publications, both of the monographs and of less detailed reports, are not part of the survey methodology and are not discussed here.

1. GENERAL SURVEY PROCEDURES

The Council of Jewish Federations (CJF) established and supports a National Technical Advisory Committee on Jewish Population

Studies (NTAC). At the time the NJPS was planned, the NTAC consisted of researchers who worked for the CJF or local Jewish federations and outside demographers and statisticians interested in Jewish issues. The NTAC endorsed an initial recommendation of the October 1987 World Conference on Jewish Demography in Jerusalem to conduct a U.S. National Jewish Population Survey (NJPS) in the spring and summer of 1990. The CJF concurred in this recommendation and agreed to support such a survey.

The choice of 1990 was a deliberate one since it placed the survey at about the same time as the 1990 U.S. Census, thereby insuring maximum comparability between the Jewish survey data and census statistics. Further, the time period chosen for the conduct of the detailed interviews—late spring and early summer—both corresponded to the timing of the Census and is a time when most college students can be reached in their families' residences or other dwelling places that are more permanent than dormitories or other college housing. The interviewing period is also the time that most Sunbelt residents are in their more permanent homes.

The NTAC had independently come up with 1990 as the logical period for the survey as part of more general considerations of appropriate survey methodology. In a series of meetings in the decade leading up to 1990, the NTAC had discussed the many aspects of planning and implementing a Jewish Population Study and had submitted the following recommendations to the CJF:

- *That a large scale survey of the Jewish population be conducted in 1990.*

- *Data collection should be by telephone.* Over the past twenty to thirty years, survey researchers had demonstrated that the quality of responses to inquiries over the telephone were, for almost all subjects, about the same as for face-to-face interviews. Response rates to telephone surveys are generally lower than in face-to-face interviews, but the cost of telephone surveys is so much lower that the NTAC felt that the substantial cost advantage of a telephone survey more than compensated for the adverse effect on quality of a lower response rate.

- *A sample of 2,000 to 2,500 Jewish households should be selected by random digit dialing (RDD), without any use of Federation or other lists of Jewish households.* RDD gives all households with telephones in the United States (both Jewish and non-Jewish) a known chance of selection into the sample so that lists are not necessary. Furthermore, it was the NTAC's judgment that the effort involved in trying to construct a national list, and the likely small percentage of U.S. Jews that would be on the list, would make the construction of the list counterproductive. It should be noted that households without telephones were not intended to be covered in the survey. In 1990, about 7 percent of U.S. households did not have telephones. However, the percentage is undoubtedly much lower for Jewish households, and the NTAC did not believe their omission would have any detectable effect on the quality of the survey results. The survey also was to omit the nonhousehold population, principally persons in nursing homes, long-term hospital units, religious institutions, military barracks, and prisons. College students in dormitories (as well as those in private residences) were to be covered in the survey, usually as members of their parents' households.

- *Data should be collected only for the civilian population living in households,* omitting the institutional and other nonhousehold population. The survey thus would exclude those in prisons, hospitals, nursing homes, hotels, religious institutions, and in military barracks. Estimates of the relatively small number of Jews in such places were added to the survey results for the estimate of the total number of Jews in the United States. However, their characteristics would not be reflected in the breakdowns of the totals by age, sex, etc.

- *A screening questionnaire that defines and identifies Jewish households should be administered to the sample of telephone households.* Since random digit dialing produces a sample of all U.S. telephone households, non-Jewish households would then be dropped and Jewish households retained for the survey.

- *That the survey include a wide variety of topics.* The NTAC developed a broad set of questions designed to shed light on the demographic, social, and economic characteristics of the Jewish population, and to provide information on items of specific Jewish concern, such as intermarriage,

Jewish education, philanthropy, observances of Jewish rituals and practices, synagogue membership, utilization of social services, volunteerism, attitudes to certain issues of Jewish concern, etc. The questions were divided into two groups: (a) ones for which reasonably accurate information for all household members could be provided by any adult in the household (e.g., age, education, observance, etc.) and (b) questions for which the accuracy of proxy responses would be in doubt (e.g., attitudes). For the first set of questions, data would be obtained for all members of the sample households. For the second group, the NTAC recommended that one adult be selected at random in each sample household and that the sample for these items should be considered as consisting of only the selected persons.

• A second, and independent, partition of the questions was also made. In order to reduce the considerable interview length, the questionnaire was divided into a "core" component, to be asked in all sample households, and "modules" to be asked in subsamples of households. More specifically, respondents were randomly allocated to three equal subsamples, and each subsample was assigned one of the three following areas of inquiries:

1. Jewish identity

2. Social services

3. Philanthropy

• *After the survey information was collected, weights should be inserted into the data file.* The weights should be constructed so that when they are used in tabulations of the survey data, they provide approximately unbiased estimates of the U.S. Jewish population in each category shown in the tabulations.

• *The individual responses to the survey questionnaire as well as the appropriate weights should be entered onto a computer tape.* Copies of the tape would be available for researchers interested in making detailed studies of particular aspects of Jewish life.

• *A high priority was put on speed of data processing, tabulations of the data, and publication of the major results,* first in a summary report highlighting the major findings in the survey, and then in a series of analytic studies focusing on particular topics.

- *That the survey be conducted outside of CJF or its member organizations.* More specifically, that a contract be let by competitive bidding to a company experienced in the conduct of such statistical studies.

The CJF approved the NTAC recommendations, provided a budget for the survey, and asked the NTAC to make the necessary arrangements. A Request for Proposals (RFP) that described the work to be done, the procedures outlined above, and the scope of work was prepared and distributed to interested statistical and market research companies. A subcommittee of the NTAC reviewed the proposals submitted by organizations that were interested in carrying out the survey, and selected the ones that were judged best. These organizations were invited to make personal presentations of their plans and their experience in such activities before the subcommittee. A contract was then awarded to a team consisting of ICR Survey Research Group and Marketing Systems Group (also known as Genesys Sampling Systems). The Marketing Systems Group was responsible for the sample selection and all weighting and estimation phases of the project. ICR was responsible for all other aspects of the survey, from questionnaire pretesting through data collection, coding, and data tape preparation.

The choice of ICR and Marketing Systems Group was based on a number of factors: understanding of the requirements of the study, the reputation of the team in doing high-quality work, experience with large-scale telephone sample surveys, an existing staff of experienced telephone interviewers and a system for training and supervising them, a capable statistician to oversee the sampling and related activities, and cost. A main, and overriding advantage of the team, was the fact that they carried out, for other sponsors, a weekly RDD national household sample survey of 2,000 households. They agreed to add the screening questions that identified Jewish households to the questionnaire then in use. It was estimated that the approximately 100,000 households screened over the course of a year would supply the 2,500 responding Jewish households desired in the final sample.

(The screening actually covered more than a year, and consisted of over 125,000 households which yielded over 5,000 households that indicated the presence of a Jewish member.) By attaching the screener questions to an existing national sample survey, the NJPS was able to avoid the expense of selecting and interviewing the very large sample needed to locate 2,500 Jewish households. Instead, the survey incurred only a fairly modest marginal cost of the added time to administer the screening questions. If the NJPS had to pay the entire cost of selecting and screening more than 100,000 households, the additional cost probably would have been well over $1,000,000.

An additional advantage of using the ICR's ongoing weekly survey was that it provided flexibility in achieving the desired sample size. The amount of screening necessary to achieve a sample of 2,500 Jewish households could only be approximately estimated in advance. With the weekly samples screened by ICR, a cumulative tally of Jewish households could be kept, and the weekly samples terminated before the end of the year if fewer than 100,000 households provided the required sample size, or it could be continued for longer than a year if that was necessary.

2. SAMPLE SELECTION

The telephone numbers selected for the NJPS were based on random digit dialing (RDD), and are a probability sample of all possible telephone numbers in the United States. The sampling procedure utilized a single-stage sample of telephone numbers within known residential working banks (the first two digits of the four-digit suffix, e.g., 212-555-XXxx). Telephone exchanges were strictly ordered by census geographic variables (i.e., Division, Metro/Non-Metro, Central City/Suburban, etc.) creating a sample frame with fine implicit geographic stratification. This procedure provides samples that are unbiased and in which all telephones have the same chance of selection. Since the random digit aspect allows for the inclusion of unlisted and unpublished numbers, it protects the samples from "listing bias"—the unrepresentativeness of telephone samples that can occur if the distinctive households whose telephone numbers are unlisted and unpublished are excluded from the sample. The RDD sample is referred to as the "screening sample." It consisted of 125,813 households that were asked whether any household member was Jewish. (See Section 4 for specific questions.) All qualified Jewish households were followed up with requests for the detailed interviews.

The household sample selection was accompanied by an automated scheme for scheduling callbacks for telephone numbers at which there was no response to the initial call. A three-callback rule was followed—the timing of the callbacks was scheduled by the computer to cover various times of the day, but within a narrow time frame. This narrow time frame was required by the short field period for each weekly survey. There were actually two weekly sample surveys, with 1,000 households in each survey. One weekly survey ran from Wednesday evening through Sunday evening; the second from Friday evening through Tuesday evening. The initial call and callback schedule ensured a minimum of two week-end attempts (if necessary) on each sample number.

The tight time schedule for the screening interviews undoubtedly reduced the response rate, as compared to a survey with more time for callbacks. (For example, persons on vacation during the survey week were never given an opportunity to respond.) However, the NTAC believed that the advantages of using an ongoing survey for screening outweighed the disadvantages.

3. PRESURVEY OPERATIONS

Two major sets of activities preceded the data collection. They consisted of the development and testing of the survey questions, and the interviewer training and briefing.

3.1. Development and Testing of Survey Instruments

Three stages of data collection were planned: screening, recontact and in-depth interviewing. The questionnaires for all three phases were initially developed by the NTAC. These documents were then edited, reformatted, and programmed for CATI interviewing by ICR staff. The development phase included several questionnaire drafts and a series of "live" pretests.

CATI stands for Computer Assisted Telephone Interviewing. It is a system in which the questionnaire has been entered into a computer, each interviewer is provided with a computer screen and keyboard, and the questions to be asked appear on the screen instead of having to be read from a paper questionnaire. The responses are entered directly into the computer. In addition to speeding up the data processing, CATI has the capability of carrying out editing for consistency and completeness of data and flexibility of operations. Almost all large-scale telephone surveys are now done by means of CATI.

All interviewing in both the Screening, Recontact/Validation, and the Main Study Phases were conducted by professional interviewers by means of computer-assisted telephone interviewing. From an interviewing standpoint, the CATI system removes the potential for interviewer error relative to skip patterns and possible response options. Moreover, the CATI system provides inherent response editing capabilities relative to both range edits and conditional requirements based upon prior responses. Computerized questionnaire control allows interviewers to better establish rapport with respondents and concentrate on responses rather than attempting to contend with the extreme complexity of the Recontact and Main Study questionnaires.

Finally, CATI capabilities allowed for access to up-to-the-minute interviewing production measures including production rates, refusal and refusal conversion rates, and results of dialing attempts.

In each pretest, personnel from NTAC and ICR monitored interviews as they were being conducted. Any unforeseen deficiencies in question content, sequencing, and nomenclature were corrected during this stage. In most cases, indicated changes were incorporated immediately, providing pre-test capabilities during the same pretest session.

The final CATI questionnaires were reviewed and tested extensively by both NTAC and ICR personnel prior to "live" interviewing. In addition, the pretest data served as a "live" test of output, data format, edit checks, etc.

3.2. Interviewer Training and Briefing

All interviewers selected to work on the 1990 NJPS were personally briefed, trained, and supervised during all hours of interviewing. In addition to participating in the standard ICR ten-hour interviewer training session, all interviewers who worked on the survey participated in a detailed briefing session developed specifically for this study.

This special briefing included an item-by-item discussion of each question and module contained in the interview; a discussion of special respondent "handling" for specific interview situations, including providing the CJF's telephone number to respondents who questioned the authenticity of the survey and suggesting that the CJF be called; and a review of areas and issues relating to Jewish heritage including customs, holidays, and proper pronunciation of Hebrew words and phrases that interviewers would be likely to encounter during the course of the study. In addition to the briefing, written interviewer aids were provided and made available during all hours of interviewing.

4. ORGANIZATION OF DATA COLLECTION ACTIVITIES

For approximately one year preceding the survey, beginning in April 1989, ICR conducted Stage I of the National Jewish Population Survey. This entailed incorporating a series of four screening questions into its twice weekly general market telephone surveys. The screening questions determined Jewish qualification and thus were the basis for the recruitment of households. The four screening questions in Stage I were asked in the following order:

1. What is your religion?
   If not Jewish, then . . .
2. Do you or anyone else in the household consider themselves Jewish?
   If no, then . . .
3. Were you or anyone else in the household raised Jewish?
   If no, then . . .
4. Do you or anyone else in the household have a Jewish parent?

This screening stage of the survey obtained information on the religious preference of 125,813 randomly selected adult Americans and the Jewish qualification of their respective households. It was determined initially that 5,146 households contained at least one person who qualified as "Jewish" or Jewishly affiliated as determined by the screening questions. Stage II, the inventory stage, consisted of attempts to recontact Jewish households to requalify potential respondents and solicit participation in the 1990 NJPS. The households classified as Jewish in the last three months of screening were omitted from Stage II because the Stage III interviewing was to follow so closely. Stage II included 4,208 households. During Stage II, a number of households that were initially classified as Jewish dropped out of the survey sample due to changes in household composition or to disqualification based upon further review.

Stage III, the final interviewing stage of the survey, yielded a total of 2,441 completed interviews with qualified respondents. The statistics reported here are drawn from these households. Through a process of scientific weighting procedures utilizing all 125,813 Stage I interviews, the sample of Jewish households represents about 3.2 million American households nationally.

The survey interviews collected information about every member of the household. Thus, the study was able to ascertain important personal information about 6,514 persons in the surveyed households. Appropriate weighting procedures indicate that the number of persons in the surveyed households represents about 8.1 million individual Americans, a number of whom are not themselves Jewish, reflecting the mixed composition of the households in the Jewish sample.

5. DATA COLLECTION:
FIRST TWO PHASES—SCREENING AND RECONTACT AND VALIDATION

5.1. Phase I: Screening

The entire screening phase was conducted as part of the ICR Survey Research Group's twice weekly telephone omnibus survey. The use of a telephone omnibus vehicle as opposed to a custom survey has obvious cost advantages; on the other side, there may be trade-offs relative to response rates, length of field period, placement of the screening questions on Jewish identity within the ever changing instrument, etc. However, these were thought to be small.

As mentioned earlier, 125,813 screeners were completed for this project. Although no formal disposition of call results is available, it is known that the proportion refusing to participate in any given weekly survey averages about 45 percent. In order to assess the potential bias resulting from this response rate, two separate analyses were conducted. They are described in Section 9.

5.2. Phase II: Recontact and Validation

The second phase of the study was conducted with respondents from Jewish households identified during the initial Screening Phase. This phase was designed to validate the initial screening process; to initiate contacts with qualified households to explain the purpose of the study and gain cooperation; and to provide a means of keeping in touch with the qualified respondents given the extended time period between the initial screening and final interview.

The primary informational objectives of the Recontact/Validation Phase were as follows:

1. Validate that the respondent/household was, in fact, Jewish;
2. Explain the purpose of the call and encourage respondents to participate in the in-depth Study during the summer of 1990;
3. Collect detailed household data relating to age, sex, and relationship of each household member, and type of residence and location; and
4. Request and secure a third party reference to assist in the future recontact for the in-depth Study.

Recontact Phase interviewing was conducted over a 52-week period, from 7 April 1989 through 2 April 1990. The process was continuous, with most recontacts occurring within two weeks of the initial qualification in the Screening Phase.

Upon successful recontact, the household member who participated in the Screening Phase was asked to reverify the Jewish character of himself/herself and other household members relative to:

- Being Jewish;
- Considering himself/herself Jewish;
- Being raised Jewish; and
- Having a Jewish parent.

Respondents were asked to participate in an in-depth Main Study Phase interview to be conducted at a later date. This recruitment included an explanation of the study, the size of the study, an explanation of how and why they were selected to participate, and the naming of CJF as the study sponsor.

Substantial efforts were made to "convert" respondents who refused to participate. Respondents who refused to participate at the introduction or during the interview itself were recontacted by specially trained interviewers. These interviewers used specially developed and proven techniques to convert refusals into participants. In some cases, alternative respondents within a given household were recruited to participate. In addition to specially trained interviewers, letters of explanation were mailed to refusals in an effort to establish credibility for the study and, in turn, to increase likely participation.

A household inventory of requalified Jewish households was created; this roster of household members included age and sex, along with each member's relationship to the primary contact person. Specifically, four questions were asked about each household member:

1. Name;
2. Age and sex:
3. Relationship to the respondent; and
4. Religious qualification.

Additional information relating to household characteristics was also requested; specifically, the type of household unit (e.g. multiple family, single unit, apartment, etc.) and whether this particular unit was the primary residence or a seasonal or similiar recreational dwelling.

Finally, information about third-party references (i.e., a relative or close friend) was requested for use in the event that respondents could not be reached at their original location. This third-party information was utilized to "track" the original respondents during the final phase of interviewing.

Not every Jewish household identified in the Screening Phase was included in the Recontact Phase. Specifically, households identified during the final three months of Screening were excluded because of the rather short time until onset of the full

National Survey; it was thought that the risk associated with alienating respondents by attempting multiple contacts over a very short period of time outweighed the few households likely to be lost due to relocation.

In total, 4,208 Jewish households identified in the Screening Phase were included in the Recontact Phase. The results of attempted recontact are shown in table A.1. It should be noted that there was no strict callback rule, but rather "nonrespondent households" were continually recycled, with many receiving 20 attempts or more.

Over 81 percent of the screened and qualified households were successfully contacted and reinterviewed; of these, 15.5 percent did not requalify and 6.3 percent disavowed knowledge of the previous interview. Just over 9 percent refused the Recontact interview.

None of the original respondent households were excluded from the 1990 Survey based on results of the Recontact Phase; the purpose here was to facilitate tracking of respondents and increase ultimate cooperation, not to requalify, validate, and reject sample households. Although the Recontact data were retained, all sample households (including those that failed to qualify in Phase II) regardless of the outcome were again attempted during the Final Phase of interviewing.

Table A.1
Results of the Recontact Validation Phase

	Number	*Percent*
Requalified and willing to participate	2,124	52.1
Requalified and not willing	316	7.5
Not requalified	652	15.5
No such respondent	266	6.3
Refused at start	315	7.5
Refused during interview	75	1.8
Language barrier	27	0.6
Nonworking	135	3.2
Nonhouseholds	20	0.5
No Contact	278	6.6
Total	4,208	100.0

6. PHASE III: MAIN STUDY—DATA COLLECTION

In the spring and summer of 1990, the third and final phase of data collection was undertaken. The survey instrument itself was initially developed by the NTAC, jointly pretested with ICR, and prepared for CATI interviewing by the ICR.

In the Main Study Phase, households that were identified as being Jewish in the screening phase were recontacted between May 8, 1990, and August 12, 1990, in an effort to complete the in-depth, detailed information requested on the Jewish character of the household, its members and related issues. Due to the considerable interview length (approximately 30 minutes), the questionnaire was divided into two parts: the "core" questionnaire and three shorter questionnaire "modules."

The core questionnaire was asked of all respondents. In addition to this core, respondents were randomly assigned to one of three groups and asked a series of more detailed questions relating to one of the following areas of inquiry (referred to as modules):

1. Jewish identity
2. Social services
3. Philanthropy

The Screening Phase had identified a total of 5,146 Jewish households over more than fifteen months of interviewing, and surveying a total of over 125,000 households. As table A.2 shows, 49 percent of these resulted in completed Phase III interviews; just over 15 percent refused to participate; and in only 13 percent of the cases was it impossible to contact any household members.

The most difficult and puzzling result however, was the roughly 18 percent of respondents and/or households which failed to requalify; all of these respondents were recontacted a second time during Phase III, and all failed to validate their replies in the Screening Phase. Sections 7 and 9 contain a discussion of this group of respondents and describe how they were used in estimating the size of the Jewish population.

It was also a standard practice to attempt conversion of all refusals, so that all of this group represents "double refusals." All telephone numbers reported as "nonworking" were verified and attempts to secure new numbers were made, although this was not

Table A.2
Results of the Main Study Phase

	Number	*Percent*
Nonworking	366	7.1
Nonhousehold	63	1.2
No Answer/Busy	191	3.7
Respondent no longer there	23	0.4
Answering machines	101	2.0
Refused at start	670	13.0
Refused during interview	126	2.4
Language barrier	21	0.4
Ineligible	146	2.8
Not requalified	908	17.6
Deleted/Not used interviews	25	0.5
Completed Interview	2506	48.7
Total	5146	100.0

very successful. There was no limit on number of followup attempts, which explains the relatively low proportion of "no answer" and "busy" sample dispositions (< 4%).

7. WEIGHTING PROCEDURES

7.1. Overview of Weighting Procedures

After the survey information was collected and processed, each respondent was assigned a weight. When the weights are used in tabulations of the survey data, the results automatically provide estimates of the U.S. Jewish population in each category shown in the tabulations.

The weighting method first insured that key demographic characteristics of the adult population of the total weighted sample of the 125,813 screened responding households matched the most current estimates of these demographic characteristics produced by the Census Bureau. The weighting procedure automatically adjusted for noncooperating households, as well as for those who were not at home when the interviewer telephoned and for households that did not have telephones or had multiple lines.

A second step in the weighting was carried out on the questionnaires completed in the recontact and validation phase and the main study phase of the study. This step made the weighted totals of completed questionnaires in each phase of the survey conform to the geographic and demographic profile of Jewish households at the earlier phases.

In addition, a separate weighting routine was established for each of the modules that was based on a subsample of the full set of Jewish households, so that the weighted total of each module corresponded to the full sample.

7.2. Detailed Description of Weighting

There were four stages in the preparation of the screening sample weights. First, households with more than one residential telephone number were assigned weights designed to compensate for their higher probabilities of selection—one-half for households with two telephone numbers, and one-third for households with three or more numbers. Secondly, cooperating households were poststratified, using 18 geographic strata—9 Census Divisions, and 2 categories for in or out of metropolitan areas. In the third stage, a weight was derived by poststratifying the weighted counts of the population in the sample households, using geographic-demographic strata, to the best current estimates of those strata. The strata comprised Census Region (4), age by sex (12), education of respondent (3), and race, i.e., white or other (2). The fourth stage was geographic poststratification at a state, metropolitan statistical area (MSA), or county level, depending on the size of the area. Individual counties with 75,000 or more households became individual strata. The remaining counties were grouped by individual MSAs or when necessary linked to a larger county (over 75,000 households) within the same MSA. Counties outside MSAs were grouped at the state level.

Following the weighting processes described above, the completed screener interviews were classified by their initial level of Jewish qualification and the results of the subsequent data collection efforts. During the various interviewing phases, a significant number of Jewish households that were initially considered qualified, subsequently became classified as non-Jewish. The largest

Table A.3
Qualified Jewish Households in Screener by Reporting Status in Validation Interview

Reporting status of later interviews	Total	Basis of qualification in screener			
		Religion	Consider	Raised	Parents
Known Jewish households	1,896,000	1,167,000	460,000	80,000	189,000
	100.0%	61.6	24.2	4.2	9.9
Refused Phase III	506,000	242,000	176,000	29,000	59,000
	100.0%	47.9	34.8	5.8	11.6
Other nonresponse	563,000	200,000	246,000	29,000	88,000
	100.0%	35.4	43.8	5.1	15.7
Not qualified	789,000	128,000	466,000	57,000	138,000
	100.0%	16.2	59.0	7.2	17.5
Total	3,753,000	1,737,000	1,347,000	195,000	474,000
	100.0	46.3	35.9	5.2	12.6

proportion of these households were originally qualified because the respondents or others in the households "considered" themselves to be Jewish. Table A.3 details weighted respondents by the basis for qualification and response category in the Phase II follow-up interview.

The critical issue was how to treat the "not qualified" in estimating the total number of Jewish households. The extreme alternatives were to ignore the requalification information altogether, essentially treating the "not qualified" as refusals; or to take the additional information at "face value" and reduce the estimates of Jewish households by 789,000, to just under 3 million.

Of course, there were a wide range of options in between. To aid in the evaluation of this situation, a DJN (Distinctive Jewish Name) analysis was conducted on the respondents qualified through the screening process. The first step in this process was obtaining a reverse match for these telephone numbers; for each telephone number corresponding to a household that was listed in the white pages of any U.S. telephone directory, the name and address of the subscriber was obtained. The surnames were then matched against a data file of distinctive Jewish surnames provided by the NTAC. The results are shown in table A.4.

As is evident from table A.4, the Not Qualified segment exhibits strikingly different proportions of DJN's from the other groups. Based on this and related information, the determination was made that all respondents originally qualified on the basis of Religion were most likely Refusals, and should remain as qualified Jewish households; conversely, among the other groups, the

Table A.4

Percentage of Sample with Distinctive Jewish Surnames (Base = Qualifiers with a Located Surname)

Reporting status in later interviews	Basis of qualification in screener				
	Total	Religion	Consider	Raised	Parents
Known Jewish household	16.7	23.3	5.6	10.5	4.8
Refused Phase III	13.8	20.0	8.0	9.5	7.8
Other nonresponse	10.9	21.2	4.9	6.7	3.8
Not qualified	2.6	8.6	1.5	0.0	1.6

unweighted ratios of DJN's indicated a likely true qualification rate of 17.5 percent.

Based on these assessments, the estimated Jewish households were adjusted to those shown in table A.5. The impact of these adjustments were to reduce the estimates of Jewish households from 3.753 million to 3.208 million, a reduction of about 14.5 percent.

The adjustments to the weighted estimates of Jewish households in table A.5 required a two-phase adjustment to the weighted dataset:

1. The indicated proportions of Not Qualified respondents needed to be weighted downward to the indicated totals, while non-Jewish households required a compensatory weight to maintain Total Household in the entire Screening Sample.

2. The completed Phase III interviews were then weighted to the estimates of Total Jewish Households, for analyses based on Jewish households only.

The first step was accomplished by stratifying based on Census Division, and within Division, by (1) non-Jewish Qualifiers; (2) Households qualified in the screener as Jewish based on other than Religion, who became "not Qualified in Phase III; and, (3) all other Jewish households. The second group represents those respondents whose estimate of Jewish affiliation was to be adjusted in this process. The revised weights were substituted in the individual data records, completing reconciliation of the full Screener Data set.

The procedure described above was carried out for the full sample and is therefore applicable to the core questionnaire that was administered to all sample households. However, each sample data record also includes a module weight in addition to the household and population weights for the core questions. The weighting procedure for the modules duplicated that of the previous section: a poststratification scheme incorporating census region and level of Jewish qualification. A simple expansion factor, to weight each module's sample total in each cell was computed, multiplied by the household weight, and incorporated into the sample record.

Table A.5
Final Estimates of Jewish Households Reflecting Adjustments to "Not Qualified" Call Results

Reporting status in later interviews	Total	Basis of qualification in Screener			
		Religion	Consider	Raised	Parents
Known Jewish HH	1,896,000	1,167,000	460,000	80,000	189,000
	100.0%	61.6	24.2	4.2	9.9
Refused Phase III	506,000	242,000	176,000	29,000	59,000
	100.0%	47.9	34.8	5.8	11.6
Other Nonresponse	563,000	200,000	246,000	29,000	88,000
	100.0%	35.4	43.8	5.1	15.7
Not Qualified	244,000	128,000	82,000	10,000	24,000
	100.0%	52.4	33.6	4.1	9.9
Total	3,208,000	1,737,000	963,000	148,000	360,000
	100.0%	54.1	30.0	4.6	11.2

Separate population weights were also developed for the statistics obtained from the randomly selected adult in each household. Essentially, these weights incorporated the household weights multiplied by the number of adults in the sample households.

8. APPLICATION OF WEIGHTS

Given the character and complexity of the survey instrument itself, a determination as to which of the weights described above to utilize for a particular statistic is not always apparent. The following explanation and examples should help in eliminating uncertainties.

Household weights should be used for developing estimates in the following types of situations:

1. Where the analysis, table, or distribution being produced is clearly based on household demographics. Examples include:

   • The number of households by level of Jewish qualification;

   • Distributions of households by number of children, number of adults, number of Jewish adults, age of oldest member, or household income distributions.

   • Household distributions based on qualification of one or more members; such as "are you or any member of your household currently a member of a synagogue or temple?"

2. Where the analysis or distribution utilizes variables constructed from the roster of household members. Examples include:

   • Age or educational attainment of all household members or subsets of all members.

   • Country of origin, or employment status, of all household members or adult household members.

The population weights are applicable only in those situations where the respondent answers to a specific question about himself or herself, and are to be utilized to represent all adult members in Jewish households. For example:

- Opinions about various public issues.
- Distributions of Jewish religious denomination, or Jewish ethnicity.
- Personal attendance at Jewish religious services.

In certain rare situations users may need to devise their own weighting schemes to establish a fully weighted sample base. This is most likely to occur when the adult members of a sample household exceed the number for which data was requested. For example, detailed information as to marital status was requested for only four members 18 years of age and older. If a particular sample household had five members, there are a number of options depending upon one's objectives and the characteristics of the household:

- A balance line of "not-reported" could be incorporated into the tables being produced.
- The simplest weighting method would be to weight each of the four responses by 1.25 in addition to application of the household weight. Depending, however, upon the characteristics of the member for whom no data is available, alternative approaches might prove more desirable.
- If the missing number's data represented one of three adult children, a better approach might be to weight the data for the two children for which data is present by 1.5, while keeping the parent's weight at 1.0.
- Alternatively, one could compensate for the missing member information on an overall basis. For example, one could categorize all qualified members by age, sex, region, etc., using the household weights; categorize those for which data was reported in a similar matrix using the household weight; and finally computing a weight for each cell which would increase the base of those responding to the weighted total in the first matrix.

In most cases, the bias created by simply ignoring the small discrepancies will be minimal. However, the user needs to make these decisions on a case-by-case basis, possibly trying alternative methods and comparing the results.

Finally, the module weights should obviously be used for tabulations of items in any of the modules regardless of whether simple totals of module items are tabulated or there are cross-classifications with other nonmodule items.

9. ACCURACY OF DATA

9.1. Nonsampling Errors

All population surveys are subject to the possibility of errors arising from sampling, nonresponse, and respondents providing the wrong information, and the NJPS is no exception. The response rate to identify potential Jewish households was approximately 50 percent. This is lower than most surveys that make efforts to insure high quality· strive to achieve. (The low response rate was partially caused by the contractor's need for each set of sample cases assigned for interview to be completed in a few days. This made intensive followup in the screener impractical.) The concern over the effect of nonresponse on the statistics is not so much on the size of the nonresponse since this is adjusted for in the weighting, but on the likelihood that nonrespondents are somewhat different from respondents. Although variations in response rates by geography, age, sex, race, and educational attainment were adjusted for in the weighting, there was still the possibility that Jews and non-Jews responded at different rates.

To test whether this occurred at an important level, the telephone numbers of approximately 10,000 completed interviews and for about 10,000 nonrespondents were matched against telephone listings to obtain the household names, and the percentage of each group having distinctive Jewish names was calculated. The percentage for the completed cases was 1.38 percent and for the nonrespondents was 1.29. The difference between the two is well within the bounds of sampling error. Although distinctive Jewish names account for a minority of all Jews, this test does provide support for the view that nonresponse did not have an important impact on the reliability of the count of the Jewish population.

In regard to errors in reporting whether a person is Jewish, previous studies indicate that the errors are in the direction of understating the count of the Jewish population, although the size of the understatement does not seem to be very large. A particular concern in the NJPS was the fairly large number of cases where respondents in households reporting the presence of one or more Jews in the screening operation, reversed themselves in the detailed interview. Of all households reported as having Jews in the screener, 18 percent were reported as nonqualified in the detailed interview. There was a possibility that this was a hidden form of refusal, rather than errors in the original classification of the households or changes in household membership.

A test similar to the one on refusals was carried out for the nonqualified households. The telephone numbers for the 5,146 households who were reported as Jewish in the screening interview were matched against telephone listings, and those with distinctive Jewish names (DJN) were identified. The detailed results of the match are reported in Section 7. They can be summarized as follows: In households that reported themselves as Jewish in the detailed interviews, 16.8 percent had DJN's. The rates were slightly smaller for refusals (13.9 percent) and for those who could not be contacted (10.9 percent). However, the percentage was only 2.9 percent for households who were reported as not Jewish in the detailed interview. It is, of course, possible that DJN households are less reticent than others in acknowledging to a telephone interviewer the fact that all or some of the household members are Jewish, but the evidence is that underreporting did occur, but not to a very serious extent. An adjustment in the weights of about 8 percent was made to account for the unreported Jews in the estimates of the total number of Jews. Since questionnaire information was not obtained for them, the statistics on characteristics of Jews may be subject to small biases if the Jewish nonqualifiers are very different from those who responded.

As mentioned earlier, other studies have reported that there is some understatement of reporting of Jewish heritage in interviews surveys. No adjustments were made for such possible understatement since firm data on its size does not exist. As a result, the estimate of the size of the Jewish population is probably somewhat on the low side.

It is not possible to quantify the effects of the relatively high nonresponse rates, the possibility that some respondents might have deliberately misreported their religious affiliations, errors arising from misunderstanding of the questions, or other problems in the data. As indicated above, the test done with the presence of Distinctive Jewish Names did not detect any important problems. Furthermore, comparisons of the estimates of total Jewish population with the results of local area surveys carried out in or near 1990, did not show any important discrepancies. The screener questionnaire that inquired about Jewish affiliations also identified other major U.S. religious groupings, and estimates of their membership corresponded reasonably well with independent estimates of the membership.

Consequently, all of the tests we were able to carry out failed to turn up any major problems in the data. However, it seems reasonable to assume that persons who did not respond are somewhat different from respondents, and the other potential sources of error must also have had some impact. When comparisons are made, either over time, or among subgroups of Jewish persons (e.g., between those with a relatively high level of Jewish education and others, persons with synagogue affiliation and unaffiliated, etc.), it would be prudent to avoid analyses or explanations of small differences, even if they are statistically significant. However, the evidence is that large and important differences do reflect real phenomena, and can be relied on.

9.2. Sampling Variability

Sample surveys are subject to sampling error arising from the fact that the results may differ from what would have been obtained if the whole population had been interviewed. The size of the sampling error of an estimate depends on the number of interviews and the sample design. For estimates of the number of Jewish households, the sample size is 125,813 screened households. The screened sample was virtually a simple random sample. As a result, it is very likely (the chances are about 95 percent) that the number of Jewish households is within a range plus or minus 3 percent around the estimate shown in this report. For estimates of the Jewish population, the range is slightly higher since sampling variability will affect both the estimate of the number of Jewish households and of the average number of Jews in those households. The 95 percent range is plus or minus 3.5 percent. These ranges are the limits within which the results of repeated sampling in the same time period could be expected to vary 95 percent of the time, assuming the same sampling procedure, the same interviewers, and the same questionnaire.

Unfortunately, due to the complex nature of the sample design and weighting method used in estimating the characteristics of the

Jewish population, it is not possible to give a simple formula that will provide estimates of the standard errors for all types of estimates. To begin with, there are three basic samples embedded in the survey:

1. The household sample can be considered as the equivalent of a simple random sample of 2,441 households.

2. For population statistics based on data reported for all household members, the sample size is 6,514. However, for most estimates of this type, the standard errors will be greater than what would be achieved with a simple random sample of 6,514 because of the presence of intraclass correlation, that is the tendency of household members to be more alike than would be the case of persons chosen at random. The intra-class correlation introduces a design effect that should be superimposed on the simple formula for the standard error.

3. Population statistics based on data reported for only one household member, selected at random, are also based on a sample size of 2,441. However, since the chance of selection of any person depends on the number of adults in the household the sample is not equivalent to a simple random sample of 2,441. The varying probabilities of selection also create a design effect.

The standard error of an estimate of a percentage can be approximated by:

$$\sqrt{D.p.(1-p)/Rn}$$

where p is the estimated percentage, D is the design effect, R is the proportion of Jews in the segment for which percentages are computed, and n is the sample size, that is, 2,441 or 6,514. When percentages are computed of all Jewish households or persons, R is equal to 1; when the base of the percentage is a subgroup of all households or persons (e.g., households observing certain rituals, all females, persons in a particular age group), the value of R is the fraction of all households or persons in that subgroup.

The value of D is 1 for household statistics. For population statistics, the value will depend on the item being estimated. Although it is possible to calculate an estimate of the value of D

for each item (or alternatively, a relatively unbiased estimate of the standard error), we assume most analysts will not want to make the fairly extensive effort needed for such calculations. Guidelines for approximating D follow.

- As stated earlier, D can be considered equal to one for household statistics.

- For items based on data reported for all household members, D will be in the range 1 to 2.7. It will be close to 1 for percentages based on a subset of the Jewish population (e.g., adult males, currently widowed persons, persons born abroad, disabled, etc.) At the other extreme, the value will be close to 2.7 on items for which household members are likely to have similar characteristics (e.g., the percentage of Jews who belong to conservative congregations). The 2.7 is the average size of Jewish households, and when D has this value, the effect on the standard error is to treat the statistic as a household item with a sample size of 2,441 rather than a population item. For other types of percentages, the value of D will be somewhere in the 1 to 2.7 range; the more alike members of a household are likely to be, the greater should be the value of D used in the calculations.

- The value of D is about 1.2 for items based on data reported for only one adult in the household. This design effect reflects the effect on sampling errors of having varying probabilities of selection, depending on the household size. For example, adults living in one-adult households will have twice the chance of selection as those in two-adult households, three times the chance as those in households containing three adults, etc.

It should also be noted that the value of n is lower for items in the modules asked for a subsample of respondents than for other items. Since the modules are based on a one-third subsample, the sample size of 2,441 and 6,514 are reduced to 814 and 2,171. When the sample sizes used in the base of percentages are obtained by simply counting the number of records used in the calculations, the count automatically provides the value of Rn, and it is unnecessary to calculate R, or to be concerned over whether or not the item is one of the modules.

Questions on Migration in the NJPS-1990 Questionnaire

52. In what year did (NAME) move to this
current address?

_____   [RECORD YEAR]
97 Always lived here   GO TO Q. 61
98 Don't know
99 Refused

53. In what year did (NAME) move into his/
her current city or town?

_____   [RECORD YEAR]
97 Always lived here   GO TO Q. 61
98 Don't know
99 Refused

54. Just before (NAME) moved into your
residence, where did he/she live?
[READ LIST]

1 Same city/town in this state   GO TO
2 Different city/town in this state   Q.57
3 Different state   GO TO Q. 55
4 Other country   GO TO Q. 56
D (DO NOT READ) Don't know   GO TO
R (DO NOT READ) Refused   Q. 58

A full copy of the questionnaire is available from: Research Department, Council of Jewish Federations, 730 Broadway, New York, NY 10003.

55. What state was that?
[USE STATE CODES; IF U.S. STATE, GO TO Q. 57.]

_____

D DON'T KNOW   GO TO
R Refused   Q. 58

56. What country was that/ [USE COUNTRY CODE.]

_____

D Don't know   GO TO
R Refused   Q. 58
[IF COUNTRY IS NOT USA, SKIP TO Q. 58]

57. What was the zip code of the previous address?

_____   [RECORD ZIP CODE]
97 There were no zip codes at that time
98 Don't know
99 Refused
[IF ANSWER TO Q. 53 IS 1984 OR EARLIER,
DO NOT ASK Q. 58, 59, or 60]

58. Where was (NAME) living five years ago, in May 1985?
[READ LIST]

1 Same house or apartment   GO TO
2 Different house or apartment in the Q. 61
   same city or town
3 Different city or town in this state
4 Different state   GO TO Q. 59
5 Different country   GO TO Q. 60
D (DO NOT READ) Don't know   GO TO
R (DO NOT READ) Refused   Q. 61

59. What state was that?
[USE STATE CODES; IF U.S. STATE, GO TO Q. 61.]

_____

D Don't know
R Refused

60. What country was that?   [USE COUNTRY CODE.]

_____
D Don't know
R Refused
[QUESTIONS 61–76 ASKED FOR RESPONDENT ONLY.]

61. What is the zip code of your current residence?

_____   [RECORD ZIP CODE]
D Don't know
R Refused

62. Is this residence owned or rented by you or someone living in your household?

1 Owned
2 Rented
D Don't know
R Refused

63. Do you think it is very likely, somewhat likely or not at all likely that you will move within the next three years?

1 Very likely
2 Somewhat likely
3 Not at all likely   GO
D Don't know   TO
R Refused   Q. 67

64. If you were to move, do you think it would be within this state, to another state or to another country?

1 Within this state   GO TO Q. 67
2 To another state   GO TO Q. 65
3 To another country   GO TO Q. 66
D Don't know   GO TO
R Refused   Q. 67

65. What state would that be?
[USE STATE CODE; IF U.S. STATE, GO TO Q. 67.]

_____
D Don't know
R Refused

66. What country would that be?[USE COUNTRY CODE.]

_____

D Don't know
R Refused

67. Do you generally spend more than two months of the year
     away from your present residence?

1 Yes
2 No   GO
D Don't know   TO
R Refused   Q. 71

67a. Is that mostly in one place, or in multiple places?

1 One place
2 Multiple places
D Don't know
R Refused

68. In what state do you spend most of your time?
     [USE STATE CODE; IF A U.S. STATE IS SPECIFIED,
     GO TO Q. 70.]

_____

D Don't know
R Refused

69. In what country do you spend most of your time?
     [USE COUNTRY CODE.]

_____

D Don't know
R Refused

70. Do you or your family own a residence in this place?

1 Yes
2 No
D Don't know
R Refused

APPENDIX C

Tables Showing Unweighted Number of Cases by Migration Status and Age

Table C.1
Number of Unweighted Cases by Lifetime Migration Status and Age:
Core Jews and Peripheral Population, Respondents Only

Lifetime Migration Status	18–44	Age 45–64	65+	Total
		Core Jews		
Nonmigrant	190	98	74	362
Intrastate	343	137	63	543
Interstate	565	236	165	966
International	80	35	51	166
Total	1,178	506	353	2,037
		Peripheral Population		
Nonmigrant	36	15	5	56
Intrastate	85	27	6	118
Interstate	115	40	14	169
International	19	6	4	29
Total	255	88	29	372

Note: Some cases are missing from this table because migration status is unknown.

Table C.2
Number of Unweighted Cases by Five-Year Migration Status and Age:
Core Jews and Peripheral Population, Respondents Only

| Five-Year Migration Status | Age | | | Total |
	18–44	45–64	65+	
Core Jews				
Nonmigrant	776	444	321	1,541
Intrastate	191	30	15	236
Interstate	186	28	15	229
International	18	3	—	21
Total	1,171	505	351	2,027
Peripheral Population				
Nonmigrant	186	73	26	285
Intrastate	34	10	2	46
Interstate	34	6	1	41
International	2	—	—	2
Total	256	89	29	374

Note: Some cases are missing from this table because migration status is unknown.

Table C.3
Number of Unweighted Cases by Lifetime Migration Status and Age:
Core Jews and Peripheral Population, Individuals

	Age			
Lifetime Migration Status	*18–44*	*45–64*	*65+*	*Total*
	Core Jews			
Nonmigrant	378	181	125	684
Intrastate	380	193	67	640
Interstate	836	435	269	1,540
International	146	86	88	320
Total	1,740	895	549	3,184
	Peripheral Population			
Nonmigrant	155	42	17	214
Intrastate	221	56	20	297
Interstate	391	144	45	580
International	77	30	9	116
Total	844	272	91	1,207

Note: The fewer number of cases reported for lifetime migration compared to five-year migration is due to the number of individuals for whom state of birth is unknown.

Table C.4
Number of Unweighted Cases by Five-Year Migration Status and Age:
Core Jews and Peripheral Population, Individuals

Five-Year Migration Status	Age			Total
	18–44	45–64	65+	
	Core Jews			
Nonmigrant	1,319	839	532	2,690
Intrastate	292	56	24	372
Interstate	276	49	26	351
International	31	6	1	38
Total	1,918	950	583	3,451
	Peripheral Population			
Nonmigrant	614	240	82	936
Intrastate	155	27	9	191
Interstate	148	19	4	171
International	13	1	—	14
Total	930	287	95	1,312

Note: The fewer number of cases reported for lifetime migration compared to five-year migration is due to the number of individuals for whom state of birth is unknown.

APPENDIX D

Construction of Ritual Index

The Ritual Practices Index is a composite of five practices: Seder attendance, lighting Chanukah candles, lighting Shabbat candles, maintaining *kashrut* (defined as having separate dishes and buying kosher meat), and fasting on Yom Kippur. Since these practices vary in intensity, from once a year to daily observance, they were weighted differentially in the construction of the index.

- Seder attendance, lighting Chanukah candles, and fasting on Yom Kippur received a weight of 2 if performed always or usually, 1 if performed sometimes, and 0 if never performed.
- Lighting Shabbat candles was weighted 4 for always/usually, 2 for sometimes, and 0 for never.
- Kashrut was given a weight of 6 if respondent reported always/usually and 0 otherwise.
- The index had a range of 16 to 0.

When tested through cross-tabulation by the denomination of respondent, the pattern was consistently in the expected direction. Orthodox respondents scored the highest, with two-thirds scoring in the 9 to 16 range. Those reporting themselves to be just Jewish had the highest proportions scoring either 0 or 1 through 4.

It is not possible from the data set to disaggregate which ritual the respondent personally performs and which is performed by others in the household. Nor does it seem necessary to do so since correlations between pairs of rituals fall within a relatively narrow range (about .4000 and .6000), indicating that the individual-level ritual (fasting on Yom Kippur) is not differentially related to other rituals. The one exception is kashrut, which has lower correlation values (between.1600 and.3000, except for a higher correlation with lighting Shabbat candles). It is nonetheless included in this study because kashrut is an important form of normative behavior in Judaism despite the fact that it is not standard practice among Reform Jews.

Even when the Ritual Index is constructed without kashrut as one of its components and its scale is reduced to a range of 0 to 10, with 8–10 being a high score, the relation of the Ritual Index to mobility remains the same. For example, whereas 71 percent of those scoring 0 on the index were nonmigrants, this was true of 79 percent of those with medium and high scores. Conversely, levels of migration are generally lower among those scoring high on the index. This is especially true of intrastate migration; the relation is not as clear for interstate mobility.

The relation of score on the Ritual Index (without kashrut) and future mobility is strong and clear. A higher percentage of persons scoring high on the index indicate no plans to move compared to those with low scores. As is true when the full index is used, however, this relation changes with age, so that among the elderly, more of those with a high score indicate it very likely they will move compared to those scoring low.

NOTES

CHAPTER 1.
INTRODUCTION

1. An in-depth analysis of the migration material from the 1970/71 survey is in process (Rebhun, forthcoming).

2. A detailed description of the methodology is provided by Joseph Waksberg in appendix A of this volume.

3. A differential weighting scheme was developed by NJPS, depending on whether the information was collected for each individual or only from the respondent as representative of adults in the household. In our analysis, we distinguish between lifetime and five-year migration patterns. Since the lifetime analysis encompasses each individual in the household, we use the weights for individuals. Because many of the characteristics and behaviors we analyze in conjunction with five-year migration are available only for the respondent or household, for the five-year analyses, we use the household weights. While these different weighting systems may result in somewhat different inflated numbers for the various migrant categories, tests indicate that the relative distributions and underlying patterns are very similar.

CHAPTER 2.
NUMBERS, DISTRIBUTION, AND MOBILITY

1. The *American Jewish Year Book* (Kosmin and Scheckner, 1991) estimated a total of 5,981,000 Jews in the United States in 1990, more than the 5.5 million estimated by the NJPS-1990. The *AJYB* estimates use counts provided by local communities, some based on recent surveys, others on federation lists, and still others on "guesstimates." As definitions of who is to be counted as a Jew and as the use of empirical methods for obtaining the local estimates become more standardized, it is expected that the state, regional, and national estimates reported by the *AJYB* will conform more closely to those based on national samples such as NJPS. Compared to NJPS-1990, *AJYB* estimated more Jews lived in the Northeast (51 percent) and fewer in the Sunbelt regions (38 percent). See tables 2.2 and 2.3.

2. For purposes of assessing the metropolitan residence of the Jewish population, this analysis relies on the NJPS data which classified households into five metropolitan residence categories, equivalent to those used by the U.S. Census, based on the location of the household's telephone exchange. The categories are: (1) living within the central city of the metropolitan area; (2) living outside the central city, but within the same county as the central city; (3) living in a suburban county of the metropolitan areas; (4) living in a metropolitan area with no central city; and (5) living in a nonmetropolitan area. In the text, categories 2 through 4 are refered to as "suburban."

3. For example, for various Florida communities surveyed between 1982 and 1993, Sheskin (1993) found that the percentage of part-year residents among the Jewish population varied between 2 percent in Orlando and 48 percent in Palm Springs.

CHAPTER 3. THE IMPACT OF MOBILITY ON REGIONAL DISTRIBUTION

1. Thanks to Bethany Horowitz, UJA-Federation of New York, for providing special tabulations.

CHAPTER 4. SOCIOECONOMIC DIFFERENTIALS

1. Age standardization eliminates the extraneous source of variation among groups due to differences in age composition. It indicates what the distributions would be (education in this case) if all subgroups being compared had the same age composition but retained their own age-specific education distribution (Shryock, Siegel, and Associates, 1976: 164–65 and 179–80).

2. Analyses of education and occupational differentials using NJPS-1970/71 were restricted to males.

3. Occupation for persons retired at the time of the survey refers to their major occupation while they were in the labor force.

4. For details on the methodology employed, see A. Goldstein, S. Goldstein, and Guo, 1990.

5. Computer space restrictions for the model preclude inclusion of divorced and widowed.

CHAPTER 5.
DIFFERENTIALS IN JEWISH IDENTIFICATION

1. Ritual bath used for purification for religious purposes.

2. For current purposes, because of the small number of cases, Reconstructionists are combined with Conservative.

3. We recognize that the ritual index includes both household and individual characteristics, but believe that their combination is justified since the household provides the ritual context in which the individual functions.

4. For an explanation of the construction of the Ritual Index, see appendix D.

5. Low level of Jewish education is defined as less than three years in any type of school or 3–5 years of Sunday school only; medium level is 3–5 years of supplementary or day school or 6 or more years of Sunday school; high level includes 6 or more years of supplementary or day school.

CHAPTER 6.
COMMUNITY INVOLVEMENT

1. Although NJPS-1990 inquired about membership in Jewish community centers, which are local, this question was asked of only a subset of the total sample. It does not, therefore, yield enough cases once migration is taken into account, and cannot be used in this analysis.

2. In the analysis which follows, the terms *non-Jewish organizations* and *secular organizations* will be used interchangeably.

3. Only the model incorporating both five-year migration status and future moves is used here.

CHAPTER 7. INFORMAL NETWORKS

1. Each component of the index has been given a score of 0 to 2. No Jewish friends equalled 0, some friends equalled 1, and most or all Jewish friends equalled 2. Similarly, a neighborhood rated as not at all Jewish scored 0, somewhat Jewish rated 1, and very Jewish rated 2. If the Jewishness of the neighborhood was deemed not at all important by the respondent, it was coded 0; if somewhat important, 1; and if very important, 2.

REFERENCES

American Jewish Year Book. 1900. "Jewish Statistics." Vol. 1. Philadelphia: Jewish Publication Society of America.

Axelrod, Morris, Floyd J. Fowler, Jr., and Arnold Gurin. 1967. *A Community Survey for Long Range Planning: A Study of the Jewish Population of Greater Boston.* Boston: Combined Jewish Philanthropies of Greater Boston.

Berger, Gabriel. 1990a. "Can We Increase American Volunteering?" *Research Notes 4* (November). Waltham, MA: Cohen Center for Modern Jewish Studies, Brandeis University.

———. 1990b. "Is American Jewish Volunteerism Lower Than Average?" *Research Notes 4* (February). Waltham, MA: Cohen Center for Modern Jewish Studies, Brandeis University.

Berger, Gabriel, and Gary A. Tobin. 1989. "Involvement in Jewish Organization: Shifting the Debate Among Policymakers." *Journal of Jewish Communal Service 66* (Fall):44–55.

Chenkin, Alvin. 1972. "Jewish Population in the United States, 1971." *American Jewish Year Book, 1972* (Vol. 73). Philadelphia: The Jewish Publication Society of America, pp.384–392.

Cohen, Renae, and Sherry Rosen. 1992. *Organizational Affiliation of American Jews: A Research Report.* New York: The American Jewish Committee.

Cohen, Steven M. 1988. *American Assimilation or Jewish Revival?* Bloomington: Indiana University Press.

———. 1983. *American Modernity and Jewish Identity.* New York: Tavistock Publications.

Council of Jewish Federations. 1994. "Preliminary Results of CJF List Enhancement Survey" (November), draft report.

DaVanzo, Julie, and Peter A. Morrison. 1981. "Return and Other Sequences of Migration in the United States." *Demography 18* (February):85–101.

de Vaus, D. 1982. "The Impact of Geographical Mobility on Adolescent Religious Orientation: An Australian Study." *Review of Religious Research* 23:391–403.

DellaPergola, Sergio. 1991. "New Data on Demography and Identification Among Jews in the U.S.: Trends, Inconsistencies, and Disagreements." *Contemporary Jewry* 12:67–97.

Drucker, Peter. 1994. "The Age of Social Transformation." *Atlantic Monthly* 274 (November):53–80.

Edelman, Lily. 1974. "A Call to Action: Projects and Proposals." *Jewish Heritage* 15 (Winter):19–30.

Eisen, Arnold M. 1993. "An All Volunteer Jewry." *Hadassah Magazine* 74 (June–July):18–20.

Elazar, Daniel. 1993. "The New Geo-Demographics of American Jewry." *Jerusalem Newsletter* 278 (July). Jerusalem: Jerusalem Center for Public Affairs.

Eldridge, Hope T. 1965. "Primary, Secondary, and Return Migration in the United States." *Demography* 1:212–219.

Fisher, Alan. 1994. "Los Angeles Jews Not Leaving City." *Wilstein Bulletin* (Fall):7, 11.

Fishman, Joshua A. 1963. "Moving in the Suburbs: Its Possible Impact on the Role of the Jewish Minority in American Community Life." *Phylon* 24:146–153.

Fishman, Sylvia B., and Alice Goldstein. 1993. *When They Are Grown They Will Not Depart: Jewish Education and the Jewish Behavior of American Adults*. Waltham, MA: Cohen Center for Modern Jewish Studies, Brandeis University.

Fowler, Floyd J., Jr. 1977. *1975 Community Survey; A Study of the Jewish Population of Greater Boston*. Research Report 8. Boston: Combined Jewish Philanthropies of Greater Boston.

Frey, William H. 1993. "The New Urban Revival in the United States." *Urban Studies* 30 (May):741–774.

Friedman, Peter, and Bruce Phillips. 1994. "The 1990 Chicago Metropolitan Area Jewish Population Study." *Contemporary Jewry* 15:39–66.

Gerber, Israel J. 1974. "Circuit Riding Rabbi." *Jewish Heritage* 15 (Winter):38–43.

Glazer, Nathan, and Daniel P. Moynihan. 1963. *Beyond the Melting Pot*. Cambridge: M.I.T. Press.

Gober, Patricia. 1993. "Americans on the Move." *Population Bulletin* 4 (November):2–40.

Goldberg, Nancy. 1988. "Project Newcomer." *Federation (RI) Voice* (September).

Goldscheider, Calvin. 1990. "The Unaffiliated Jew in America: Sociological Perspectives." *Humanistic Judaism* 18 (Spring):15–22.

———. 1986. *Jewish Continuity and Change: Emerging Patterns in America*. Bloomington: Indiana University Press.

Goldscheider, Calvin, and Sidney Goldstein. 1988. *The Jewish Community of Rhode Island: A Social and Demographic Survey, 1987*. Providence: The Jewish Federation of Rhode Island.

Goldstein, Alice. 1990. "New Roles, New Commitments? Jewish

Women's Involvement in the Community's Organizational Structure." *Contemporary Jewry 11* (Spring):49–76.

Goldstein, Alice, and Sylvia B. Fishman. 1993. *Teach Your Children When They Are Young: Contemporary Jewish Education in the United States.* Research Report 10. Waltham, MA: Cohen Center for Modern Jewish Studies, Brandeis University.

Goldstein, Alice, Sidney Goldstein, and Shenyang Guo, 1991. "Temporary Migrants in Shanghai Households, 1984." *Demography 28* (May):275–291.

Goldstein, Sidney. 1992. "Profile of American Jewry: Insights from the 1990 National Jewish Population Survey." *American Jewish Year Book, 1992,* Vol. 92. Philadelphia: The Jewish Publication Society of America, pp.77–173.

———. 1991. "American Jews on the Move." *Moment 16* (August):24–28, 49–51.

———. 1990. "Jews on the Move: Implications for American Jewry and for Local Communities." *The Jewish Journal of Sociology 32* (June):5–30.

———. 1987a. *A 1990 National Jewish Population Study: Why and How,* Occasional Paper No. 1988–04. Jerusalem: Institute of Contemporary Jewry, The Hebrew University of Jerusalem.

———. 1987b. "Demography of American Jewry: Implications for a National Community." *Parsippany Papers III.* New York: Council of Jewish Federations.

———. 1982. "Population Movement and Redistribution Among American Jews." *The Jewish Journal of Sociology 24* (June):5–23.

———. 1981. "Jews in the United States: Perspectives from Demography." *American Jewish Year Book, 1981,* Vol. 81. Philadelphia: The Jewish Publication Society of America, pp. 3–59.

———. 1971. "American Jewry, 1970: A Demographic Profile." *American Jewish Year Book, 1971,* Vol. 72. Philadelphia: The Jewish Publication Society of America, pp. 3–88.

———. 1968. *A Population Survey of the Greater Springfield Jewish Community.* Springfield, MA: Jewish Community Council.

———. 1964. *The Greater Providence Jewish Community: A Population Survey.* Providence: General Jewish Committee.

———. 1958. *Patterns of Mobility 1910–1950.* Philadelphia: University of Pennsylvania Press.

Goldstein, Sidney, and Calvin Goldscheider. 1968. *Jewish-Americans: Three Generations in a Jewish Community.* Englewood Cliffs, NJ: Prentice Hall.

Goldstein, Sidney, Calvin Goldscheider, and Alice Goldstein. 1988. "A Quarter Century of Change: Rhode Island Jewry 1963–1987" *Rhode Island Jewish Historical Notes 10* (November):93–114.

Goldstein, Sidney, and Alice Goldstein. 1983. *Migration and Fertility in Peninsular Malaysia*, Report No. N-1860.AID. Santa Monica, CA: The Rand Corporation.

Goldstein, Sidney, and Barry Kosmin. 1992. "Religious and Ethnic Self-Identification in the United States 1989-90: A Case Study of the Jewish Population." *Ethnic Groups* 9:219-245.

Hansen, Kristin A. 1991. *1990 Selected State of Birth Statistics for States*, CPHL-121. Washington, D.C.: U.S. Bureau of the Census.

Horowitz, Bethamie. 1994. "Findings from the 1991 New York Jewish Population Study." *Contemporary Jewry* 15:4-25

———. 1993. *The 1991 New York Jewish Population Study*. New York: United Jewish Appeal—Federation of Jewish Philanthropies of New York, Inc.

Israel, Sherry. 1987. *Boston's Jewish Population: The 1985 CJP Demographic Study*. Boston: Combined Jewish Philanthropies of Greater Boston.

Jaret, Charles. 1978. "The Impact of Geographical Mobility on Jewish Community Participation: Disruptive or Supportive?" *Contemporary Jewry* 4 (Spring/Summer):9-20.

The Jewish Population Study of the Greater Kansas City Area. 1979. Kansas City.

Kfari, January 1990. Burling, VT: Conference on Judaism in Rural New England.

Klass, Tim. 1994. "Rural Jewish Communities Are Vanishing." Associated Press Release, 26 August.

Kosmin, Barry. 1992. "Counting for Something: The Why and Wherefore of the CJF 1990 National Jewish Population Study." *Journal of Jewish Communal Service* 68 (Summer):292-298.

Kosmin, Barry, Sidney Goldstein, Joseph Waksberg, Nava Lerer, Ariella Keysar, and Jeffrey Scheckner. 1991. *Highlights of the CJF 1990 National Jewish Population Survey*. New York: Council of Jewish Federations.

Kosmin, Barry, and Seymour P. Lachman. 1993. *One Nation Under God: Religion in Contemporary American Society*. New York: Harmony Books.

Kosmin, Barry, and Paul Ritterband, Eds. 1991. *Contemporary Jewish Philanthropy in America*. Savage, MD: Rowman and Littlefield.

Kosmin, Barry, Paul Ritterband, and Jeffrey Scheckner. 1987. "Jewish Population in the United States, 1986." *American Jewish Year Book, 1987* (Vol. 87). Philadelphia: The Jewish Publication Society of America, pp. 164-176.

Kosmin, Barry, and Jeffrey Scheckner. 1992. "Jewish Population in the United States, 1991." *American Jewish Year Book 1992* (Vol. 92). Philadelphia: Jewish Publication Society of America, pp. 261-281.

————. 1991. "Jewish Population in the United States, 1990." *American Jewish Year Book 1991* (Vol. 91). Philadelphia: Jewish Publication Society of America, pp. 204–224.

Kritz, Mary M., and June Marie Nogle. 1994. "Nativity Concentration and Internal Migration Among the Foreign-born." *Demography 31* (August):509–524.

Lazerwitz, Bernard. 1978. "An Estimate of a Rare Population Group: The U.S. Jewish Population." *Demography 15* (August):389–394.

Lazerwitz, Bernard, J. Alan Winter, and Arnold Dashefsky. 1988. "Localism, Religiosity, Orthodoxy, and Liberalism: The Case of Jews in the United States." *Social Forces 67* (September):229–242.

Lebowitz, Barry D. 1975. "Migration and the Structure of the Contemporary Jewish Community." *Contemporary Jewry 2* (Fall/Winter):3–9.

Lenski, Gerhard. 1963. *The Religious Factor*. Garden City, NY: Doubleday.

Lieberson, Stanley, and Mary C. Waters. 1988. *From Many Strands: Ethnic and Racial Groups in Contemporary America*. New York: Russell Sage Foundation.

Liebman, Charles S., and Steven M. Cohen. 1990. *Two Worlds of Judaism: The Israeli and American Experiences*. New York: Yale University Press.

Linfield, H.S. 1931. "Statistics of Jews." *American Jewish Year Book* (Vol. 33). Philadelphia: Jewish Publication Society of America, p. 276.

Long, Larry. 1988. *Migration and Residential Mobility in the United States*. New York: Russell Sage Foundation.

Longino, Charles F. 1994. "From Sunbelt to Sunspots." *American Demographics 16* (November):22–31.

Luckmann, Thomas. 1967. *The Invisible Religion*. New York: Macmillan.

Marks, Barry. 1975. "Small Town Jewry: A Rabbi's Perspective." *Sh'ma 5*:210–213.

Massarik, Fred. 1992. "Knowledge About the U.S. Jewish Populations: Retrospect and Prospect 1970–2001." *Journal of Jewish Communal Service 68* (Summer):299–305.

————. 1974. "Jewish Population in the United States, 1973." *American Jewish Year Book, 1974–75* (Vol. 75). Philadelphia: The Jewish Publication Society of America, pp. 295–302.

Massarik, Fred, and Alvin Chenkin. 1973. "United States National Jewish Population Study: A First Report." *American Jewish Year Book 1973* (Vol. 74). Philadelphia: The Jewish Publication Society of America, pp. 264–306.

Mayer, Albert J. 1970. *Columbus Jewish Population Study: 1969*. Columbus,OH: Jewish Welfare Federation.

————. 1966a. *The Detroit Jewish Community. Geographic Mobility:*

1963–1965, and Fertility—A Projection of Future Births. Detrtoit: Jewish Welfare Federation.

———. 1966b. *Milwaukee Jewish Population Study, 1964–1965.* Milwaukee: Jewish Welfare Fund.

Maynard, Betty J. 1974. *The Dallas Jewish Community.*

Merton, Robert K. 1957. *Social Theory and Social Structure.* Glencoe, IL: The Free Press.

Moore, Deborah Dash. 1994. *To the Golden Cities.* New York: The Free Press.

Morrison, Peter A. 1971. "Chronic Movers and the Future Redistribution of Population: A Longitudinal Analysis." *Demography 8* (May):171–184.

Mott, Frank L., and Joyce Abma. 1992. "Contemporary Jewish Fertility: Does Religion Make a Difference?" *Contemporary Jewry 13*:74–94.

Mott, Frank L., and Susan H. Mott. 1994. "Columbus Ohio Jewry: An American Microcosm?" *Contemporary Jewry 15*:67–96.

Neugeboren, Jay. 1994. "Where Do We Live Now?" *Tikkun 9*:53–56ff.

New York Times. 6 March 1994. "New York Exports Its Talent as a Migration Tide Turns."

———. 14 November 1993. "Boomtown U.S.A."

———. 19 December 1993. "Humbled by Mean Recession, California Fights for Its Jobs."

———. 22 May 1988. "Where Rural Jews Can Get Together."

Newman, William M., and Peter L. Halvorson. 1979. "American Jews: Patterns of Geographic Distribution and Changes, 1952–1971" *Journal for the Scientific Study of Religion 18* (June):183–193.

North American Commission on Jewish Identity and Continuity. 1994. "Preliminary Reports and Recommendations of the Commission's Working Groups," draft report.

O'Malley, Sharon. 1994. "The Rural Rebound." *American Demographics 16* (May):24–29.

Packard, Vance. 1972. *A Nation of Strangers.* New York: David McKay Co.

Patinkin, Mark. 1980. "We're Hardly Pioneers but the Road Calls Us." *Providence (RI) Evening Bulletin,* January.

Phillips, Bruce A. 1993. "Regional Differences Among American Jews." In *Papers in Jewish Demography 1989,* Uziel O. Schmelz and Sergio DellaPergola, Eds. Jerusalem: Institute of Contemporary Jewry, The Hebrew University in Jerusalem, pp. 104–112.

———. n.d. "1993 NJPS Follow-up Study on Intermarriage." Unpublished statistics, Hebrew Union College, Los Angeles.

Plotnick, Michael Z. 1994. "The Seventy Faces of Community." *Sh'ma 25* (November 25):1–3.

Rebhun, Uzi. 1993a. "Community of Residence as a Determinant of

Jewish Identification in the United States." *Yahadut Zemanenu (A Research Annual)* 8:301–336 (in Hebrew).

———. 1993b. "Similarities and Dissimilarities in National and Community Surveys: The Case of American Jews," Paper presented at Eleventh World Congress of Jewish Studies, Jerusalem, June.

———. forthcoming. "Comparative and Follow-up of Demographic Processes Among American Jews: The Impact of Geographic Mobility on the Structure of the Jewish Family and on Patterns of Jewish Identity, 1970–1990." Ph.D. dissertation in process, Institute of Contemporary Jewry, The Hebrew University, Jerusalem.

Ressler, William H. 1993. "Gemorrah the Same? Community Influence on Adult Jewish Identity." *Contemporary Jewry* 14:73–93.

Rhode Island Herald. 8 May 1980. "Population Shifts Create New Problems for Jewish Federations."

Rimor, Mordechai, and Gary A. Tobin. 1991. "Jewish Fundraising and Jewish Identity." In *Changing Jewish Life: Service Delivery in the 1990s*, Lawrence I. Sternberg, Gary A. Tobin, and Sylvia Barack Fishman, Eds. New York: Greenwood Press, pp. 33–54.

Ritterband, Paul. 1986. "The New Geography of Jews in North America." *New Insights on a Changing Jewish Community*, Occasional Paper No. 2. New York: North American Jewish Data Bank, The Graduate School and University Center, CUNY.

Roof, Wade Clark. 1993. *A Generation of Seekers.* New York: Harper Collins.

———. 1976. "Traditional Religion in Contemporary Society: A Theory of Local-Cosmopolitan Plausibility." *American Sociological Review* 41 (April):195–208.

Rosen, Harry R. 1970. "Jewish Population Survey 1970." *Toledo Jewish News* (April):17.

Rosenwaike, Ira. 1989. "Migration Patterns of the Elderly: The Case of the American Jewish Population." *The Journal of Aging and Judaism* 3 (Spring):116–127.

"Serving Isolated Congregations." 1991. *United Synagogue Review* 43:25.

Sheskin, Ira. 1994. "Jewish Identity in the Sunbelt: The Jewish Population of Orlando, Florida." *Contemporary Jewry* 15:26–38.

———. 1993. *The Jewish Federation of Greater Orlando Population Study: Comparison Table Report.* Orlando: Jewish Federation of Greater Orlando.

———. 1992. *The Sarasota-Manatee Jewish Federation Community Study.* Sarasota: The Sarasota-Manatee Jewish Federation.

———. 1987.*The Jewish Federation of Palm Beach County Demographic Study.* West Palm Beach: Jewish Federation of Palm Beach County.

————. 1982. *Population Study of the Greater Miami Jewish Community*. Miami: Greater Miami Jewish Federation.

Shryock, Henry S., Jacob S. Siegel, and Associates. 1976. *The Methods and Materials of Demography*. New York: Academic Press, Inc.

Sidney Hollander Memorial Colloquium. 1987. *The Emergence of a Continental Jewish Community: Implication for the Federations*. Collected Papers. New York: Council of Jewish Federations.

Tobin, Gary A. 1993. "Issues in the Study of the Urban and Regional Distribution of Jews in the United States." In *Papers in Jewish Demography 1989*, Uziel O. Schmelz and Sergio DellaPergola, eds. Jerusalem: Institute of Contemporary Jewry, The Hebrew University, pp. 66–75.

————. 1989. "The Locating of JCCs in Modern Jewish Communities." *JWB Circle 46* (January–February):6–9.

Union of American Hebrew Congregations (UAHC). 1994. "Small Congregations Programming." New York: Small Congregations Department, Union of American Hebrew Congregations.

U.S. Bureau of the Census. 1991. "Geographic Mobility: March 1987 to March 1990." *Current Population Reports*, Series P–20, No. 456. Washington, D.C.: Government Printing Office.

————. 1982. "Nonpermanent Residents by States and Selected Counties and Incorporated Places: 1980." *Supplementary Report, 1980 Census of Population*. PC80-S1–6. Washington, D.C.: Government Printing Office.

————. 1961. *1960 Census of Population*, Vol.1, *Characteristics of the Population*. Washington, D.C.: Government Printing Office, pp.1–16.

————. 1958. "Religion Reported by the Civilian Population of the United States, March 1957." *Current Population Reports*, Series P–20, No. 79. Washington, D.C.: Government Printing Office.

Verbit, Mervin F. 1971. *Characteristics of a Jewish Community: The Demographic and Judaic Profiles of the Jews in the Area Served by the Jewish Federation of North Jersey*. Paterson, NJ: Jewish Federation of North Jersey.

Waite, Linda, and Judith Sheps. 1994. "The Impact of Religious Upbringing and Marriage Markets on Jewish Intermarriage." Paper Presented at the Annual Meeting of the Population Association of America, Miami, May.

Welch, Michael R., and John Baltzell. 1984. "Geographic Mobility, Social Integration, and Church Attendance." *Journal for the Scientific Study of Religion* 23(1):75–91.

Westoff, Charles F. 1964. *A Population Survey*. Cherry Hill, NJ: Jewish Federation of Camden County.

White, Michael J. 1987. *American Neighborhoods and Residential Differentiation*. New York: Russell Sage Foundation.

Woocher, Jonathan. 1990. *Jewish Affiliation: An Agenda for Research.* New York: American Jewish Committee.

Zimmer, Basil G. 1955. Participation of Migrants in Urban Strucures." *American Sociological Review* 20 (April):218–224.

SUBJECT INDEX

NAMES INDEX

Long, Larry, 42, 139, 147, 153
Longino, Charles F., 107
Luckman, Thomas, 4

Marks, Barry, 8
Massarik, Fred, 15, 41
Mayer, Albert J., 11, 12
Maynard, Betty J., 17
Moore, Deborah Dash, 2
Morrison, Peter A., 69
Mott, Frank L., 195, 229, 293
Mott, Susan H., 229, 293
Moynihan, Daniel P., 13

Neugeboren, Jay, 2
New York Times, 86, 112, 312
Newman, William M., 42, 48
Nogle, June Marie, 154
North American Commission on Jewish Identity, 330

O'Malley, Sharon, 49

Packard, Vance, 3
Patinkin, Mark, 2
Phillips, Bruce A., 70, 211, 229
Plotnick, Michael Z., 99

Rebhun, Uzi, 89, 371
Ressler, William H., 6
Rhode Island Herald, 312, 315
Rimor, Mordechai, 266
Ritterband, Paul, 42, 48, 266, 309

Roof, Wade Clark, 4
Rosen, Harry R., 12
Rosen, Sherry, 211
Rosenwaike, Ira, 323

Scheckner, Jeffrey, 39, 48, 113, 371
Sheps, Judith, 189
Sheskin, Ira, 7, 22, 64, 66, 67, 166, 187, 216, 224, 229, 285, 372
Shryock, Henry S., 100, 372
Sidney Hollander Memorial Colloquium, 24
Siegel, Jacob S., 100, 372

Tobin, Gary A., 21, 22, 23, 24, 211, 266, 325

U.S. Bureau of the Census, 39, 47, 63, 137, 138, 148, 157
Union of American Hebrew Congregations (HUAC), 329

Verbi, Mervin F., 17

Waite, Linda, 189
Waters, Mary C., 293
Welch, Michael R., 9
Westoff, Charles F., 11
White, Michael J., 293
Winter, J. Alan, 228
Woocher, Jonathan, 211

Zimmer, Basil G., 7